Special Praise for *Real Hope, True Freedom*

"Dr. Milton Magness and Marsha Means's new book, *Real Hope, True Freedom: Understanding and Coping with Sex Addiction,* provides an important resource for individuals and families caught in the snares of sexual addiction. Rich with examples taken from the lives of addicts and their families, supported by the latest scientific research, attentive to the role of faith and spirituality in recovery, and organized through a series of candid and frequently asked questions from those living with sex addiction, this book is essential material for a wide range of readers, from sex addicts themselves, to their spouses and families, to those in the pastoral and counseling professions who seek accessible resources for their congregants and clients. Ultimately, because this book offers understanding and insight into an often unspoken, yet epidemic addiction in our society, the reader discovers that real hope and true freedom can come from breaking the cycle of addiction and committing to a disciplined and lifelong recovery process."

Mark A. Heckler, PhD
President, Valparaiso University

"In *Real Hope, True Freedom*, Milton S. Magness and Marsha Means provide an incredibly balanced, state-of-the-art book that enriches the field of sex addiction. Therapists, clergy, and clients are given brain research, in addition to helpful tools for spiritual and sexual health, and recovery models that are very practical."

Ralph H. Earle, MDiv, PhD
Author, President and Founder
Psychological Counseling Services, Ltd.

"There is a tremendous amount of useful information in *Real Hope, True Freedom*, much of it presented in Q&A format—questions posed by individuals dealing with their own or a loved one's sexual addiction, and answered by the authors. As such, the book can be read start-to-finish, or piecemeal as questions arise, allowing individuals with pressing issues to find an immediate answer before looking at sex addiction as a whole or at topics that may be more secondary to them. Though Magness and Means are Christian-based in their approach, the material in this book applies equally to pretty much anyone dealing with sex addiction, regardless of his or her belief system."

Robert Weiss, MSW
Author of *Sex Addiction 101: A Basic Guide to Healing
from Sex, Porn, and Love Addiction*

"No question we live in a sexually saturated culture. This has contributed to many problems and aided the deterioration of our homes and lives. What God has intended as something beautiful, man has tangled into a mess. Dr. Magness is an expert in helping to untie these knots. As you read this book allow him to guide you on the path to purity and clarity."

Gregg Matte
Pastor, Houston's First Baptist Church

"Milton and his co-author Marsha take sex addiction beyond telling the world that sex addiction is a treatable problem. The book's power lies in identifying real client questions that appear in treatment and then answering them in a language both therapist and client can learn from. Well done."

Brenda Schaeffer, PhD
Author of *Is It Love or Is It Addiction?*

"Is there hope? Absolutely! Magness and Means provide much-needed answers to the tough questions every sex addict and partner ask in the early stages of discovery, disclosure, treatment, and recovery. *Real Hope, True Freedom* is an essential guidebook on the path to healing and wholeness."

Vicki Tidwell Palmer, LCSW, CSAT
Author of *Moving Beyond Betrayal: The 5-Step Boundary Solution for Partners of Sex Addicts*

REAL HOPE,
TRUE FREEDOM

REAL
HOPE
TRUE
FREEDOM

Milton S. Magness, DMin
and Marsha Means, MA

UNDERSTANDING AND COPING
WITH SEX ADDICTION

CENTRAL RECOVERY PRESS

LAS VEGAS

Central Recovery Press (CRP) is committed to publishing exceptional materials addressing addiction treatment, recovery, and behavioral healthcare topics, including original and quality books, audio/visual communications, and web-based new media. Through a diverse selection of titles, we seek to contribute a broad range of unique resources for professionals, recovering individuals and their families, and the general public. For more information, visit www.centralrecoverypress.com.

Publisher: Central Recovery Press
             3321 N. Buffalo Drive
             Las Vegas, NV 89129

22 21 20 19 18 17   1 2 3 4 5
Library of Congress Cataloging-in-Publication Data
Names: Magness, Milton S., author. | Means, Marsha, 1948-
Title: Real hope, true freedom: understanding and coping with sex addiction
/ Milton S. Magness, DMin, and Marsha Means, MA.
Description: Las Vegas: Central Recovery Press, 2017.
Identifiers: LCCN 2016032625 (print) | LCCN 2016034071 (ebook) | ISBN
9781942094302 (paperback) | ISBN 9781942094319 (e-book)
Subjects: LCSH: Sex addiction--Treatment--Popular works. | Sex
addicts--Family relationships. | BISAC: FAMILY & RELATIONSHIPS / Marriage.
| PSYCHOLOGY / Psychopathology / Addiction. | PSYCHOLOGY / Interpersonal
Relations.
Classification: LCC RC560.S43 M23 2017 (print) | LCC RC560.S43 (ebook) | DDC
616.85/833--dc23
LC record available at https://lccn.loc.gov/2016032625

Photo of Milton S. Magness by Gittings. Used with permission.

Photo of Marsha A. Means by Juan Ezequiel Nuñez. Used with permission.

Every attempt has been made to contact copyright holders. If copyright holders have not been properly acknowledged please contact us. Central Recovery Press will be happy to rectify the omission in future printings of this book.

Publisher's Note: This book contains general information about sexual addiction and its effects on relationships. The information is not medical advice and should not be treated as such. Central Recovery Press makes no representations or warranties in relation to the information in this book. If you have specific questions about any medical matter discussed in this book, you should consult your doctor or other professional healthcare provider. This book is not an alternative to medical advice from your doctor or other professional healthcare provider. Our books represent the experiences and opinions of their authors only. Every effort has been made to ensure that events, institutions, and statistics presented in our books as facts are accurate and up-to-date. To protect their privacy, the names of some of the people, places, and institutions in this book have been changed.

Author's Note: The approach used in this book reflects the treatment model that is used at Hope & Freedom Counseling Services as well by Certified Hope & Freedom Practitioners (CHFP) who have been trained in the Hope & Freedom treatment model.

Cover design and interior design and layout by Sara Streifel, Think Creative Design.

To Gerald and Gayle

Who have worked tirelessly to help men and women

overcome the adverse impact of sex addiction,

and model restoration for other couples

FREEDOM

HOPE

TABLE OF CONTENTS

PREFACE

When people ask me what kind of work I do, I'm never quite sure how to respond. And when I do (always as briefly as possible), they often squirm in discomfort. On occasion when a man has asked me follow-up questions, I've simply handed him my card and suggested he look at my website. Then, if after looking, he's still interested, he can give me a call. As you may have guessed, those calls never come. The term sex addiction makes them uncomfortable.

The topic of sex addiction makes us all uncomfortable. Especially if we don't understand what it means (and does not mean), how it starts in one's life, how it impacts the lives it touches, and how to heal the wounds that usually fostered it in the first place.

Maybe I should simply introduce myself as a story bearer. We've all seen torchbearers for the Olympic Games on TV. But instead of a flame, I carry women's stories tucked in the recesses of my heart. Hearing these stories and carrying them in my heart has taught me many things. I'll share some of those lessons as I answer the many questions women have submitted for this book. But I want to share three of them here.

Pain Does Not Bow to Psychological Criteria

Women's stories have taught me that the psychological criteria used to diagnose sex addiction do not matter to the heart. When your life is shattered because the one to whom you've entrusted your heart has sought emotional or physical gratification outside your relationship, you really don't care whether a professional would label him a "real sex addict." Fairly regularly, a new woman will say to me: "The counselor gave him a test and told me he is not a sex addict; does that mean I shouldn't hurt? Is there something wrong with me for feeling this way?"

No, there is not something wrong with you. When vows, commitments, and treasured connections are violated between a man and his partner, it hurts. It makes no difference to a broken heart whether or not his behavior meets the required diagnostic criteria for sex addiction. Loss is loss. Pain is pain. And it's all experienced as trauma, with or without a professional's blessing.

There Are Treasures in the Trauma Chest

Treasures in the trauma chest? Are you crazy? I can almost hear women thinking these words as we approach this topic in groups. Granted, it's an idea that may come further along the healing path for some than for others. Yet, many women realize fairly early on that buried beneath all the heartache, loss, and change their partner's addiction brought to their lives, there *are* buried treasures.

What might those treasures be? Most gain a new understanding of themselves, their gifts, their strength, their courage, their tenacity, as well as their ability to love, to forgive, and to dust themselves off and begin again. They gain the ability to allow others to have their own feelings without losing *their* own peace. They gain the ability to grow healthy boundaries. And they gain empathy they could never have known without this shattering experience. Strikingly, couples who make it to the other side, still together, all say they have gained a relationship they would never have known if they'd been spared this challenging journey.

An Opportunity for Adventurous Growth

While most of us can compare this "adventure" to falling down the rabbit hole in an Alice-in-Wonderland-like experience, once the disorientation clears, with the help of a guide, we soon realize we must roll up our sleeves and go to work building new emotional muscles. If we're to survive, and to eventually thrive, it's going to require hard work and growth!

This is my favorite part of being a story bearer. I'm given the joy and the privilege of being invited into women's stories as they begin to write a different future based on their new growth. And as the weeks pass, I have a front row seat as they grow and strengthen new emotional muscles.

Most can only see their growth and progress in the rearview mirror. But in time, all realize how far they've come. And some even say it's been worth all the pain for what they've gained from this devastating experience.

My sisters on this journey are amazing. And so are their stories. What a privilege to be granted a season of sharing in their stories and lives, then to carry them in my heart for the rest of my days.

These are just three of the rich lessons being a story-bearer has taught me. My hope for you, dear Reader, is that as you keep taking baby steps along your own trajectory of healing and growth you will make these— and many more—discoveries. And, that in the bottom of *your* trauma chest you too will find beautiful buried treasures.

Marsha Means

HOPE

FREEDOM

ACKNOWLEDGMENTS

When I first began offering Three-Day Intensives that focused on restoring relationships damaged by sex addiction, I did not realize how many couples would want to participate in these programs. For many years I did my best to accommodate as many couples as my schedule would allow. But one therapist cannot meet the needs of all couples. Additionally, I realized that unless I trained other therapists in my treatment model, the Hope & Freedom Intensive Program would end whenever my career comes to an end.

Over the past several years, I have trained a small number of outstanding therapists to become Certified Hope & Freedom Practitioners (CHFP). I looked for deeply skilled sex addiction therapists who would come to Houston and learn my treatment model while working with several couples in Hope & Freedom Intensives. What I did not expect was how much I was going to learn from this group. I sit in awe of them and of their commitment to help couples restore their relationships. In every case, the teacher became a student during the training.

I have read glowing success stories from many couples who attest that their relationships have been saved by CHFPs. Each week these incredible therapists are giving couples a second chance. I am privileged to be associated with them. Rather than list them all here, I would encourage you to go to www.FindACHFP.com to read about them and their work.

Publishers can make or break authors. I want to thank all of the talented and dedicated people at Central Recovery Press for their work and commitment to this project. This is my second book with CRP and I am finding again that working with them has been an absolute pleasure. From my first contact with Executive Editor Nancy Schenck, to the guidance of Eliza Tutellier and Valerie Killeen, to the marketing genius of Patrick Hughes, and especially to the many hours of work with my gifted editor, Dan Mager, I have been privileged to be able to associate with the best publishing team anywhere.

Milton S. Magness

INTRODUCTION

The Canadian Rockies are filled with some of the most breathtaking beauty in the world. I spend as much time as possible here, enjoying multiple sports year round. At the same time, winters at my Canadian home can be dangerously cold and bleak.

There are times when the temperature plunges to minus thirty degrees or even colder. Snow comes a foot or more at a time. Nights are long and the days may be as brief as eight hours or less. Many of our friends suffer months-long depression every winter as they battle seasonal affective disorder (SAD) due to the lack of sunlight.

When the temperature plunges, simple errands outside can become life threatening. Going to the grocery story demands planning and multiple layers of clothing to remain healthy. Floors are covered in grit tracked in by snow boots, and mudrooms are littered with all manner of footwear and more coats than will comfortably fit.

In the midst of some of the harshest weather, there is a beautiful phenomenon. When the temperature plunges, the accumulated snow compacts forming transparent crystals. These crystals cover the snowfields but are invisible in low light conditions. However, when the sun comes out, the snow shimmers like it is studded with diamonds. The temperature may still be extremely cold and there may yet be several more months of harsh weather ahead, but the glimpse of diamonds in the snow brightens an otherwise unremarkable day. The glistening crystals are one of the most beautiful sites during winter.

Sex addiction is a condition that has decimated countless lives and destroyed many families. The path of destruction caused by sex addicts is mind-numbing. This book takes a frank look at sex addiction and the devastation it causes. We look at the tremendous damage sex addicts cause to others, especially to their partners. This is also a book of hope. In the midst of the destruction, some individuals and some couples find their way out and get their lives back on track, finding new life, new hope, and renewed relationships on the other side of addiction.

To be fair, we do not know how many sex addicts and partners do well after recovery. There are no statistics to indicate how many marriages survive sex addiction. Certainly, many sex addicts never stop acting out, many partners never fully heal from the trauma caused by their partners' sex addiction, and many marriages end as a result of sex addiction.

However, we do know there are sex addicts that become fully healthy. They stop all of their acting out and change their other problematic and unhealthy behaviors. Though sex addiction will remain with them throughout life, they are able to regain much of what they lost as a result of their active addiction and live in integrity.

There are also partners that find true healing after the trauma of being in a relationship with a sex addict. Some of these partners are still in that relationship and others have moved on in their lives without their sexually addicted spouse. The healing journey often takes years but can happen through diligent work.

We have had the privilege of working with couples whose relationships survived sex addiction. These fortunate couples often find that their relationships are better after recovery from sex addiction than they ever were before the discovery of sexual acting out. Although this is far from the norm, their stories are important, and a number of them are included at the end of this book. Although this book does not try to soften the impact of sex addiction, it is our hope that while reading it, you will glimpse some diamonds in the snow.

The working title for this book was "Why Did He Do It? Why Can't She Get Over It?" These questions are at the nexus of understanding and coping with sex addiction. Sex addiction is real. It is not something dreamed up by Hollywood to help celebrities dodge responsibility for their inappropriate actions or to explain a lapse in judgment. Sex addiction is not just liking sex or even just liking sex a lot. This has nothing to do with sex drive, libido, or hormones.

Sex addiction is a debilitating disorder that conservatively affects 3–6 percent of the population. It is epidemic in America. That figure is based on those who have sought treatment in the USA for sex addiction. When you add to this number the partners/spouses and children of sex addicts, the number of people whose lives are directly impacted by sex addiction reaches as high as 30 million!

Since most sex addicts are men, this book speaks of addicts in the masculine and partners of sex addicts in the feminine. However, women can also be addicted to sex. Regardless of gender, this book gives direction to addicts, their partners, and those who love them.

This book is written in part to address frequently asked questions (FAQ) that have been supplied by others—primarily sex addicts and their partners. These questions were generated by more than 270 people who completed questionnaires sent to those who signed up for the Hope & Freedom newsletter and via links posted on several websites. These respondents contributed over 4,000 questions. In part, because there are so many questions and concerns shared by people exposed to sex addiction, quite a few of these questions were similar in nature. Approximately 190 of them are directly addressed in this book.

Many of these questions are posed and answered directly throughout this book, and many more are addressed within the narrative. Most of the remaining questions that were contributed on the questionnaires are duplicates of, or similar to, other questions already asked. Appendix A: Finding Frequently Asked Questions (FAQs) and Answers at a Glance will allow you to prioritize the areas and questions that are of greatest immediate interest to you and give you the opportunity to focus on other areas later.

I am very pleased to have Marsha Means as my coauthor for this book. Marsha's outstanding work with wounded partners of sex addicts has brought hope to many women who did not know where to turn. She and I have worked collaboratively with many clients over the past decade. The insights she contributes to this book further help partners navigate the stormy waters of healing and show them how to move from wounded to healthy, from pain to joy, and from fearful to hopeful.

Some of the time when Marsha and I use the pronoun "I" for the sake of clarity, we will insert our name in parentheses. In those cases, we are relating our own experiences or our own point of view. The "we" pronoun indicates either collaborative writing or a point of view that we share.

This book is the fourth in the Hope & Freedom Series. It is my firm belief that sex addiction is not only treatable, but that sex addicts can live free from all acting-out behaviors—forever. It is also possible for relationships that have been badly damaged by sex addiction to heal and be completely restored. I have the privilege of working with couples each week, many of whom had previously given up on their relationships. Through the hard work of recovery by both partners, these couples have been able to rebuild their relationships.

Hope can be yours today. Freedom comes only through persistent, unrelenting recovery.

Milton S. Magness

PART ONE

THE AVENUE TO ADDICTION

FREEDOM

HOPE

CHAPTER 1

THE ROLE OF FAMILY OF ORIGIN

Wilson's Story

"Shut the hell up! If you open your frigging mouth again I'll shut it for you!" Wilson cowered in the corner as he did every time his dad got drunk and started finding fault with every member of the family.

"I'm sorry."

"I said shut the hell up. You're just like your mother, you sniveling coward. You'll never amount to anything."

Sometimes Wilson got hit. Other times, like tonight, he was pummeled by his father's words. He was reminded again that he was worthless, that he didn't measure up to his father's expectations and would never succeed at anything.

Wilson often deliberately became a target to keep his father occupied so his drunken rage would spare his mother and his little sister. The scars on his back and legs were not as memorable as the deep psychological wounds his father inflicted. Whatever the problem, whatever was broken, whatever was missing, Wilson knew it was his fault.

Just once he wished he could see his father sober and hear him say kind things to him. Just once he wished he could hear his father say, "I love you." But not tonight. Tonight Wilson was angry too. He thought to himself, one of these days I am going to be big and I will make you pay!

By the time Wilson was ten, he had seen pornography many times. He discovered his father's hidden stash of sexually explicit magazines. Then an older girl that lived down the street introduced him to physical sex. What Wilson realized was that as long as he was engaged in any kind of sexual behavior he didn't feel alone and unloved. He began to live for the moments when he could slip away and live in fantasy.

By age eleven, Wilson discovered masturbation by accident. He realized that if he rubbed his penis, it felt good. Every time his father started raging, Wilson would escape to the bathroom or the garage and masturbate. He could escape into fantasy and for a few moments block out his father's anger.

By his thirteenth birthday, Wilson was masturbating every day, sometimes several times a day. Regardless of the dysfunction at home, he could escape into his fantasy world of sex and, for a while, forget the daily pain of his life. He often had open sores on his penis where he had rubbed the skin off from his constant masturbation.

As Wilson matured physically, emotionally he seemed to remain stuck at ten years old. By the time he was fifteen, his father had deserted the family. Even in his absence, Wilson could hear his father's voice in his head telling him he was not good enough. When Wilson was not being sexual with himself or someone else, he nursed his rage. His anger always seemed to be just below the surface. He got in fights at school and destroyed other's property.

As an adult, Wilson continued to use sex to medicate and to escape reality. After several failed relationships, he gave up on the idea that he would ever be in a loving and fulfilling relationship. Sex partners seemed plentiful. He didn't have to pretend to care about someone in order to have sex with her. He felt like he invented the term "friends with benefits."

What Wilson had a hard time admitting was that he longed to have a special person he could love and then be truly loved by her. He scoffed at one partner who told him that he was looking to her to find the love his father never showed him. How could he still want to be loved by his father after being so abused by him?

As Wilson entered his mid-twenties, he achieved significant success as an investment banker. He thrived on work and found that people trusted him. But his professional life and his personal life were very different.

Wilson spent few evenings without being engaged in some sexual activity with someone. He began to have two depressing thoughts. First, he realized that his life was dominated by sex. He now felt alone even when he was having sex. He was always looking for the next person with whom he could start a relationship. And it didn't matter how much sex he had; it seemed like it was never enough. Second, Wilson felt he would never be able to live a monogamous life.

These thoughts and the concerns they generated were the beginning of Wilson's quest for recovery. He wanted a different life—one not dominated by sex. He yearned for a healthy relationship. He also wanted to get free from his propensity to rage when things didn't go his way.

How could he be a success in other areas of his life and have messed up his personal life so badly? Others looking at him saw him as someone who succeeded against great odds. People admired his success in business and envied his ability to carry on multiple relationships with so many women. His friends constantly fed his ego saying, "You're the man!"

Yet in his private moments, Wilson knew he didn't want to continue the shell of a life he was living. He yearned to be free from his obsessive and compulsive sexual behavior. He wanted to feel normal, but he didn't know what normal was. All he knew was the life he had lived.

Abuse during childhood does not cause addiction. However, many, many people who struggle with addiction have been abused—some physically, others verbally and psychologically, still others sexually. Abuse is the fertile soil in which addiction—in all its forms—often grows.

Abuse during the formative years of life sets a new normal; it changes the baseline for what is normal behavior. A person who has been abused may escape into sex, food, work, alcohol or other drugs, spending, gambling, high-risk sports, self-abusive behaviors (cutting, burning, etc.), criminal behavior (burglaries, theft, arson), or even violent crime. We will examine the role of abuse in the development of sex addiction a bit later. But abuse itself does not explain why someone becomes addicted. For every person who comes from an abusive childhood and becomes an addict, there are many more of similar backgrounds who never develop addiction. Another factor that often sets the stage for addiction is the presence of addiction in one or both parents.

....

Addiction seems to run in my family. Three of my four grandparents are alcoholics and my brother is a drug addict. Am I at greater risk of developing addiction?
....

Addiction is an intergenerational problem. When we study the families of addicts we often find that addiction is present in preceding generations. Although this is often the case with alcohol and other drug addictions, sex addiction may be so well hidden that an addict may not be aware of the presence of sex addiction in his parents. And when it comes to grandparents, even if compulsive sexual acting out occurred, often such behaviors become the closely held family secrets. Family histories are frequently sanitized in an attempt to preserve the illusion of an ideal family.

The most reliable risk factor for future addiction is a family history of addiction. For alcohol and other drugs, we know that the transmission of addiction is part genetic and part environmental. There is speculation that there may be a genetic component to sex addiction, but as of yet there is no scientific data to back that up. However, a variety of environmental factors seem to provide fertile ground from which sex addiction can rise.

Boundaries

When we hear the word "boundaries," we may think in terms of sports where there are clear indicators on the court or field of play as to what is in bounds and what is out of bounds. Families have boundaries as well. Boundaries let us know who is responsible for various tasks, how family members interact with each other, what behaviors are acceptable, and what behaviors are not acceptable. There are three broad categories of boundaries in families: clear, rigid, and defuse.

In families with *clear boundaries*, children have an established bedtime as well as clearly defined rules by which they live. Adults live by agreed upon guidelines in the way they behave and how they interact with each other. There may be times when exceptions are made to a boundary such as allowing a child to stay up past bedtime on a special occasion. There is clarity on what the boundaries are and when and why exceptions are made.

In families with *rigid boundaries*, there are no exceptions made to family rules. Rigid boundaries lead to isolation and a breakdown in communication. There is an atmosphere of either indifferent detachment or of tension and anger. Physical abuse may be present in these families.

Families with *defuse boundaries* do not have an understanding of where one person's role and rights end and the role and rights of others begin. Parents are overly involved in every aspect of a child's life. Husbands and wives have few if any individual pursuits. Children may be allowed to do what they want. Enmeshment is the norm.

Being raised in a family that does not have clear boundaries is one of the factors that can predispose a person to developing addiction.

Attachment

Attachment refers to the emotional bonds that connect one person to another. Attachment disorder is an umbrella term that describes a person's inability to develop normal, healthy bonds with other human beings. Healthy attachment bonds develop in early childhood and are the result of being raised in a nurturing environment. An attachment disorder may develop because of a number of factors, including moving frequently over a short period of time, changing caregivers often, the absence of one or more primary caregivers, unresponsive caregivers (such as a child crying and there is no one responsive to his or her cries), or profound neglect.

When a person is a sex addict and also suffers from an attachment disorder, he or she may turn to casual sexual relationships hoping for the neurochemical reinforcement that is present in a committed relationship. (Neurotransmitters, the source of this reinforcement, are chemical messengers that, among other things, regulate mood.) He may have an inability to rebound from disappointments or criticism. Consequently, he may look for acceptance from someone who is willing to be sexual with him—even if he has to pay for it.

I think that my mother's trauma and my father's inability to deal with it greatly affected their relationship with me. Is it possible that this lack of bonding contributed to the development of my sex addiction?

Yes, it is possible. It is healthy to recognize the possibility that the lack of attachment may have contributed to your sex addiction. If your parents were not emotionally available to you then that certainly has had a negative impact on your life. The question now is what are you going to do about it? You can choose to believe that you will always sexually act out because of the unresponsive parenting you received. Or, you can engage a skilled sex addiction therapist who has expertise in working with adults who have attachment disorders. We will look more at treatment in Part Two.

CHAPTER 2

ABUSE

Abuse is often a factor in the development of addiction. Abuse can take many forms including sexual, physical, psychological, and religious abuse. Neglect intersects with abuse when there is a failure to protect children from being abused by others.

Sexual Abuse

Jed's Story

Jed's sexual acting out started when he was in grade school. When asked about his first sexual experience, he recalled that it took place on a campout with two other boys his age. Others had picked on him for as long as he could remember because he had some physical characteristics that were more common to girls than to boys. Jed welcomed the opportunity to go camping with two other boys because it seemed like he was being accepted as one of the guys, even though these boys were among those who had ridiculed him the most.

When evening came, the boys ganged up on him and forced him to engage in sexual acts against his will. As the night progressed he participated without being forced. That was the beginning of a lifelong fascination with forced sex. Through the years he spent thousands of hours fantasizing about being forced to be sexual. Sometimes he envisioned himself as the one forcing someone else to be sexual against his or her will.

As an adult, Jed sought out pornography involving bondage, discipline, and sadomasochism (BDSM). He started seeking out people he could pay to engage in BDSM behaviors and to abuse and humiliate him. Jed felt his sex life was a bit twisted, but until he got into therapy he never made the connection between his early sexual abuse and his sexual proclivities as an adult.

....

When I was ten, I found some soft-core porn magazines hidden in my father's dresser . . . I would sneak them out and masturbate to the images every time I was home alone. How do I stop feeling guilty about doing that?

....

First, it is crucial for adults to recognize that having pornography that can be found by children is a covert form of child sexual abuse. Children are naturally curious. They will check out every nook, cranny, and "secret" place in their environment. If pornography is in the home, at some point a normal curious child will likely find it.

Unfiltered and unsupervised access to the Internet also puts children at risk of being exposed to pornography. The average age of first exposure to Internet pornography has commonly been reported to be age eleven. There is some evidence that this number is decreasing to as young as nine. However, protecting children from harmful Internet sites at home is not enough since access to the Internet is ubiquitous.

The original question concerned guilty feelings you have over childhood behavior. Healing begins with realizing that you were a child with a normal curiosity about sex. As an adult, it is time to recognize that you were a child and forgive that ten-year-old boy for doing things that ten-year-old boys do.

Physical Abuse

A person who is physically abused in their formative years is at risk of developing addiction or multiple forms of addiction as a coping mechanism.

I was brutally whipped by my father many times until I was a teenager. Could this abuse be partly responsible for my sex addiction?

Although we can never conclusively point to one factor or even multiple factors as the definitive cause for the development of sex addiction, we do know that physical abuse can contribute to it. Abuse like you describe is terrifying. Children may spend increasingly longer periods in fantasy to escape an abusive environment. Sexual fantasies are normal. Yet when a person spends hours a day indulging sexual fantasies, he or she is well on the way to developing sex addiction.

Both of my parents used to slap me a lot when I was a child. I don't remember acting out sexually until I was about fifteen. Why didn't I develop sex addiction earlier?

You said you don't remember acting out sexually when you were much younger. What is your understanding of what constitutes sexual acting out? You may not have physically acted out until you were fifteen, but I wonder how much of your time was spent in sexual fantasy before that. Many people become caught up in fantasizing about sex long before acting out physically.

We know that not everyone who is abused develops addiction. The best we can do is to recognize that there are a variety of contributing factors.

Psychological Abuse

Helen's Story

Helen's earliest memories were of her mother telling her that she would never amount to anything. She was constantly being compared to her sisters and told that she wasn't as smart or as pretty, and that no one would ever want to marry her. By the time Helen entered high school, she had already had many sex partners. She was determined to prove her mother wrong and found there were many people who wanted to be with her and be sexual with her. As an adult, Helen could look back on a long string of failed relationships. With each failure, she heard her mother's voice in her head mocking her.

When Helen entered treatment for sex addiction, she learned that the hardest work she had to do involved changing the way she thought about herself. With the help of a skilled therapist, she was able to develop a new script for her thoughts and came to believe that she was a person of worth and value. Helen also found she was able to stop her acting out and live in true sexual sobriety. Two years into recovery she met and subsequently married a man who was himself a recovering alcoholic. They have now been married for ten years and believe that the success of their marriage is due to the commitment each of them has to their own recovery.

We recall the children's rhyme, "Sticks and stones may break my bones but words will never hurt me." Not only is this not true, we know that psychological abuse inflicted by unkind words can cause even more damage than physical abuse. Psychological abuse, also referred to as mental or emotional abuse, can contribute to the development of depressive and anxiety disorders, and post-traumatic stress disorder (PTSD), as well as addiction. Emotional abuse can take many forms and can include anything from verbal abuse and constant criticism to more subtle tactics, such as intimidation, manipulation, and refusal to ever be pleased.

Sometimes those who are being psychologically abused may not even know it. They may think what they are experiencing is normal—as in the case of an abused child who has not known anything else. Other examples of psychological abuse include efforts to control and dominate, shame, blame, accuse, judge, humiliate, degrade, abandon, neglect, and the "silent treatment." Children who are psychologically abused may be threatened, cursed, called names, yelled at, mocked, and ignored.

As with other forms of abuse, it is important for the person who has been abused to know that it is not his or her fault. He or she did not cause it. The abuse is the result of the issues and insecurities of the abuser. Behaviors that lead to addiction may be the way a person escapes the pain of his or her abuse.

Religious Abuse

Religious abuse involves using religion to control or manipulate someone. It is the mistreatment of a person who is seeking spiritual guidance, and may include harassment, intimidation, fear, and guilt trips. Religious teachings may be well-intentioned but taken to extremes or used as a weapon to pressure a person into certain behaviors. The extremes of religious abuse are clear in cases of sexual abuse by priests.

A less well-known example of religious abuse is when an elder of a church pressures a mentally ill person not to take medication but instead to pray harder. Another example is when people are threatened with going to hell or perdition if they engage in certain behaviors. Religious leaders as well as parents may use shame to pressure people to throw away music or books that are thought to be evil. Children are frequently taught in absolutes and that it is wrong to question dogma. They learn that they are not to think for themselves but to accept without question what they are taught. Religious leaders can be authoritarian and narcissistic. Often a very high level of trust is placed in their words, which congregants often accept without question.

Have you been the victim of abuse? It may be helpful to go back through your life, especially the first eighteen years, and make a list of incidents of abuse by category. What kind of abuse occurred? Who was the abuser? How old were you when it happened? How did you feel at the time of the abuse? How do you feel now?

Having a history of abuse does not excuse addiction but it may help explain it. You did not intend to become a sex addict. Yet, a variety of circumstances in your early life worked together to make you vulnerable to addiction.

FREEDOM

HOPE

CHAPTER 3

ADDICTION AND
THE BRAIN

When I (Milton) first attended graduate school in the 1970s, I was taught that the brain was pretty much set at birth. It was believed that people were born with a large but limited number of brain cells and that number decreased through the years. Further, it was thought that neuropathways were already fully developed and would change little throughout life.

However, we now know that, just as with other parts of the body, we produce new brain cells (known as neurogenesis) throughout our lives. An article in the scientific journal *Cell* gives evidence that 700 new neurons are added to the hippocampus daily corresponding to an annual turnover of 1.75 percent of the neurons in that part of the brain.[1] Neurogenesis is good news in that it helps restore healthy brain function and improve the quality of life for people with a variety of disorders and aids recovery from addiction.

When it comes to understanding addiction and recovery, of even greater importance is neuroplasticity—the brain's ability to reorganize itself by forming new neural connections throughout life. A research study showed that the hippocampus—the part of the brain that holds

---

1   K. L. Spalding, "Dynamics of Hippocampal Neurogenesis in Adult Humans," *Cell* 153, no.6 (2013): 1219–1227.

spatial representation capacity—of London taxi drivers was significantly larger than that of London bus drivers. Scientists at University College, London conducted Magnetic Resonance Imaging (MRI) scans of sixteen London cabbies and found that the hippocampus was significantly larger than that of the fifty control subjects. They also found that the hippocampus was more developed in cab drivers who had been driving for forty years compared to those who had driven for a shorter period of time.[2] The scientists theorized that since bus drivers travel the same route every day, they do not exercise that part of the brain as much as taxi drivers who have to navigate different routes constantly.

Psychiatrist Jeffrey Schwartz, regarded as one of the leading experts in the field of neuroplasticity, coined the term "brain lock" to describe both obsessive-compulsive behavior and a treatment plan based in neuroplasticity he developed for obsessive-compulsive disorder (OCD) patients. He said persons with OCD can self-treat their condition using four steps:

1. **Relabel** the obsessive thoughts and compulsive urges as obsessions and compulsions, not as real thoughts.

2. **Reattribute** the obsessive thoughts to a brain malfunction called OCD.

3. **Refocus** on a wholesome, productive activity for at least fifteen minutes.

4. **Revalue** the entire obsession and compulsion group as having no useful meaning in your life.[3]

Although sex addiction is not the same as OCD, certainly many of the behaviors in sex addiction and other forms of addiction involve obsessive thinking and compulsive behaviors. As George Koob, director of the National Institute on Alcohol Abuse and Alcoholism in Bethesda, Maryland, put it,

> A lot of people think addiction is what happens when someone finds a drug to be the most rewarding thing

---

2   F. Jabr, "Cashe Cab: Taxi Drivers' Brains Grow to Navigate London Streets," *Scientific American*, December 8, 2011, http://www.scientificamerican.com/article/london-taxi-memory/.

3   J. M. Schwartz, *Brain Lock: Free Yourself from Obsessive-Compulsive Behavior* (New York: Regan Books, 1997).

they've ever experienced. But drug abuse is not just feeling good about drugs. Your brain is changed when you misuse drugs. It is changed in ways that perpetuate the problem. The changes associated with drug use affect how addicts respond to drug cues, like the smell of a cigarette or the sight of a shot of vodka. Drug abuse also changes how other rewards, such as money or food, are processed, decreasing their relative value.[4]

Nikolaas Tinbergen, a Nobel Prize-winning ethologist, coined the term "supernormal stimuli." He found that he could create stimuli that were far stronger than the natural stimuli that cause certain animal behaviors. For example, he constructed plaster eggs and found that birds would choose to sit on eggs that were larger and more vividly colored than their own eggs. Some of the eggs were so large that birds had a hard time remaining on them without sliding off. He also found that certain territorial fish would more vigorously attack wooden fish models that were painted more vividly. In one study he constructed cardboard dummy butterflies with more defined markings and found that males would prefer to try to mate with them than real females.[5] This may help explain why sex addicts might be more interested in watching pornography than being sexual with a partner in a committed relationship.

Things we see clearly affect our brains. Pornography triggers brain activity in sex addicts that is similar to that triggered by drugs in drug addicts. Cambridge neuroscientist Valerie Voon conducted a study to see what changes take place in the brains of people with and without compulsive sexual behavior.[6]

The study used Functional MRI (fMRI) to assess nineteen subjects with compulsive sexual behavior and nineteen healthy subjects as they viewed sexually explicit videos compared with non-sexually exciting

---

4   B. Brookshire, "Addiction Showcases the Brain's Flexibility," *Science News: Magazine of the Society for Science & the Public*, August 5, 2014, https://www.sciencenews.org/blog/scicurious/addiction-showcases-brain-flexibility.

5   G. Ciotti, "Supernormal Stimuli: This Is Your Brain on Porn, Junk Food, and the Internet," *Huffington Post*, July 17, 2014, http://www.huffingtonpost.com/gregory-ciotti/supernormal-stimuli-this-_b_5584972.html?utm_hp_ref=tw.

6   V. Voon, T. B. Mole, P. Banca, et al., "Neural Correlates of Sexual Cue Reactivity in Individuals with and without Compulsive Sexual Behaviours," *PLOS ONE* 9, no. 7 (2014), e102419.

videos. Dr. Voon concluded, "there are clear differences in brain activity between patients who have compulsive sexual behavior and healthy volunteers."[7]

Sex addicts who are married or are in committed relationships know that viewing pornography negatively affects their desire to be sexual with their partner. Young and otherwise healthy men who suffer from sex addiction may find it difficult to be aroused by their partner. Often, they go to physicians to see if there is a medical problem only to find out that they are in good health and there is no medical reason for them to have erectile difficulties. They may take testosterone and drugs for erectile dysfunction to counter the problem even after determining the problem is not physical. The use of pornography and the fantasies reinforced by masturbating to pornography has altered their brains.

Therapists and physicians, specifically urologists, have long known there is a link between pornography use and brain function. A fascinating aspect of the Voon study is that it provides, for the first time, scientific evidence of a link between pornography use and erectile dysfunction. The researchers found that participants "experienced diminished libido or erectile function specifically in physical relationships with women (although not in relationship to the sexually explicit material)."[8]

Within the sex addiction therapy professional community, there is a lot of discussion about this study. Caution abounds not to make too much of any single study and to understand the limitations of neuroimaging studies. However, evidence continues to mount that the brains of sex addicts are altered by their compulsive sexual activity.

There is increasing evidence that the brain registers all pleasures or rewards in the same way, whether they originate with alcohol or other drugs, food, or sex. In the brain, pleasurable experiences facilitate the release of the neurotransmitter dopamine, which influences the brain's system of reward-related learning. This system has an important role in sustaining life because it links activities needed for human survival (such as eating and sex) with pleasure and reward. The brain's reward pathway includes those areas involved with motivation and memory as well as pleasure. As a result, the more pleasurable an experience is, the

---

7   Ibid.
8   Ibid.

more powerful the memory of it tends to be, and the more motivated the individual is to repeat it.[9]

In another study, sixty-four men between the ages of twenty-one and forty-five were given brain scans using MRIs. The researchers found that the subjects who watched pornography often had a smaller striatum—an important part of the brain's reward system involved in sexual arousal. The study's lead researcher, Simone Kühn, said, "That could mean that regular consumption of pornography more or less wears out your reward system."[10] He surmised that study subjects who watch a lot of pornography need increasing stimulation to experience the same amount of pleasure or reward.[11]

Such research disproves the argument of pornography advocates that porn is just an expression of a high sexual desire. Those who use pornography most have less response to sexual images, and therefore, less sexual desire. They consume more and more pornography in order to get a brain-reward response.

As a person's reward circuitry becomes increasingly dulled and desensitized by drugs, nothing else can compete—food, family, and friends lose their relative value, while the ability to curb the need to seek and use drugs progressively vanishes. Ironically, and perhaps cruelly, eventually even the drug loses its ability to produce pleasure, but the compromised brain leads addicted people to continue to pursue it anyway as the memory of the drug and the pleasure it no longer produces becomes more powerful than the drug itself.[12]

Gradually scientists are gathering evidence that the changes in the brain brought about by drug addiction are also taking place in the brains of sex addicts. While this does not give sex addicts an excuse for their acting out, it does help explain why someone who otherwise makes good decisions will engage in behavior that causes such harm. Why, for example, would a physician engage in unprotected intercourse

---

9   Helpguide.org, "Understanding Addiction: How Addiction Hijacks the Brain," accessed September 20, 2016, http://www.helpguide.org/harvard/how-addiction-hijacks-the-brain.htm.

10   S. A. Kühn, "Brain Structure and Functional Connectivity Associated with Pornography Consumption, the Brain on Porn," JAMA Psychiatry, 71, no. 7 (2014): 827–834.

11   Ibid.

12   National Institutes of Health, "The Brain: Understanding Neurobiology—The Essence of Drug Addiction," accessed September 20, 2016, https://science.education.nih.gov/supplements/nih2/addiction/guide/essence.html.

with a prostitute? Why would a minister who is entrusted with the spiritual guidance of his flock be sexual with parishioners? Why would a successful executive engage in sexual behavior with subordinates that he knows could result in a sexual harassment lawsuit? The only thing that explains such effectively insane behavior is that sex addiction has significantly changed brain functioning—including reasoning and decision-making.

Evidence continues to mount that addiction-based changes in the brain warrant classifying addiction as a brain disease. A recent article in the *New England Journal of Medicine* concluded that neuroscience continues to support the brain disease model of addiction and that neuroscientific research offers new opportunities for the prevention and treatment of substance addiction and behavioral addiction related to food, sex, and gambling, and may also improve our understanding of the processes involved in voluntary behavioral control.[13] It notes that "the concept of addiction as a disease of the brain challenges deeply ingrained values about self-determination and personal responsibility that frame drug use as a voluntary, hedonistic act."[14] While classifying addiction as a brain disease may be understandably upsetting to partners of sex addicts who believe their partners may use the "disease card" as an excuse for their behavior, viewing sex addiction through the lens of a disease model has important implications for the treatment approaches we use.

---

13 N. D. Volkow, "Neurobiologic Advances from the Brain Disease Model of Addiction," *The New England Journal of Medicine* 374, no. 4 (2016): 363–371.

14 Ibid.

CHAPTER 4

OTHER RISK FACTORS

The Genetic Component

IS THERE AN "ADDICTION GENE"?

We know genetics likely play a role in the development of alcoholism.[15] Although there is speculation that genetics may also play a role in the development of sex addiction, there is as yet no clear scientific evidence to support this. Although genetics may make some people more susceptible to developing addiction, susceptibility does not translate to inevitability.

Furthermore, genetics alone cannot explain addiction. Environmental and social factors also play a role. Even when addiction is kept secret, as is typically the case with sex addiction, people with active addiction tend to be preoccupied, emotionally unavailable to their families, and frequently absent physically in order to pursue their addiction. Addicts are often so self-absorbed they are not able to give their children the care and attention they need. Children may never see evidence of a parent's addiction but the consequent neglect, lack of emotional and often physical availability, and perhaps the imposition of demanding standards and harsh discipline may set the stage for addiction to develop as those children grow.

---

15 National Institute on Alcohol Abuse and Alcoholism, "Genetics of Alcohol Use Disorders," accessed September 20, 2016, http://www.niaaa.nih.gov/alcohol-health/overview-alcohol-consumption/alcohol-use-disorders/genetics-alcohol-use-disorders.

Psychological Risk Factors

....

My therapist said I should see a psychiatrist. Why would he suggest that?

....

Being evaluated by a psychiatrist prior to or at the beginning of recovery is generally recommended. This is part of the "due diligence" process to either confirm or rule out other problems that may impact problematic sexual behavior. The presence of certain conditions may help explain a wide variety of behaviors including compulsive sexual behavior. Psychological risk factors include attention deficit hyperactivity disorder, mood disorders like depression and bipolar disorder, obsessive-compulsive disorder, anxiety disorders, and personality disorders.

Attention Deficit Hyperactivity Disorder (ADHD)

....

My wife is convinced I have ADHD. Could this cause my sex addiction?

....

ADHD does not cause sex addiction, but ADHD and sex addiction often co-occur. Persons with ADHD have a stimulus-seeking brain. They seek out things that are stimulating or novel. They may have difficulty reading a book if the subject matter is not particularly stimulating or if a plot develops slowly. When a person has ADHD, they may tend to procrastinate and be good at starting projects but not good at finishing them.

Persons with ADHD have multiple, even racing thoughts that can shift their interest from one subject to another in rapid succession. As their thoughts move from subject to subject they may find themselves stuck in the limbo of inaction. One physician described his ADHD by saying, "bright shiny objects distract me."

So how does ADHD play into sex addiction? Sex is the ultimate stimulation. Fantasizing about sex may occupy hours of a person's time. Because pornography is so visually stimulating and there is so much of it available online, someone with ADHD can easily view pornography for hours at a time.

Video games provide much the same stimulation. Some sex addicts with ADHD spend hours playing video games before venturing into sexually oriented Internet activities. Before they are aware of it, they may be totally engrossed in a wide variety of sexually oriented Internet activities.

....

Will taking my medication for ADHD eliminate the need for me to attend twelve-step meetings?

....

No. Treating all co-occurring disorders is necessary for a person to have the greatest chance of success in recovery.

Mood Disorders

....

What part does depression play in sex addiction, and how does sex addiction affect depression?

....

Substance addiction and depression frequently co-occur. One third of people with major depressive disorder engage in substance abuse.[16] In the absence of studies related specifically to sex addiction, we assume the rate of co-occurring depression and sex addiction may well be as high. Our considerable experience working with sex addicts shows this to be true. Additionally, we know that the development and pursuit of sexual acting-out behaviors may predispose a person to developing significant depression. The cycle feeds on itself because sex addicts may seek relief from their depression by acting out sexually, and in the aftermath of compulsive sexual acting out, people often experience depression.

The presence of depression may make it difficult for some and impossible for others to remain sexually sober. (Sexual sobriety is achieved when one is able to live free from all of the problematic sexual behaviors that have brought harm to the addict and/or other people.) It is imperative for sex addicts who recognize symptoms of depression to be evaluated by a psychiatrist. Although any physician can diagnose and treat depression, the advanced diagnostic skills of a psychiatrist are most helpful in treating it. Treating depression will not curb sex addiction but it will make it possible for a person to engage in a successful recovery process.

---

16 L. Davis, A. Uezato, J. M. Newell, and E. Frazier, "Major Depression and Comorbid Substance Use Disorders," *Current Opinion in Psychiatry* 21, no. 1 (2008): 14–18.

I have been diagnosed with bipolar disorder. How does this impact my sex addiction?

Bipolar disorder is a mood disorder characterized by periods of elevated moods (mania) and periods of depression. To be diagnosed with Bipolar I a person needs to have at least one manic episode. Bipolar II is diagnosed if there is at least one hypomanic (literally "lesser mania" or "below mania") and one major depressive episode.

When a person with bipolar disorder has a manic episode, he or she may engage in extravagant shopping or enter into outlandish commercial ventures. He or she may also seek sexual adventures. A sex addict with bipolar disorder may be more inclined to engage in even higher risk sexual behavior during a manic episode than when there is no mania present. Bipolar disorder is a serious mental health disorder and usually requires mood-stabilizing medication prescribed by a psychiatrist.

Narcissism

Raymond's Story

Raymond is a born risk taker. He thrives on adventure and enjoys the accolades that he gets from telling others about his adventures: flying, diving, racing, hang gliding, rock climbing—whatever will get the adrenaline pumping.

He found that the more risks he took with his sexual acting out, the greater the high he experienced. On several occasions, he arranged for one of his partners to be in the same restaurant while he was having lunch with his wife. He surreptitiously made eye contact with her across the restaurant and even arranged to have her meet him by the restroom where he briefly kissed her.

On another occasion, he invited a neighbor and her husband to have dinner with him and his wife. He had been grooming this woman for months with overly friendly conversations and suggestive comments. During dinner, he removed his shoe and ran his foot up and down her legs. He was thrilled when he saw her blush and then grin.

As far as Raymond was concerned, he felt he could get away with just about anything. Raymond felt entitled to all of the fun that he wanted. He even told himself that if his wife were ever smart enough to catch him, he would not stop his acting-out behavior. He believed that she would never leave him.

....

I'm sure my husband is a narcissist. Is narcissism related to sex addiction?

....

The term narcissist comes from a character in Greek mythology—Narcissus—who fell in love with his own reflection in water. Sex addicts are very narcissistic in that they are self-centered and self-absorbed. What matters most to them is what they want and what makes them feel good in the moment.

Actually most individuals have some narcissistic traits, and to a degree these are healthy. It is important to look out for ourselves and our interests, to care about our appearance, to want to be successful in our careers, and to have others think well of us. In recovery, both sex addicts and wounded partners will necessarily exhibit some healthy narcissism where they place their own recovery above other interests.

While narcissism is a common factor in sex addiction, many partners seem to want to diagnose their sex addict partner with Narcissistic Personality Disorder, which is much more extreme and which I believe is seldom the case. I would strongly encourage you to leave all diagnosing to trained professionals.

Narcissistic and Other Personality Disorders

Narcissistic Personality Disorder (NPD) is a mental disorder in which people have an inflated sense of themselves and their own importance, along with a powerful need for admiration. Those with NPD give little consideration to the needs of others. They have a lack of empathy for other people, seeing themselves as special, unique, and unlike "ordinary" people. People with NPD tend to see themselves as victims and are offended by the slightest criticism. They often believe that the world owes them simply because of who they are. But, behind this mask of confidence is a fragile self-esteem. They often use people and love things, instead of loving people and using things. They tend to ignore boundaries and view people as objects to be exploited. According to the Diagnostic and Statistical Manual of Mental Disorders (DSM-IV-TR) NPD is diagnosed in between 2 percent and 16 percent of the population in clinical (treatment) settings.[17] The DSM-IV-TR suggests that between .5 percent and 1 percent of the general population has NPD, and that more men are diagnosed with NPD than women.[18]

If your husband is a sex addict and has NPD, it is unlikely that he will be willing to get help for either condition. He will likely see his extracurricular sexual behavior as something he is somehow owed. If he is willing to get help and sincerely shows *through action* that he is willing to do whatever it takes to restore your relationship, I believe that is evidence that, however narcissistic he may be, he does not have NPD.

What is empathy and how do I do it?

Empathy is the ability to put yourself in someone else's place and feel what they are feeling. It is the epitome of "walking in someone else's shoes." Empathy is very different from sympathy. Sympathy is feeling sorry for another's hurt or pain. Without empathy it is impossible to understand how someone else feels or what her or his experience is like.

If you are a sex addict, to have empathy for your partner, imagine how you would feel if your situations were reversed. How would you feel if you found out that she had been secretly engaged in the same behaviors as you? What would be going on in your mind if you found your world crumbling down around you? How would you feel if her behavior threatened to take away everything that you hold dear?

Society has imposed a certain definition of what it means to be a man. Being tough, resilient, unmoved by hardship, and never shedding tears may be some people's idea of masculinity, but such emotional detachment is poison to an intimate romantic relationship.

Empathy is related to "emotional intelligence," a term frequently used to describe a person's ability to tune in to and understand the feelings, motivations, and desires of others. Empathy can be learned. When you see your partner is sad, put aside your own feelings and ask yourself

---

17 American Psychiatric Association, *Diagnostic and Statistical Manual of Mental Disorders*, 4th ed. Text Revision (Arlington, VA: 2000).

18 Ibid.

what might she be feeling. Make it a priority to develop a deeper understanding of emotional intelligence. Give your all to studying empathy and how you can increase your awareness of others' feelings.

How did I become a sex addict?

It is usually impossible to identify specific causes for any individual's sex addiction. A number of the factors covered earlier may be involved. This question is located in the section on narcissism because, for some, the quest to find out why they became a sex addict is just another expression of their narcissism. This group believes they are so special that surely something extraordinary happened to them that can explain their sex addiction. However, the bottom line can be as simple as having had a difficult, challenging childhood and having coped with stress and emotional pain in unhealthy ways that became patterns and led to unhealthy decisions and actions. Regardless of the family background, through repetition unhealthy actions involving sex become habituated into the obsessive and compulsive patterns that lead to addiction. In general, this is how most people become sex addicts—there need not be anything especially unique about them or their background.

If I think my husband may have a personality disorder or some other form of mental illness, what should I do?

If there are signs of mental illness or mental instability, I strongly recommend getting a full battery of psychological testing by a clinical psychologist. The testing should include a Millon Clinical Multiaxial Inventory (MCMI-III) and Minnesota Multiphasic Personality Inventory-2 (MMPI-2), as well as other assessments and a clinical interview that will help a qualified professional make a formal diagnosis. Whenever possible, if a personality disorder or any other form of mental illness is suspected, it is important that this be either confirmed or ruled out through a comprehensive assessment process before proceeding with sex addiction treatment. The assessment results will help determine the best course of treatment.

I think I may have an abnormally high sex drive. Could my sexual behavior be a hormonal problem?

Persons who have abnormally high levels of sex hormones (androgens), or very high levels of certain neurotransmitters, such as dopamine, serotonin, or norepinephrine, may display an unusually high sex drive, known as hypersexuality. Additionally, some medications (such as dopamine agonists that are used to treat Parkinson's disease and restless leg syndrome) may cause hypersexual behavior. The presence of any of these factors needs to be considered prior to beginning sex addiction treatment.

True sex addiction has nothing to do with the level of a person's sex drive. Sex addicts can be obsessed with having sex or trying not to have sex. They may go from one sexual relationship to another, carrying a feeling that they cannot get enough sex. Some have sexual behavior so out of control they are physically exhausted from their sexual exploits and yet still feel that they must find someone else to be sexual with or perhaps masturbate to the point of injury. For them, too much sex is not enough. This is a hallmark of sex addiction; not an abnormally high sex drive.

CHAPTER 5

THE ROLE OF PORNOGRAPHY

Gregory's Story_____

Gregory had always been fascinated by technology. He loved computers and the access they granted him to the Internet. As a researcher for a top pharmaceutical company, he worked long hours staring into computer screens. By accident, he discovered pornography and found that he liked having brief diversions throughout the day. He rationalized that he was able to concentrate better after he indulged in what he called a bit of "recreational Internet use."

His world began coming apart when he was summoned to human resources and presented with a printout showing the number of hours he had been looking at pornography over the previous four months. He was astounded to learn that he was averaging more than five hours a day on porn sites, and some days as much as seven hours—all of it on work time.

Gregory has been out of work for the past two months and hopes to be able to get back into research with another company. Now, his days are spent searching the Internet for a job. To break up the boredom of that task, he occasionally seeks out pornography sites. He says that porn is not really a problem and that he can quit it if he wants. Gregory was appalled when his wife found his pornography stash on their computer and suggested that he may be addicted. He is sure that he is not an addict and has promised to stop.

Many, many people like Gregory believe that pornography is not harmful. They maintain this belief in spite of losing jobs, relationships, and self-respect. When evidence of their out-of-control behavior is presented to them they excuse it as a temporary problem.

According to Porn Hub, in 2015, 4,392,486,580 hours of pornography were viewed on the Internet. Pornography was streamed at a rate of seventy-five gigabytes per second. That's the equivalent of filling all of the available storage space on all smart phones sold in 2015 with pornography. Further, nearly 88 billion pornography videos were viewed. Averaged out, that's enough for every person on Earth to view twelve porn videos![19]

The Barna Group conducted a nationwide survey for ProvenMen.org[20] (a Christian-based organization) that included 1,000 households in the US. Ninety-two percent of those beginning the survey agreed to continue to the targeted questions. Here are some of the highlights of the study:

- Approximately two-thirds (64 percent) of US men view pornography at least monthly.

- The number of Christian men viewing pornography virtually mirrors the national average, and Christian men watch pornography at work at the same rate as the national average.

- Broken down by age:

  ⬧ Eight in ten (79 percent) men between the ages of eighteen and thirty view pornography monthly.

  ⬧ Two-thirds (67 percent) of men between the ages of thirty-one and forty-nine view pornography monthly.

---

19 Porn Hub, "2015: Year in Review," January 6, 2016, http://www.pornhub.com/insights/pornhub-2015-year-in-review.

20 J. Hesch, "2014 ProvenMen.org Pornography Addiction Survey," ProvenMen.org, 2014, http://www.provenmen.org/2014pornsurvey/pornography-use-and-addiction/#addiction.

❖ One-half (49 percent) of men between the ages of fifty and sixty-eight view pornography monthly.

• One-third (33 percent) of men between the ages of eighteen and thirty either think that they are addicted or are unsure if they are addicted to pornography.

• 18 percent of all men (approximately 21 million) either think that they are addicted or are unsure if they are addicted to pornography.

• More than four in ten men (44 percent) believe they should either view pornography less often or were unsure if they should view it less.[21]

What about you? How often do you view pornography? How many times have you tried to stop and failed? How many times have you promised your wife that you would quit only to be caught again in the same behavior?

Pornography can destroy your life. The more a person watches it, the more he feels he needs it. This is the essence of the addiction dynamic. The phenomenon of *tolerance* builds as images/videos that previously satisfied are no longer good enough. Immediate pleasure becomes more illusive over time. Images that once repulsed a person may become the norm as he searches for the perfect image to feed his fantasies as they progress. Satisfaction is increasingly difficult to come by and ever more short-lived.

Some men search for hours for a video that satisfies their particular sexual desires. They may employ programs that crawl the Internet in search of pornography that they save and catalog on multiple hard drives totaling many terabytes. Some have collected more pornography than they could view in a lifetime yet they continue searching, hoping to find some pornographic offering that will make them feel whole. Sadly, some of those who use such programs have been arrested for possessing child pornography, even though they were unaware their pornography crawlers had saved this illegal material.

---

21 Ibid.

Pornography can have such a hold on people that some lose job after job due to accessing porn at work. Others forfeit educational opportunities because pornography monopolizes their time and attention. Married men may be so addicted to pornography that they no longer find being sexual with their wives satisfying. It is often shocking to women to find out that their husbands are addicted to pornography because they express little or no desire to be sexual with their wives.

Recent research indicates that teens and young adults use pornography more than other groups. Young adults, ages eighteen to twenty-four, are both more likely to actively seek porn regularly and more likely to come across porn more often. Fifty-seven percent report seeking out porn at least once or twice a month, compared to 37 percent of teens, 43 percent of older Millennials, 41 percent of Gen-Xers, and 17 percent of Baby Boomers.[22]

Some people try to argue that pornography can be good for relationships or that within certain parameters pornography has value. Others say that pornography is helpful in that it can be a tool for sex education. A growing amount of data proves this is not the case.

The pornography industry has coalesced around themes of violence and female degradation.[23] Rather than educating people about healthy sexuality, pornography depicts sexuality as being base, degrading, and abusive. It is no wonder that people of all ages who regularly consume pornography have distorted views of sexuality.

A study was conducted of 487 college men between the ages of nineteen and twenty-nine to see if the pornography themes of violence and female degradation guided their sexual experiences. The results of the study indicate that the more pornography the men consumed, the more likely it was that they would request their partners to participate in activities they viewed. The study also found that the men would deliberately conjure up those pornographic images to maintain arousal during sex, and that the greater the use of pornography, the less the men enjoyed sex with their partners.[24]

---

22 Barna Group, "Teens & Young Adults Use Porn More Than Anyone Else," *Research Releases in Culture & Media*, January 28, 2016, https://www.barna.com/research/teens-young-adults-use-porn-more-than-anyone-else/#.V-MAjzsXb-0.

23 C. Sun, A. Bridges, J. A. Johnson, and M. Ezzell, "Pornography and the Male Sexual Script: An Analysis of Consumption and Sexual Relations," *Archives of Sexual Behavior*, 45, no. 4 (2016): 983–994, doi:10.1007/s10508-014-0391-2.

24 Ibid.

Two additional studies were conducted that involved nearly 2,000 college-age men. The study wanted to see if pornography had any impact on the practice of "hooking up"—that is, engaging in casual, high-risk sex with relative strangers. The studies found that the greater the study subject's use of pornography, the higher the incidence of hooking up.[25]

Is addiction to pornography different from sex addiction?

The short answer is no—addiction to pornography is simply a form of sex addiction. Sometimes people try to minimize their behavior by saying they "only" have an addiction to pornography. Sex addiction has many expressions and can take many forms. It is progressive and one type of sexual acting out often progresses to another.

Those who believe their addiction is not as bad as that of other people because their compulsive behavior has thus far been confined to viewing pornography need to take a more objective look at the consequences of their actions. Sex addiction, even when confined to viewing pornography, results in many of the following losses:

- Loss of integrity and transparency. Sexual acting out takes place in secret. In chasing an increasingly illusive "high," sex addicts descend into a world of secrets and hidden behaviors. They build a world filled with lies and deceit to cover their compulsive sexual behavior.

- Loss of or decrease in intimacy within a committed relationship. Partners of sex addicts often complain that there is little or no mutual sexual expression. Once sex addiction has been discovered, partners of sex addicts are genuinely perplexed, for their partner was not being sexual with them.

- Loss of time. As sex addiction progresses, more and more time is spent in pursuit of gratification through acting-out behaviors.

---

25 S. R. Braithwaite, G. Coulson, K. Keddington, and F. D. Fincham, "The Influence of Pornography on Sexual Scripts and Hooking Up among Emerging Adults in College," *Archives of Sexual Behavior* 44, no. 1 (January 2015): 111–123, doi: 10.1007/s10508-014-0351-x.

- Loss of self. Sex addicts are often filled with feelings of shame and regret. Promises are made to oneself that problem behaviors will not be repeated—followed by the repeated breaking of such promises. Feelings of self-loathing may predominate sex addicts' thoughts. These feelings spill over into relationships with partners, children, coworkers, and friends.

- Loss of community. Isolation is one of the hallmarks of addiction. In order to get the time needed to engage in acting out, sex addicts gradually pull themselves away from people with whom they were once close. Often, they have no true friends.

- Loss of connection with one's children. Sex addicts are often mentally and emotionally absent, even when they are physically present with family.

- Loss of interest in things that once brought joy and pleasure. Hobbies and other interests are common casualties of sex addiction. Many sex addicts complain that they are overworked and do not have time for the things they enjoyed in the past. In truth, the voracious appetite of their addiction has stolen their availability.

- Loss of serenity—individually and within the family system. Any semblance of internal peace or serenity is displaced by preoccupation, cravings, obsessive thoughts, and compulsive behaviors. Peacefulness in the family is replaced by quarreling or stressful silence. Tension is present whenever there is an active sex addict in the home. Children may think they are unloved because sex addicts seem to be on edge whenever they ask questions. Partners may feel marginalized because sex addicts are consumed with themselves and their own interests.

- Loss of reputation (sometimes). The consumption of pornography, while usually done in secret, often becomes public when discovered by others. Coworkers and wounded partners may take delight in telling others of the disturbing images discovered. Teachers, physicians, clergy, and other helping professionals lose credibility when their pornography viewing habits are made public. Some cannot continue in their chosen profession because of the damage to their reputation.

- Loss of jobs (sometimes). In an age where companies carefully monitor employees' computer use, it is still surprising that many people continue to take the risk of viewing pornography at work on company computers. Even those who use their own electronic devices find that employers take exception to using company time to indulge in pornography.

- Loss of freedom (sometimes). There are people in prison today because their pornography use included child pornography. Possessing child pornography is against the law, and local, state, and federal law enforcement continues to engage in campaigns to protect minors from exploitation and abuse. Targeting those who use child pornography is one of the tactics used in this battle. As of this writing, California enacted a law (AB-1775) requiring therapists to report clients who report viewing even one image of child pornography. Other states are now considering similar legislation.

  The unfortunate aspect about these laws is that people who seek the help of therapists to get free from sex addiction may place themselves in legal jeopardy if they discuss having viewed child pornography. To counter this, therapists who treat sex addiction are amending their informed consent agreements to warn clients that such admissions will result in a mandated report to the appropriate authorities.

- Loss of life (sometimes). As losses mount, depression grows. Some sex addicts become acutely desperate as the consequences of sex addiction mount and their world crumbles. Suicide may seem like a way out, and some people take their own lives. If you ever feel that the solution is to end your life, reach out to a therapist, call 911, or contact the National Suicide Prevention Hotline at 1-800-273-TALK (8255). If you are outside the United States, go to www.iasp.info or www.befrienders.org.

Trying to draw a distinction between sex addiction and "only" being addicted to pornography is another form of denial—a futile attempt to convince oneself and others that the addiction is manageable and benign. Sex addiction is a monster that wants to consume everything that is of true value.

Can pornography cause erectile dysfunction (ED)?

While there are no scholarly studies or definitive research to indicate this, the experience of many sex addicts is that there is indeed a link between their erectile difficulties and their consumption of pornography. These individuals report that while they are able to get an erection and masturbate while looking at pornography, they cannot get an erection with their partner. These reports come from young men as well as older men.

An increasing number of therapists and physicians report that their patients suffer from erectile dysfunction with no identifiable medical reason for it. So far, there are no studies that can prove that pornography causes erectile dysfunction. But we do know that 30 percent of men eighteen to thirty years of age complain of erectile dysfunction.[26] While there may be a lack of empirical data that proves pornography can cause erectile dysfunction, there are numerous online forums where young men openly discuss their pornography use and the difficulty they have being able to be sexual with another person.

Those who suffer from erectile dysfunction will want to seek out the help of a urologist to rule out any physical/medical problems. In the absence of research that verifies a link between pornography and ED, we are left with the experiences of many sex addicts who report a return to normal erectile function after getting into recovery and stopping all pornography use.

Can pornography harm my marriage?

Many partners have told me (Milton) that they feel their husbands are being unfaithful by looking at pornography. This is difficult for many men to comprehend because they feel that, as long as real people are not involved, they are not being unfaithful. During disclosures, it often comes out that men whose acting out is confined to pornography use and compulsive masturbation are having very little sex with their wives.

---

26 A. Mialon and A. Berchtold, "Sexual Dysfunctions among Young Men: Prevalence and Associated Factors," *Journal of Adolescent Health* 51, no. 1 (July, 2012): 25–31.

These women are frequently shocked to find out that there was a lot of sex going on—selfish, self-satisfying sex—that doesn't involve them.

As this manuscript was being prepared to go to press, professors Samuel Perry and Cyrus Schleifer from the University of Oklahoma, presented the results of a longitudinal study on the effects of pornography on divorce, to the American Sociological Association. Their research sought to learn whether those who began using pornography during the study period experienced any difference in divorce rate compared to those who did not use pornography. They found that, "Beginning pornography use between survey waves nearly doubled one's likelihood of being divorced by the next survey period, from 6 percent to 11 percent."[27]

A Further Note on Pornography

Contrary to how many people rationalize their use of pornography, it is not victimless. Although some of the women and men portrayed in pornographic pictures or videos participate voluntarily and profit from it, many who participate in the porn industry are looking for a way out of their problems and are desperate enough to subject themselves to degrading circumstances. They may be addicted to drugs and need money to feed their addiction. Some live in parts of the world where human life is cheap and they can never hope to make more than a few dollars a day. The promise of what may be more money than they have ever seen to participate in pornography can be a powerful lure.

It is common for those who participate in a single pornographic film or video to be so devastated from the degradation and loss of self-respect that they quit the adult film industry altogether. Yet, the damage has already been done to their sense of self. They cannot take back the images of themselves, now forever on the Internet; forever fearful they could be discovered in the future by someone they love.

Pornography passively promotes prostitution. Even though much of the pornography available today can be viewed for free, the models used to produce pornography are generally paid for sexual acts—this is the heart

---

27 Samuel Perry, et al., "Till Porn Do Us Part? Longitudinal Effects of Pornography Use on Divorce," paper presented at 111th Annual Meeting of the American Sociological Association, Seattle, August 22, 2016, http://www.eurekalert.org/pub_releases/2016-08/asa-bpu081616.php.

of prostitution. Viewing any pornography supports an industry focused on exploiting vulnerable women, men, and children. It is interesting that even some people who are the most vocal in denouncing the exploitation of others will minimize the contribution they make with regard to victimizing others through their own use of pornography.

CHAPTER 6

THE PROGRESSION OF SEX ADDICTION

Julian's Story_____

Julian did not set out to become a sex addict. He remembers learning to masturbate at age ten after a classmate told him how. He was soon masturbating daily and multiple times on some days. Julian did not see his first pornography until he was almost out of high school. He said he was hooked from the first video he watched and could not seem to get enough.

When he married at age twenty-three, Julian was sure he would be able to stop masturbating and viewing pornography. For a few years, he seemed to have his sexual desires under control. He and his wife had an active and satisfying sex life.

Julian stumbled onto a website that had classified listings of people who offered sexual services through spas, massage parlors, modeling studios, and photography studios. On a lark, he decided to take his camera to a photography studio, hoping he could take photos of a nude woman. Instead he found the studio was just a cover for a brothel, and that day he engaged his first prostitute.

Trying to keep this new behavior to a minimum, Julian determined that he would not spend more than $100 a month on it but soon *he was finding ways to stretch his budget and was making multiple visits to prostitutes each month. Recently, Julian was arrested after he agreed online to pay for sex from a girl who said she was sixteen but was very mature for her age. Subsequent to his arrest, Julian's wife filed for divorce. He is now awaiting trial being charged with the solicitation of a minor.*

Not every sex addict will progress to illegal behaviors. In fact, most sex addicts do not ever commit a sexual offense—that is engage in sexual behavior that includes rape, incest, or sex with minors. Yet, the reality is that sex addiction is a progressive chronic intimacy disorder in which the addictive behaviors, the amount of time devoted to the addiction, and the risks taken generally escalate over time. One sexual behavior often leads to another and sometimes to whole new categories of acting out.

Sex addiction frequently takes a person to a depth of depravity and personal degradation that he or she would not have believed possible. As the addiction progresses addicts stand on a precipice, measure the jump, and invariably underestimate how far they will fall.

Masturbation

At the risk of offending Shakespeare enthusiasts, "To masturbate or not to masturbate. That is the question." The recovery community is divided on whether masturbation is a problematic behavior for sex addicts. Sex addiction therapists are also in disagreement as to whether masturbation can or should be a part of life for a sex addict who is in recovery.[28]

....

There is a lot of talk about whether masturbation for sex addicts is healthy or not. If your spouse is all right with masturbation and you are both open about it, is it okay?

....

Partners would certainly prefer their sexually addicted partner masturbate rather than engage in sex with other people. Early in

---

28 For a more thorough discussion on masturbation, see the chapter "Day 27: The 'M' Question," in M. Magness, *Thirty Days to Hope & Freedom from Sexual Addiction: The Essential Guide to Beginning Recovery and Preventing Relapse* (Carefree, AZ: Gentle Path Press, 2010).

recovery, both sex addicts and their partners may not have any problem with masturbation.

With masturbation, one partner uses sexual energy on himself or herself that could be focused on the couple. When I ask recovering couples how often they have sex with each other and whether the frequency is about right or they wish it were more or less frequent, most respond that they wish they were sexual more often. In virtually all of these couples, before recovery the sex addict was masturbating several times a month to as many as several times a day, with most addicts endorsing masturbation two to three times a week. The easiest solution for these couples was to eliminate or significantly reduce sex with self so the available sexual energy can be focused on the relationship.

Partners of sex addicts may suggest that masturbation is okay when fantasizing about the spouse. However, sex addicts are still objectifying and reducing their partner to a sex object. It's important to be aware that sex addicts in recovery often struggle with their thoughts to keep fantasy—even about one's partner—from leading to other forms of acting out.

....

As a sex addict, how do I determine if masturbation is healthy or not?
....

Proponents would say that masturbation may be healthy if fantasy is not the fuel for it. Others would say that it is healthy if it only happens with a certain frequency. Still others suggest that masturbation is fine so long as pornography is not involved.

One of the core beliefs of sex addicts is that sex is their most important need. Looking for rationalizations to continue to masturbate is another expression of a sex addict's need to keep the focus on sex. Preoccupation with masturbation is indication enough that this activity has elevated importance.

Is masturbation helpful in maintaining healthy thoughts or does it exacerbate problem thinking—as characterized in the twelve-step phrase, "stinking thinking"? Has masturbation led to greater sexual intimacy with your spouse or caused you to isolate more?

Occasionally, chronic masturbation leads to physical problems, such as premature ejaculation (PE). In such cases, simply discontinuing masturbation may not be enough to correct PE. There are numerous approaches that may help PE, including applying a small amount of benzocaine or other topical anesthetic to the glans of the penis.

It's important to have your condition evaluated by a urologist to rule out any medical problems and learn about medical options, including taking certain medications used for treating depression (like SSRIs, selective serotonin reuptake inhibitors) that have the side effect of inhibiting sexual arousal. A next step would be to see a sex therapist knowledgeable about sex addiction. Sex therapists can suggest other options that may be helpful in treating PE.

....

In recovery from sex addiction, when is masturbation considered a relapse?

....

Sex addicts in recovery must decide what behaviors are problematic for them. There are twelve-step fellowships (like Sexaholics Anonymous) that strictly define any sex outside of a marriage, including masturbation, as a breach of sobriety. Other fellowships encourage each sex addict to define sobriety for himself.

There are advantages and potential pitfalls to each approach. There is structure and a degree of comfort in having the fellowship or group determine what is healthy and what is not, including what constitutes a relapse. Sometimes the members of these fellowships adopt positions that closely parallel religious teachings familiar to them. As a result, they perpetuate a taboo or "thou shalt not" approach to some forms of sexuality that made these activities more attractive in the first place and may have been a factor in the development of sex addiction for some.

Critics of twelve-step fellowships that give each member the responsibility to determine for himself or herself what is healthy or unhealthy, and in turn what constitutes sobriety, rightly point out the potential to use such personal definitions to avoid accountability.

Ultimately, each person has to take a candid look at masturbation and the extent to which it enhances or hinders his recovery. Regardless of what twelve-step fellowship one attends, each recovering person has to decide for himself or herself how recovery will be approached.

Same Sex Behaviors

When it comes to sex addiction, questions concerning same-sex acting-out behaviors are common.

....

I just found out my husband has been having sex with men. I am more devastated by this than by learning he's had sex with many female prostitutes. How can I compete with a man? Does this mean my husband is gay?

....

It sounds as though your husband's sexual behavior has been focused on heterosexual acting out until recently. It is entirely possible that rather than being gay your husband has continued pushing the boundaries of his acting out trying to achieve the same neurochemical high he experienced in the past but can no longer get from his old behaviors. Some heterosexual men progress to sex with other men seeking avenues of acting out that are novel or are more "forbidden" to heighten the rush they get.

With substance addiction, through the continuing use of alcohol and other drugs, addicts develop a *tolerance* so that over time an ever-increasing amount of the drug is needed to produce the same neurochemical high. Similarly, sex addicts have to continually ramp up the intensity of their acting out in order to get the high they seek. For example, sex addicts who concentrate on pornography may start out with porn that primarily depicts nudity and the suggestion of sexual behavior. This may progress to harder core pornography that includes actual and varied sex acts, and then to pornography that graphically illustrates various fetishes. A sex addict may gravitate toward images that once disgusted him in order to produce the desired level of sexual excitement.

Occasionally, I hear women express relief in finding out that their husbands were acting out with men. Regardless of whether a spouse sees same-sex acting out as more or less harmful to the relationship, it is important for couples in this circumstance to get help from a sex addiction therapist to work through the complicated issues involved.[29]

Does sex addiction lead to homosexuality?

There are no studies to even suggest that this could be true.

Does past sexual abuse impact gender preference in sex addiction?

Sex addicts who were sexually abused as children may reenact the trauma they experienced through their sexual acting out. Those abused by someone of the same sex may reenact those sexual experiences later in life, and yet not have a physical attraction to people of the same sex.

Trauma reenactment occurs subconsciously. Sometimes trauma victims seek to repeat their exact trauma. It is crucial that people caught up in reenacting their traumatic experiences get help from a skilled therapist to work through these repetitive compulsions.

My husband condemns inter-racial relationships, same-sex relationships, and viewing child pornography. Now I find out these are his acting-out behaviors. Can you explain this contradiction?

It sounds like your husband is torn between beliefs he learned early in life and attractions he has developed. As noted earlier, when sex addiction progresses addicts pursue forms of sexual acting out that are different or more "forbidden" to heighten the high they get. It's also helpful to understand that one of the ways people try to deflect attention from their own behavior is to loudly condemn the same behavior in others. Additionally, your husband may think that his condemnation of these behaviors will help him to stop them.

If indeed your husband views child pornography, it is imperative that this behavior stops immediately. If he is in possession of child

---

29 www.findachfp.com, www.sash.net, and www.sexhelp.com list therapists who specialize in working with sex addicts and their families.

pornography, even a single image or single video, he runs the risk of being arrested and prosecuted.

Sexual Offending

Some people may confuse the term sex addict with sex offender. This unfortunate misperception only adds to the stigma surrounding sex addiction and prevents many people from facing their addiction. Sex offenders are individuals who have committed actual crimes, such as involvement with (including viewing) child pornography, sexual behavior with minors, sexual assault/rape, or incest. However, sex addiction is very different from sexual offending and the vast majority of sex addicts do not ever commit a sexual offense. Of course, there are occasional examples of sex addicts who have committed sexual offenses. Moreover, most sex offenders do not meet the clinical criteria for sex addiction. Rather, sex offenders tend to have deep-seated mental disorders that require specialized treatment and continual monitoring throughout life.

My husband is a sex addict and now I am worried he may harm my teenage daughter. Is she at risk?

Although there is no correlation between sex addiction and sexual offending, in the abstract, it is impossible to know whether she is at risk or not. Is she a biological daughter or a step-daughter? Statistically speaking, it is less likely for a father to perpetrate on a biological daughter. However, since you raise the question of risk, have you noticed any specific behavior on the part of your husband or your daughter that makes you concerned?

Your job as a parent is to protect your children from harm. If your concern continues, you may want to consult with a professional. Healthy boundaries between your daughter and your husband are important, including appropriate dress and avoiding any sexual talk or jokes.

The progression of sex addiction is fueled by factors that include denial and self-deception, minimization, terminal uniqueness, and procrastination.

Denial and Self-Deception

Sex addicts lie—a lot. They lie to their spouses. They lie to their other family members. They lie to their friends. Often, they even lie to their therapists. But the greatest lies are the lies they tell themselves. Addicts of all varieties have advanced skills at self-deception. For a sex addict, lying to oneself is as common as lying to others.

Denial is a psychological defense mechanism that helps protect people from too much anxiety and emotional pain. Denial is different from dishonesty. Denial operates at an unconscious level outside of one's awareness, whereas people know when they are lying or otherwise being dishonest. In our society there is stigma attached to every form of addiction. No one wants to be thought of by others, or admit to oneself, that he or she is an addict. Addicts live in denial as long as they can deflect the truth about their addiction. Even when faced with evidence of their addiction, sex addicts typically do all within their power to deny it—to themselves as well as to others. They may even deny they participated in particular behaviors when irrefutable evidence to the contrary exists.

Minimization

Minimization is another defense mechanism sex addicts employ. Through minimizing sex addicts attempt to discount the frequency and severity of their acting-out behaviors. They may compare their behavior to others and conclude that they are not "as bad" and therefore are not sexually addicted. For example, those who act out with pornography may respond that they are not sex addicts because they have not been sexual with people. Those who act out in strip clubs or massage parlors may claim they are not sex addicts because they have never had an affair. Sex addicts who have had multiple affairs may believe they are not sexually addicted because they have never paid for sex.

Terminal Uniqueness

Even after sex addicts get past their denial and minimization and begin to come to terms with the reality of their addiction they may resist going to twelve-step meetings, working with a therapist, entering treatment, and engaging in a process of recovery, believing they are "not like other sex addicts." They may think they are smarter, not as depraved, or more disciplined than other sex addicts.

When they finally agree to get help, many sex addicts continue to struggle with denial, minimization, and resistance. If a therapist recommends inpatient treatment, a sex addict may believe that his uniqueness qualifies him for a shorter or less intensive treatment program. When he does begin attending twelve-step meetings and hears about the importance of getting a sponsor, he believes he doesn't need one. If he does get a sponsor who strongly suggests following the standard recommendation for those new to twelve-step recovery to attend ninety meetings in ninety days to help establish a foundation of sobriety, he concludes that he only needs to attend one or two meetings a week. Such individuals want to believe they are so special that they can figure out a better way of doing recovery than following a program that has worked for multitudes of other people.

The term used to describe this condition in twelve-step programs is "terminal uniqueness." This is another expression of the narcissism that contributed to the development of their sex addiction. Sex addicts have to work through these faulty beliefs before they can fully engage in recovery.

Procrastination

When will recovery begin? Or for those supposedly in recovery, when will they get serious enough to take the actions necessary to change their attitudes and behavior and stop their acting out more permanently? The Spanish word mañana best captures the procrastination of some sex addicts. Although the word can be translated as tomorrow, it is understood that action is being put off until sometime in the unspecified future. That may mean tomorrow but more likely it will happen considerably later. In order to overcome their procrastination, many addicts need to be confronted directly with the consequences of putting off taking action toward recovery.

Sex Addiction's Relationship to Other Forms of Addiction

Further complicating sex addiction is the fact that it may not occur by itself. Addicts may have significant challenges in other areas of life.

Alcohol and other drug addiction may co-occur with sex addiction. Some sex addicts struggle with gambling, eating disorders, shopping or spending addiction, or addiction to video games.

A desire to escape is a significant contributing factor in the development of addiction. Addiction Interaction Disorder is a term introduced by Patrick Carnes, PhD, to describe a condition where various forms of addiction are clustered together. His research indicates that addictions not only coexist but interact with one another.[30]

When multiple forms of addiction are present, addicts may focus on one at a time. If sex addiction is getting out of hand, they concentrate on stopping the sexual acting out while their addiction to gambling becomes unmanageable. If alcohol or other drugs are seen as the primary problem, sex addiction may go unchecked until the negative consequences of acting out force them to refocus.

Some twelve-step meetings for alcohol or other drug addiction may discourage members from speaking about sex addiction in those meetings. Sex addiction may be present and even be the primary addiction for many alcoholics and other drug addicts but may go undetected because the emphasis is on staying away from booze or other drugs. Some twelve-step meetings focusing on alcohol or other drugs may wink at addicts taking the so-called "thirteenth step" of hooking up with other members of the group for sexual liaisons. So long as members do not drink or use other drugs, they are considered sober or "clean." Such singleness of purpose may allow sex addiction to go undetected.

CHAPTER 7

GENERAL QUESTIONS ABOUT SEX ADDICTION

....

How common is sex addiction?

....

The Society for the Advancement of Sexual Health[31] has estimated that 3–6 percent of the population of the United States suffers from sex addiction. This percentage is based on the number of people who present for treatment. Since addicts usually avoid treatment as long as they possibly can, the actual number may be significantly higher.

Some people try to emphasize the magnitude of sex addiction by quoting statistics that are much greater, but have little foundation in research. If we take the minimum of the best estimates we have, there are at least 9.5 million sex addicts in the United States—equal to the combined populations of the states of Alaska, Montana, North and South Dakota, Wyoming, Vermont, Delaware, and Rhode Island.

If we factor in the number of spouses/partners who have been wounded by sex addicts and the children of sex addicts who have been damaged, the numbers escalate considerably. Sex addiction is a huge problem in our society.

---

31 www.sash.net.

Is sex addiction a real disease?

As with alcohol and other drug addiction, sex addiction is generally treated using a "disease model." However, like gambling addiction, it is a *process* or behavioral addiction that does not involve psychoactive substances. Whereas sex addiction causes changes in the brains of those afflicted with it, and its progression resembles a disease process, its classification as a disease continues to be controversial.

Accepting sex addiction as a disease may also give some sex addicts an excuse or rationalization for their behavior. Confronted with their sexual acting out they say, "I can't help it, I have a disease." Some partners of sex addicts think that referring to sex addiction as a disease minimizes addicts' responsibility for their behavior. Although their compulsive behavior may be out of control, as stated earlier, sex addicts are always responsible for their behavior. It's most accurate to consider sex addiction a disorder.

What are the criteria for diagnosis of sex addiction?

Currently there are no definitive diagnostic criteria for sex addiction. However, most sex addiction therapists look for the following in diagnosing sex addiction:

- Preoccupation with and frequent cravings for sex
- Obsessive thoughts about sexual fantasies to the point of excluding other thoughts
- Lack of interest in activities that once were important
- Desire to spend more time alone than interacting with others
- Engaging in excessive sexual behaviors despite efforts to stop and negative consequences associated with such behavior
- Neglecting obligations like work, school, or family in order to pursue sexual interests
- Feelings of irritability when not able to engage in sexual behavior
- Escalation of the scope of sexual behaviors or time spent pursuing and participating in sexual acting out

The presence of just a few of these is enough to indicate that a person should consider receiving treatment for sex addiction.

A recently developed screening tool called PATHOS[32] is a brief questionnaire that health professionals can use to identify the presence of sex addiction. PATHOS is an acronym for six assessment questions:

P: Preoccupied—Do you often find yourself preoccupied with sexual thoughts?

A: Ashamed—Do you hide some of your sexual behavior from others?

T: Treatment—Have you ever sought therapy for sexual behavior you did not like?

H: Hurt others—Has anyone been hurt emotionally because of your sexual behavior?

O: Out of control—Do you feel controlled by your sexual desire?

S: Sad—When you have sex, do you feel depressed afterwards?

A positive response to just one of the six questions indicates a need for additional assessment with a sex addiction therapist. Answering yes to two or more is a strong indication that the person is a sex addict.

In *Stop Sex Addiction*[33] I suggested a two-question assessment:

1. Have you engaged in sexual behavior that has harmed you or others?

2. Did you repeat that behavior?

Although not all who answer "yes" to both of these questions are sex addicts, when answering honestly, all sex addicts answer yes to both. How would you answer these questions?

---

32 P. J. Carnes, B. A. Green, L. J. Merlo, A. Polles, S. Carnes, and M. S. Gold, "PATHOS: A Brief Screening Application for Assessing Sexual Addiction," *Journal of Addiction Medicine* 6, no. 1 (2012): 29–34, doi: 10.1097/ADM.0b013e3182251a28.

33 Milton Magness, *Stop Sex Addiction: Real Hope, True Freedom for Sex Addicts and Partners* (Las Vegas: Central Recovery Press, 2013).

Why is sex addiction not listed in the DSM-5?

The *Diagnostic and Statistical Manual of Mental Disorders, Fifth Edition* (*DSM-5*), is the comprehensive classification and diagnostic manual published by the American Psychiatric Association. Sex addiction was listed in the third edition published in 1980 but was removed in the fourth edition published in 1994. In preparation for the publication of the fifth edition in 2013, a committee of academic and clinical experts debated whether to include sex addiction in some form. There were several hurdles to overcome. First, the *DSM* does not use the term *addiction*. Alcohol and other drug addiction is covered under the term *substance use disorder*. The committee grappled with terms for out-of-control sexual behavior and finally settled on "hypersexual disorder." They conducted clinical trials in conjunction with several treatment centers trying to amass the data needed to have sex addiction included in the *DSM-5*. In the end, there was simply not enough data for it to be included.

Regardless of its lack of inclusion in the *DSM-5*, those who struggle with problematic sexual behavior, those whose lives are negatively impacted by sexual acting out, and those of us who strive to help them have no doubt that sex addiction is a very real disorder.

What is the difference between sex addiction and love addiction?

Sex addiction and love addiction are both disorders of intimacy. Sex addicts tend to be more interested in specific sexual acts where love addicts are more interested in having a relationship with others. Some love addicts and some sex addicts will engage in sexual behaviors with multiple partners. And some sex and love addicts never engage in sexual behaviors with others. Dr. Brenda Schaeffer has written the seminal work on love addiction: *Is It Love or Is It Addiction?*[34] I would encourage you to read it for a fuller explanation.

Love addicts look for the next relationship that is going to fill the void in their lives. They are continuously searching for an ideal person that will make their life more meaningful—that they think will make

---

34 Brenda Schaeffer, *Is It Love or Is It Addiction?* (Center City, MN: Hazelden, 2009).

them whole. As they focus on their intended target, they may be very charming and solicitous. But when love addicts are successful in their quest they typically find that the person they pursued is not the right person for them after all, and begin their search all over again. Often, love addicts will not end that relationship so as to avoid being alone, continuing it as they seek a new ideal partner.

Also, some sex addicts choose to describe their addiction as love addiction in an effort to minimize their shame and the greater stigma associated with sex addiction.

What is the difference between sex addiction and being polyamorous?

Polyamorous means "many loves." Although I (Milton) do not believe polyamory is healthy, a chief difference between it and sex addiction is in the presence or absence of honesty. Those who practice true polyamory believe in openness and transparency, including the knowledge and consent of all partners involved. Obviously, this is not the case with sex addiction, where so much of the relevant behavior is secretive and cloaked in dishonesty.

Using the label of polyamory in the attempt to dress up or rationalize sex addiction does not lessen its destructive impact on oneself or others.

Is there a relationship Between IQ and sex addiction?

There have been no published studies that indicate a relationship between a person's level of intelligence and sex addiction. In our practices, we see sex addicts with a wide range of intelligence from those who appear to have low IQs to extremely intelligent persons who have earned multiple graduate degrees. Sex addiction does not discriminate with regard to intelligence.

Is there a relationship between wealth and sex addiction?

Sex addiction does not discriminate with regard to socioeconomic status. That being said, wealthy sex addicts often maintain the belief that, because they have incomes that set them apart from the majority of people, they are not like "ordinary people," and that their wealth makes them somehow "superior." This narcissism and grandiosity can drive the expectation that they should have whatever they want; whatever gives them pleasure. When this dynamic is extended to sex, the likelihood that someone will become caught up in sex addiction is increased.

What makes it so difficult for people with sex addiction to ask for help, even when they obviously need it?

Shame, guilt, embarrassment, denial, and minimization are the greatest hindrances to seeking help for both sex addicts and their partners. The shame is often so great that many people suffering from sex addiction will never seek help until they feel as though they have no choice. When people admit they have a problem and need help, they need to take responsibility for it and actually do something about it. This is extremely scary and emotionally painful, so it's no surprise that most people avoid it for as long as they can. As more brave people step forward with the willingness to talk about their recovery and healing from sex addiction—both addicts and their partners—more of those who are suffering with this disorder will mobilize the courage to seek help.

What is the difference between guilt and shame?

Guilt is the emotional experience people have when they believe or recognize they have done something "wrong." Feeling guilt because of poor decisions you have made and because of the trail of pain and destruction you created in your sex addiction is healthy.

Guilt is an important emotion to have in recovery because it is closely related to remorse. There are people who are incapable of feeling guilt because they suffer from antisocial personality disorder sometimes referred to as sociopathy. They lack the ability to feel remorse or to express empathy. Be grateful if you feel guilt for how you have harmed yourself and others.

Shame is more characterological. Shame results from feeling there is something wrong, not just with one's actions, but with who one is as a person. It is the belief that one is somehow inherently defective. Whereas guilt produces remorse and regret, shame results in self-loathing. Put another way, guilt is an acknowledgment of having done something that is "bad." Shame is a judgment that "I am a bad person." Guilt is helpful to recovery. Shame undercuts recovery.

What is being done to educate the general public about sex addiction?

This book and the many other books written over the past few decades are part of the education process. Organizations like the Society for the Advancement of Sexual Health (SASH)[35] seek to bring awareness of the scope of sex addiction. Additionally, our websites[36] contain a great deal of material about sex addiction, the trauma of partners of sex addicts, and treatment for both addicts and partners, as well as hope for the future.

How could I have participated in behaviors that are so contrary to my faith and values?

Sex addicts who have a strong personal faith fight with their conscience much of the time. After each acting-out episode, they are filled with regret, remorse, and self-loathing. They make deals with themselves that they will never do those behaviors again. They pray and make promises they intend to honor. But, much more often than not, they end up breaking those promises and return to engaging in the same and sometimes more extreme behaviors.

Engaging in behaviors that are inconsistent with your beliefs does not nullify your faith. If it were a matter of personal faith and/or personal strength or willpower, many people would simply stop all acting out permanently. However, faith, strength, and willpower have little to do with what happens once the addictive process begins and brain chemistry changes as people become progressively caught in the

---

35 www.sash.net.

36 www.acircleofjoy.com and www.hopeandfreedom.com.

obsessive-compulsive grip of sexual acting out. The only thing that explains why people continue to engage in behaviors they desperately want to stop is that they are addicted.

A significant number of those I (Milton) work with are clergy from various faith perspectives. Without exception, each of these men are in great mental anguish knowing that their acting-out behaviors stand in opposition to everything they believe. In their desire to change, all of them increased their spiritual disciplines and prayer life. Still, they acted out—not because their faith was not strong enough, but because of their untreated sex addiction.

How does sex addiction affect a person's self-esteem?

Sex addicts who are active in their addiction often have significant problems with their self-esteem. Outwardly, they may present a persona of confidence and superiority. They may look like they succeed in every other area of life.

Their self-esteem suffers because:

- They are participating in behaviors they loathe in others.
- They recognize (at least deep down) that their behavior is not only harming themselves but others.
- They realize their many attempts to stop have been unsuccessful.
- They must live in a shadow world to keep others from knowing about their behavior.
- They habitually lie to those who mean the most to them and must continue their duplicity in order to keep their behavior hidden.

If I become successful at not acting out, will I still always be a sex addict?

Sex addiction must be treated for life. As with other forms of addiction, we speak of sex addicts as "recovering" rather than being "recovered." A person who is recovering recognizes the importance of remaining vigilant and continuing to practice taking care of oneself mentally, emotionally, physically, and spiritually throughout life in order to keep the addiction at bay. Those who believe they have recovered frequently become complacent and run the risk of returning to their problematic sexual behaviors.

There is an acknowledgment in the terms "sex addiction" and "sex addict" that this is a disorder to take seriously and needs thoughtful and ongoing recovery efforts. But, beyond the addict and his partner, such terms may stop being helpful and become pejorative. In some contexts, talking about behavior may be more useful. If a sex addict has the need to talk about the damage he has caused in his addiction, he can speak about his behaviors and how he has hurt others.

It needs to be stressed that a person always maintains a right to privacy. What and with whom one shares are strictly up to each individual. There is no obligation to tell the public, casual friends, or even close friends about one's addiction. The exception to this is when a sex addict gets into a committed relationship. Partners have a right to know about the past, as well as current struggles of someone with whom they are considering entering a relationship.

FREEDOM

HOPE

CHAPTER 8

QUESTIONS ABOUT SEX ADDICTION FROM PARTNERS

Why didn't I see the signs before? How could his addiction remain hidden for so many years? Am I a fool or naive to not have seen it earlier?

The reason you did not see signs of addiction is likely because your husband was so skilled at deceiving you. Sex addicts become masters of deception in order to keep their addiction hidden. Many partners tell me (Milton) there were absolutely no signs of addiction in their husbands, and no way they could have known. Their husbands were tidy and careful, leaving no tracks that could lead to discovery. Then one day they got sloppy and the truth was out. In these marriages, there were no "signs" and no way to know. If your marriage falls into this category, don't search for self-blame because there is no way you could have known.

And others can only see the signs with the benefit of hindsight after the sex addiction has been discovered. When the truth spills out, suddenly past behaviors and situations make sense.

Although each of us wishes we could have known and prevented the heartache and loss in the first place, all we can do is acknowledge, accept, and adapt to our new reality, going forward from where we now find ourselves.

Of course, some partners are faced with the evidence of addiction and ignore it. They see clear signs of acting out but choose not to connect the dots. This is often how denial and minimization work for partners, and it enables sex addicts to continue pursuing their addiction. However, most of the partners with whom we have worked were not in denial, being naive, or choosing not to see the addiction. They were truly deceived. In retrospect, many women see the signs of addiction and think they should have done something about it sooner. Their only error was in trusting someone that proved to be untrustworthy.

How could he have hidden the electronic tracks of his acting out so well?

Sex addicts use many techniques to hide their acting out. They erase their browsing history and erase their text messages. Many browsers offer a "private" setting that does not keep the history so that someone logging on after them will not see evidence of their Internet viewing. There are multiple smartphone apps that allow calls and texts to be sent without using the programs that are native to that phone. They may even erase these apps after use and then reinstall them later to continue clandestine conversations. Smartphones can be reset, defeating any installed blocking and tracking software. Often, sex addicts have another device that they keep secret. A hidden cell phone or a secret computer allows sex addicts to act out without using devices that a spouse may be monitoring. They may use apps like Snapchat that erases texts sent to sexual partners.

Is there anything I could have done to prevent him from being unfaithful to me?

There is absolutely nothing you could have done to prevent him from being unfaithful to you. No matter what your husband may say, he did not become a sex addict because of some deficiency or behavior on your part. No matter who he married, he would have made the same choices because the addiction is rooted in him and his story.

....

Why would my husband want to have sex with others rather than me?

....

The primary reason he had sex with others is because he is a sex addict. But other things fuel the addiction, including the high an addict gets from the illicit chase, the fact that he can have sex without emotional intimacy, the short-lived ego stroke the acting out gives him.

But I know your underlying question is really not about those things. Rather it is, "*Why was I not enough for him? Why did he go somewhere else when he could have come to me?*" Sadly, the answer is the same: it's not that he didn't love you; it's because he is an addict. Your husband may very well love you more than anything else in the world, but because he's an addict, he acts out.

....

Why does my husband prefer an unattractive prostitute to his beautiful, loving wife?

....

Those with sex addiction aren't necessarily looking for someone more attractive than their current partner. A sex addict may even consciously seek out the opposite. As their sense of shame increases, some sex addicts intentionally look for sex partners that effectively degrade them and reinforce their shame. One very successful man with unlimited financial resources admitted that his addiction ultimately led him to look for street-walking prostitutes in drug-infested parts of town. In his words, "the cheaper and the dirtier, the better."

You are right in thinking this does not make sense. Addicts do not think rationally when chasing their addiction. The only thing that matters is getting the fleeting high offered by their acting out.

Can you explain the irony of a sex addict who is unable or unwilling to have sex with his wife?

There may be several reasons a sex addict is not having sex with his spouse or committed partner. First, there may be so much sexual energy being expended in being sexual with others or himself that he simply has nothing in reserve for his spouse. Secondly, a committed sexual relationship can be very satisfying, rewarding, and fulfilling. However, for sex addicts, the neurochemical release that comes from sex within a committed relationship is much less than that achieved through sexual acting out. Sex addicts are addicted to getting a higher high whenever possible.

Another reason a sex addict may not be having sex with his spouse is related to his recovery status and efforts. In an attempt to control their acting out, some sex addicts believe the solution is to stop being sexual, period. But, while sexual abstinence for a time can be a helpful part of the recovery process, recovery should ultimately include having a healthy sexual relationship within one's marriage. We will look at this in more detail in Part Four.

Why didn't he ever think of me and our children and the damage he was causing by his acting out?

Many sex addicts report they do think about the people in their lives whom they love, but they're so caught up in their addiction they can't, or don't, stop. And others are so deep into acting out they're beyond caring. Either way, the "insanity" people in twelve-step recovery talk about so ensnares them that only the imminent or actual loss of loved ones, job, and/or loss of financial security hold a chance of bringing them back to reality. And many times they're so entrenched in their addiction, by the time they face such consequences even that great loss is not enough to stop them.

How can he prefer masturbation to having sex with me?

We have heard many women express the same sentiments. It is

important to remember that your husband's preference of masturbation over sex with you is not your fault, and may in fact have very little to do with you. When a person masturbates, he or she typically employs sexual fantasy or memories of past sexual experiences. Reliving those experiences or playing out a sexual fantasy causes a neurochemical release that creates a rush, which for some sex addicts is more intense than having sex with their spouse. Sex addicts can play out these fantasies as theater of the mind, where they are the main actor and the director. They can change the ending, as well as the supporting cast. In this theater, sex addicts act out varying parts of the play in order to get a stronger high.

In these internal plays, there are no disagreements. Financial and other life problems do not exist. Everything revolves around the sex addict. Partners are always in the mood for sex. How can you compete with that? In short, you cannot. Sex addiction has sold him the lie that his fantasy is better than real life with you.

Why did I end up in this relationship?

There's no one-size-fits-all answer to this question. We end up in the marriages we do for reasons that are unique and specific to our individual stories and needs. Many of us marry unhealthy people because they are much like the unhealthy families in which we grew up. When chaos and crisis were the norm during our youth, chaos and crisis will be our "normal" when we date. People naturally gravitate toward the familiar. Some choose a "father" figure for reasons rooted in childhood. Some marry the first man to come along to get out of the abuse in their childhood home.

But regardless of the reason, when you recognize you're in a relationship with an addict, you need to seek help, healing, and emotional growth for yourself. Then, and only then, can you begin to heal. By taking such steps and changing yourself, you disrupt the unhealthy patterns in your marriage. That opens the door for the addict to get help too, if he doesn't want to lose you.

Will my husband always feel like he needs something more?

Sex addicts chase the high that comes from acting out. The nature of addiction is that as long as it remains active, addicts (including sex addicts) will continually need "more." Some sex addicts act out, then within an hour or so, sometimes less, act out again. Sex addicts pursue sex not because they need it but because they have an insatiable desire driven by changes in their brain chemistry for more.

The good news is that if your husband gets into recovery, as his brain chemistry resets, his desires and drives will gradually normalize. Healthy sex can return to your relationship. Recovery offers the hope that not only can your relationship be restored but that your husband will find his sexual relationship with you fulfilling.

Why do so many churches seem to blame the wife instead of addressing sex addiction?

If you have had this experience in your church, it is deeply unfortunate. His sex addiction is not your fault. You have not failed in some way. Regrettably, many people lack understanding about sex addiction and some individuals and religious groups believe that if the husband is acting out sexually, there must be some deficiency in regard to his wife. This flawed thinking is shared by some clergy, as well as other helping professionals who lack knowledge about sex addiction.

Over the past several years, there are a growing number of churches that understand sex addiction and are taking steps to help both sex addicts and wounded partners. Some of these churches have counseling centers where professional counselors provide support and treatment to individuals and families affected by sex addiction. Thankfully, some seminaries are now doing a better job of equipping ministers to recognize addiction in its various forms so they can provide appropriate help when needed.

If this is an addiction and the addict's sexual acting out is compulsive, how is it that sexual liaisons are often carefully planned in advance?

Sex addicts may act out impulsively, but they are still able to plan future acting out. Disorders characterized by compulsive behavior do not prohibit advance planning. Sex addicts are similar to those addicted to alcohol or other drugs who sometime need their "fix" immediately, but at other times plan in advance to get what they want. In addition to the compulsive behaviors, sex addiction is marked by obsessive thinking. The thinking of sex addicts is dominated by thoughts of past sexual events and fantasies of future acting out. They become preoccupied with creating opportunities for being sexual.

I just found out that my husband is a sex addict. Am I in danger?

Depending on the sexual behaviors in which your husband has engaged, your health may well be in danger. One of the first things every partner of a sex addict needs to do is to be tested for sexually transmitted diseases (STDs). You owe it to yourself (and any children you have) to protect your health. Even if your husband swears he has not had sex with anyone else, you still need to take this important step. He may or may not be telling you the truth. Has he lied to you in the past? If so, how do you know he is telling you the truth now? Because dishonesty and specifically lying are inherent in addiction, it is important to err on the side of self-protection.

Often, it's only when a polygraph is a part of recovery that the addict will finally tell the complete truth. Your life is too important to risk believing what he says when his acting out is first discovered. And if you are a mother of dependent children, you must immediately prioritize your life and your health by being tested for STDs as soon as possible. I (Marsha) have actually had a former client die because of an STD her husband gave her. So please, take this important step. Insist that your husband also be screened for the full range of STDs. When the results come back, you need to see his results for yourself rather than take his word.

Even if the results of testing for both of you are negative, unless you have a system in place to verify your husband's acting out has stopped, you continue to place your health at risk when you have sex with him. In Part Four, we discuss how to get on a path to restoring your relationship in ways that provide greater certainty you are not risking your health by being sexual with your husband.

Your general health could be in danger as well. Emotional trauma is very hard on the body. Partners of sex addicts often develop autoimmune disorders, in addition to depression and anxiety disorders.

There are also other potential dangers partners of sex addicts face. Many partners are in danger of financial ruin because addicts may lose their jobs and/or spend a great deal of money on their addiction, creating debts the partner knew nothing about. Homes have been lost, and bank accounts and retirement savings have disappeared.

....

I don't like my husband going to twelve-step meetings. He tells me that many of the men there continue to act out.

....

I (Milton) can understand your concern. At the beginning of recovery it would be ideal for your husband only to be exposed to other sex addicts that are solidly in recovery, who have never had a slip or relapse, and whose behaviors are identical to his. People in twelve-step meetings share their "experience, strength, and hope." They share about their successes and their challenges and failures. However, it is valuable for your husband to hear about the experiences of men whose sexual acting may have exceeded his own, as well as those of others whose acting out may pale in comparison to his. It is also helpful for him to be faced with the reality that simply attending meetings will not keep him sober.

In meetings he will hear men talk about their struggles to remain sexually sober and hear about the setbacks of others. He will hear real life stories about what has worked and what hasn't. All of this information is instructive as he solidifies his resolve to remain in recovery. He will benefit from listening to others share about their recovery journey. Hopefully, your husband will want to emulate those who are doing well and be cautious not to repeat the mistakes of those who relapse.

It's also possible your husband is being selective in what he tells you about meetings in the hope you will take the position that he does not need to attend them. You can help him most by insisting that he is responsible for his own recovery. If he does not have a sponsor, he needs one—today.

....

Should I be concerned that female sex addicts attend some of my husband's twelve-step meetings? Isn't this like pouring gas on a fire?

....

While I (Milton) can understand your concern, the atmosphere in twelve-step meetings is not one where people are looking to hook up for sex. Most of the women I have known who attend sex addiction related twelve-step meetings are genuinely looking for recovery and sustained sobriety.

Often what women share can be very enlightening to male sex addicts who have typically been uninterested in the feelings of those they act out with or consequences for those individuals. To hear the sadness, sorrow, and even desperation of female sex addicts, which may be a mirror of what your husband experienced in his own addiction, can be eye-opening. Many men never realize their acting out partners are also very wounded, vulnerable people trying to find meaning and self-worth—only to lose it a bit more each time they act out.

....

Is there anything I could have done to prevent this?

....

There is nothing you could have done to prevent this. Remember, you are powerless over the addict, his choices, and his outcome. Even if there were warning signs prior to marriage—little flirtatious behaviors, discovering a porn stash, or unexplained absences and expenditures—most ignore them, often for what seem like viable reasons. You didn't know there was such a thing as sex addiction, he explained your discovery away—and you wanted to believe him. Or perhaps a parent, counselor, or clergy member told you, "All boys do it. Once you are married, it will stop." But it didn't.

One thing is certain: we cannot rewrite our history. However, we can learn from it and create a different present and future. If these behaviors don't fall away once an addict is in recovery, it is an indicator of where he is in his change process. As much as wounded partners want change to happen overnight, sobriety is usually progressive.

Can a sex addict ever stop?

Although the ongoing discontinuation of sexual acting out is a significant challenge for most addicts, and more don't make it than do, sexual sobriety is absolutely possible. But, the addict has to want it as much as he wants life itself. Recovery and true change require investing time and energy for group meetings, weekly meetings with his sponsor, and doing ongoing step work that's a part of his recovery program. Stopping sexual acting out comes from putting in the time and energy required to gain freedom. Recovery requires multiple changes in one's thinking, behaviors, and life. These changes affect the places he goes, the things he does, and the people he socializes with.

CHAPTER 9

IS THERE ANY HOPE?

Is there hope for me?

This is the question I hear sex addicts ask most. The answer is yes! There is great hope so long as you are willing to do the work necessary in recovery. Although many people new to recovery fail, and the odds are against them, many others are successful in recovery. If they have a setback, they learn from it. As they achieve modest sobriety milestones, they celebrate these small but important victories. They use each victory as a stepping-stone to move forward in recovery.

Not only is there hope for sex addicts, there is great hope for wounded partners. One of the most wonderful things about recovery is that there is also hope for relationships that have been badly damaged by sex addiction. We have seen many couples on the verge of divorce restore their relationships through tireless individual work in recovery and then working together to rebuild the relationship. It may be hard to believe while you are in the midst of your hurt and pain, but you can heal. And, you will heal if you are determined to take the steps necessary to recover.

At the end of this book, you can read excerpts from the stories of couples who have successfully restored their relationships after the devastation of sex addiction. We hope their stories inspire you to continue your journey. Because the journey is arduous, there are many who do not persevere and ultimately give up on their relationships. Commit now to do whatever is necessary to see your relationship restored.

Riley's Story_____

Riley liked to joke in twelve-step meetings that God got him into recovery. He said, "God was driving a black and white with flashing lights on the top." Riley's arrest for soliciting prostitutes seemed like the end of his life. For years, he was considered one of the leading citizens in his community and his church.

There were many repercussions from his arrest. In the beginning, it looked like they would all be negative. His family was devastated. Neighbors whispered about him. Parents warned their children not to go into the yard of the "dirty man." Even men he worked with whom he previously went to strip clubs with shunned him.

That was fifteen years ago. Riley's arrest brought him into recovery for sex addiction and alcoholism. He recognized that both forms of addiction were out of control in his life. Since then, he has found a freedom in recovery he never knew existed. His relationship with his wife has been restored. Once again, his church looks to him for leadership. In his neighborhood, he is thought of as the man to turn to when people need counsel.

His greatest satisfaction has come from sponsoring other men who struggle with sex addiction. He continues to attend twelve-step meetings weekly and give hope to newcomers. Through the years, he estimates that he has sponsored about fifty men. His biggest surprise came a few years into recovery when he realized that he was grateful for his arrest. If not for his arrest, his addiction would likely have remained hidden. Now, because of his recovery, he is happier than at any time in his life.

Recovery is a life-long process. Sometimes people enter recovery thinking it is a "quick fix" or they believe, "I'll work the Twelve Steps and then I'm cured." What they do not realize is that for recovery to work it must be a lifestyle. Developing a recovery lifestyle begins when a person first enters recovery and then continues for life. There is no graduation ceremony. No one reaches a place of lasting achievement that concludes the recovery process.

One of the first important realizations that comes from recovery is the quest for honesty over abstinence from sexual acting out. Honesty, integrity, and transparency come to mean as much as sexual sobriety. The integrity that comes from practicing recovery permeates every activity and every relationship throughout one's life.

Recovery is the vehicle that allows a person to strip away the false persona that clouds life and make it more difficult. In the process, recovery helps people learn who they really are underneath the addiction.

PART TWO

THE ROAD TO RECOVERY

FREEDOM

HOPE

CHAPTER 10

RECOVERY BASICS

Recovery from sex addiction is much, much more than stopping all acting out. Those who stop acting out but do not create a new life are not in recovery. They may be abstinent, but they are not in recovery—they are the equivalent of what those in recovery from alcohol refer to as a "dry drunk."

Recovery creates a life free from the insanity that reigns in active addiction. To get solidly on the road to recovery, there are some things you need to start, some things you need to stop, and some things you need to change.[37]

Things to Start

The very first thing to start is attending twelve-step meetings focused on sex addiction. There are several major twelve-step programs, including Sex Addicts Anonymous, Sex and Love Addicts Anonymous, and Sexaholics Anonymous. You can find contact information for these and other sex addiction-related twelve-step fellowships in Appendix D at the back of this book.

Begin by making a master list of all of the sex addiction-related meetings in your area for each day of the week. Some of the larger cities have meetings morning, afternoon, and evening, seven days a week.

---

37 A more thorough treatment of recovery basics is found in Milton Magness, *Thirty Days to Hope & Freedom from Sexual Addiction: The Essential Guide to Beginning Recovery and Preventing Relapse* (Carefree, AZ: Gentle Path Press, 2010).

With your list in hand, determine which will be the first meeting that you attend. In addition to face-to-face meetings, many of the major fellowships offer online and/or telephone-based meetings. Attending meetings in person, if at all possible, is preferable. That notwithstanding, online or telephone meetings can also be extremely helpful.

Those new to recovery are strongly encouraged to attend ninety meetings in ninety days. In twelve-step language this is known as doing a "ninety in ninety," and it helps build a foundation of information, understanding, and experience needed for lifelong recovery. This saturation with recovery will help you learn a new vocabulary distinctive to the recovery community. Moreover, a ninety in ninety will help you begin to develop the new neuropathways that support new healthy behavior patterns.

After completing ninety meetings in ninety days, a sound recovery program includes continuing to attend multiple twelve-step meetings weekly—for life. Many people are able to attend three or four meetings each week and still find time for other pursuits. The focus should not be on doing the minimum one can get away with, but rather on developing the strongest recovery program possible while still having time for family and work.

After starting twelve-step meetings, getting a sponsor is the highest priority. From your very first meeting, be diligent in searching for a sponsor. A sponsor is a mentor who can guide you through your recovery program. Sponsors are sex addicts in recovery who have worked the Twelve Steps and have achieved sustained sobriety. Their role is not to be your marriage counselor or your personal therapist. They will guide you down a path they have walked and are continuing to walk.

Is there another way of doing recovery instead of a twelve-step program and attending meetings? Yes, but there is nothing as effective for sex addiction as twelve-step-based recovery. I have clients ask me if I will give them a plan B that allows them not to attend meetings. My response is always the same. As serious and as devastating as sex addiction is, I will not encourage sex addicts to take any path in recovery that has proven to be less successful than the twelve-step programs.

After securing a sponsor, it is time to begin your Step work. *Working* the Steps is not the same as *reading* the Twelve Steps. For each of the Steps, your sponsor will give you assignments that may involve reading material, writing exercises, and worksheets. There is no one right way of working the Steps or a set amount of time needed for completing the Twelve Steps. Your sponsor will guide your progress.

As a useful starting point, think in terms of doing a Step a month and completing the Twelve Steps over the course of a year. Some Steps will take longer and others will need less time. There is nothing to be gained by rushing through them, but neither is there any virtue in dragging the process out over several years. Once you complete the Steps, you will start through them again and methodically work through them several times during your lifetime. Each time through the Steps will yield deeper insights that enrich your recovery and your life.

In working the Steps and attending twelve-step meetings, you will hear many references to making a spiritual connection—with yourself, with others, and with God or another Higher Power. That spiritual connection may be similar to or different from one you grew up with or with what others have. For many, this is the most difficult part of the journey. Your sponsor can be helpful in making suggestions about how you can develop the spiritual part of your life.

It is important to note that twelve-step programs are not religious, though they are spiritual in nature. It has been said that human beings have a "God-shaped hole" they try to fill with other "things." All forms of addiction can be viewed as attempts to fill this hole. Sex addicts try to fill this hole with sexual activity. Yet, only a spiritual connection with that which is greater than and beyond oneself can fill that void. The concept of a "God-shaped hole" was first identified in *Pensées*, a collection of fragments on theology and philosophy written by 17th-century French philosopher and mathematician Blaise Pascal, and published in 1669.[38]

Recovery is, in part, about becoming accountable. You are encouraged to build a support system that includes men in your twelve-step meetings. These are men you have gotten to know on a more personal basis and

---

38 Blaise Pascal, *Pensées* (1669; reprinted North Arlington, NJ: Ozymandias Press, 2016).

with whom you will have regular telephone contact. You need five men in your life who you have given permission to hold you accountable for how you live and work your recovery. This Circle of Five[39] will help you break the isolation that deepened as your addiction progressed. One member of this circle is your sponsor.

Concurrent with twelve-step program participation, many people find it helpful to begin therapy with a sex addiction therapist.[40] Professional therapy is especially helpful for those starting recovery, trying to repair a relationship damaged by sex addiction, and those who have suffered a relapse. Sex addiction therapists are skilled at doing family of origin work, which gets to the root of addiction. Healing from trauma is another potential benefit of therapy, making it an especially good choice for partners wounded by a sex addict and for those who have suffered from abuse in the past.

Group therapy is also very beneficial for sex addiction recovery. Facilitated by a trained therapist, group therapy brings people together who have experienced similar challenges in a way that facilitates learning and healing through the sharing of experience, mutual connection, and support. The fee for group therapy is typically significantly less than for individual or couples' therapy.

Things to Stop

Entering recovery will require you to stop certain behaviors. First on this list is to stop all sexual acting out. It is essential to be clear as to what constitutes acting out. This involves drawing up a sobriety contract[41] that places specific behaviors in three categories:

- **Red Light Behaviors** = Forbidden. If you engage in these you know you have acted out and have broken sexual sobriety.

- **Yellow Light Behaviors** = Dangerous. These are not acting-out behaviors per se but they are likely to lead to acting out and therefore should be avoided.

---

39 For more information about developing a Circle of Five, see Milton Magness, *Thirty Days to Hope & Freedom from Sexual Addiction: The Essential Guide to Beginning Recovery and Preventing Relapse* (Carefree, AZ: Gentle Path Press, 2010).

40 The following websites have listings of therapists who work with sex addicts: www.findachfp.com, www.sash.net, and www.sexhelp.com.

41 iRecovery app lets users develop a sobriety contract and track their recovery daily. See www.recoveryapp.com.

- **Green Light Behaviors** = Healthy. These are behaviors that promote recovery and health.

Red light behaviors begin with those behaviors most closely connected to your sex addiction that motivated you to seek recovery in the first place. If you were caught having an affair, then you include "sex outside of my marriage" as a forbidden behavior. If you lost your job because of looking at pornography at work, then you include "viewing pornography" as a red light behavior. You will need to determine where masturbation fits in your sobriety plan. Is it forbidden, dangerous, or healthy for you? Be honest with yourself and utilize your sponsor and the men in your support system in determining what helps and what hinders your recovery.

Other red light behaviors may include:

- Going to sexually oriented businesses
- Entering chat rooms
- Initiating contact with former sex partners

Yellow light behaviors include all behaviors that have led to acting out in the past or might cause you to want to act out. Perhaps that means watching "movies with sexual content." If cybersex has been a problem, then you might add "working on a computer when I am alone" as a yellow light behavior. Additional yellow light behaviors may include:

- Flirting
- Cruising parts of town where acting out has or could occur (such as intentionally going past strip clubs or areas known to be frequented by prostitutes)
- Listening to a genre of music that was closely related to your acting out or that you listened to when you were acting out
- Searching the Internet for former partners
- Missing twelve-step meetings
- Massages (if there has ever been any acting out while getting a massage or if getting a massage is triggering)

Green light behaviors include all healthy activities. This means recovery behaviors; taking care of your mental, emotional, and physical health; spiritual activities; and behaviors that deepen and strengthen your primary relationship. The following are often listed as green light behaviors:

- Attending twelve-step meetings
- Working with one's sponsor
- Going to therapy
- Attending worship or pursuing other spiritual activities
- Prayer/meditation
- Activities with one's children
- Dates with one's spouse
- Being sexual with one's spouse
- Reading
- Working out
- Eating healthy
- Getting adequate sleep

Recovery requires practicing honesty. When you enter recovery it is time to stop lying. Sex addicts lie to cover up their acting-out behavior and avoid the consequences of it. However, they may have learned to lie early in life to escape punishment for something they did or to avoid disappointing others. Sex addicts often lie about things that really do not matter but they continue to lie because they are practicing impression management, wanting to control how others see them and to present themselves as being as close to perfect as possible.

Partners of sex addicts have often told me (Milton) that dealing with lying is more difficult for them than dealing with their partner's acting out. Honesty must become so important that people in recovery tell the truth regardless of the consequences.

Similarly, a commitment must be made to stop hurting others. All destructive behavior must end. While pursuing addiction, sex addicts can be verbally abusive to their partners. This behavior sometimes reflects the way sex addicts feel about themselves. They may hate themselves because of their behavior and believe their partners must feel the same way. Sex addicts may vent their anger not only at their partners, but also at their children and their coworkers. They may assume others hold them in the same contempt and so they project their disgust onto others.

This cessation of doing harm needs to include an end to hurting oneself. Sex addicts engage in many behaviors that inflict various forms of self-harm. These include other addictive behaviors, negative self-talk, unrealistic expectations of self, and self-pity. In recovery, sex addicts can learn how to look at themselves differently and treat themselves with kindness and compassion. It is time to grant yourself the grace you have wished others would show you. You deserve to receive the gifts of recovery. You are worth the time, money, and effort that recovery will demand. This is the day to say, "Whatever it takes, whatever it costs, I deserve recovery!"

Things to Change

Entering recovery means there are many things you need to change. These include all of the things to start and all of the things to stop described earlier, but there is more to it. First, you must change your priorities. Recovery must be the most important thing in your life. Your number one priority is to do whatever it takes to recover from sex addiction—because without sexual sobriety you are likely to lose whatever else is important to you. In order to maintain that priority you must be willing to make whatever other changes are necessary. If you have attempted recovery in the past and have failed, perhaps it is time to consider entering an inpatient treatment facility or an intensive outpatient (IOP) treatment program. You can find a list of many such programs in Appendix D.

Recovery may dictate the need to change some of your friends. Are there people in your life who encourage you to engage in unhealthy behaviors? Do you have friends who have colluded with you in sexual acting out and helped to cover up your activities? Such "friends" may be threatened by your efforts to make healthy changes and—directly or indirectly—discourage your recovery. Maybe it is time for you to get a different class of friends. One of the best places to make new friends is at twelve-step meetings where members share common experiences and goals, have similar flaws, and want to live differently.

It is also time to change the way you treat your partner. Have you raged at her when you were feeling shame over your acting out? Have you blamed her for your behavior? Have you "gaslighted" her by making her doubt her memory or perception?

If you are ready to begin to live differently, now is the time for you to make your own list of behaviors and activities to start, stop, and change as you enter recovery. Take a few moments and copy the following worksheet on a separate sheet of paper. If you entered recovery before reading this book then there is a fourth list you need to include. You have already started making changes in your behavior and thinking, so add a list of things you are going to continue now that you are in recovery. Complete this worksheet for yourself—take the time you need but no more than that. Anything more than an hour or two reflects procrastination. There's no need to obsess about what to write. You already know much of what you need to do. Now you're simply putting it into words, as a precursor to putting it into actions.

Now that I am in recovery, these are the things I am going to:

START:

1. _____
2. _____
3. _____
4. _____
5. _____
6. _____
7. _____
8. _____
9. _____
10. _____

STOP:

1. _____
2. _____
3. _____
4. _____
5. _____
6. _____
7. _____
8. _____
9. _____
10. _____

Now that I am in recovery, these are the things I am going to:

CHANGE:

1. _____
2. _____
3. _____
4. _____
5. _____
6. _____
7. _____
8. _____
9. _____
10. _____

CONTINUE:

1. _____
2. _____
3. _____
4. _____
5. _____
6. _____
7. _____
8. _____
9. _____
10. _____

Recovery is something that you DO! It consists of actions you take. When a person is in solid recovery, there are multiple recovery-related activities that he does every day.

You may find the time and energy recovery requires daunting, but how much time and energy did your active sex addiction consume on a daily and weekly basis? Remember, your sex addiction is so ingrained it became a way of life. It will take considerable time and effort to overcome and change your destructive habit patterns and develop a new lifestyle.

A sample Personal Recovery Plan can be found in *Stop Sex Addiction* (Central Recovery Press, 2013), and you can download a blank Personal Recovery Plan form at www.stopsexaddiction.com/worksheets.

The Free Stuff Is Priceless

Not everyone can afford to enter inpatient treatment for thirty, forty-five, or ninety days. Every sex addict cannot afford to participate in an intensive outpatient program or even individual therapy. Although each of these helps, you do not have to spend a lot of money to gain the benefits of recovery.

Attending twelve-step meetings is free. Your sponsor will meet with you regularly and never charge you a penny. Working the Twelve Steps of recovery does not require you to cover any costs. The support offered by other recovering sex addicts is free of charge. Many recovery websites offer a host of recovery information at no cost. The YouTube channel www.GotToStopIt.com has many free videos about recovery for both sex addicts and partners.

Some people discount the value of anything that is free. Although Twelve Step recovery does not cost any money, it does demand time and energy. As with so many other things in life, the benefit you get from recovery will be in direct proportion to the effort you put into it. Do not overlook the value of these things just because they do not have a financial price tag. This free stuff is priceless!

FREEDOM

HOPE

CHAPTER 11

GENERAL QUESTIONS ABOUT RECOVERY

I have just acknowledged that I am a sex addict. How can I slow down my sex addiction?

We are glad you have taken this important step of recognizing the presence of sex addiction in your life. Your question is similar to that posed by cigarette smokers who want to decrease rather than stop smoking. Sex addiction cannot be controlled by simply decreasing sexual acting out. The only goal worth pursuing is for you to stop ALL of your sexual acting-out behaviors forever.

Recovery is not something you do a little of in hopes of feeling better. You must enter recovery completely, holding nothing back. Only when you give yourself completely to a program of recovery will you have hope of getting your life back.

How long does recovery take?

As noted earlier, recovery is a life-long process. A more useful question is, "How long will it be until I see the benefits of recovery in my life?" Some people see benefits from the very first meeting they attend. Changes in attitude and behavior can be seen from the very first day of recovery. It is possible to stop acting out today and never go back to your former behavior.

It is essential to keep in mind that the most important day of your recovery is today. Rather than being consumed by the regret of what happened yesterday or the anxiety of what might happen tomorrow, concentrate on today. Just for today, you can remain sexually sober. For today, you can do the work of recovery. Tomorrow, you just do it again. Live in today. Enjoy the fruit of your recovery today.

The change in your thinking that will more permanently support this new way of life is typically a three- to five-year process. For some it comes sooner, but for others it may take longer. Importantly, you never "graduate" to a time when you will no longer need to engage in recovery activities.

With every meeting you attend and every hour you spend doing the Step work assigned by your sponsor, you are progressing in your recovery. You are recovering and in the process of becoming the person you were created to be—a man of integrity and purpose.

Am I going to have to fight with this every day?

At first it may feel as if you are in a fight, but as you stay engaged in recovery, you will no longer have a daily struggle for sobriety—your focus will gradually shift from keeping negative behaviors at bay to filling your life with the positive pursuits.

A word of caution: there is often a honeymoon period during the first several months to the first year of recovery. This is especially so when partners discover the acting out and give an ultimatum to the addict to either get in recovery and stop all acting out or the relationship is over. This motivation is so great that many sex addicts give their all to recovery, at least in the beginning. Some find that their desire to act out decreases so dramatically that they mistakenly believe they have been "cured," and therefore can stop their recovery activities. This honeymoon period is analogous to a person being in remission from an incurable disease. The disease is not gone but is simply not currently progressing.

When a person remains totally committed to and engaged in recovery, his or her sex addiction is in remission. However, if they stop actively participating in recovery, the sex addiction usually comes back with a fury. Sex addicts who relapse often find that their acting-out behaviors during a relapse are even more destructive than they were prior to entering recovery.

A key word here is vigilance. You must remain vigilant for the rest of your life. Sex addiction will always be part of your life. But, with recovery, you can live your life free from sexual acting out and from the patterns of destructive thinking that lead to acting out. Let up on recovery and you will be pulled back toward addiction. There is no standing still in recovery. You are either moving forward in recovery or you are on the road to slipping and ultimately to relapse.

Do the cravings or urges ever go away?

As recovery progresses, cravings and urges to act out lessen in both frequency and intensity. That being said, most sex addicts with long-term sexual sobriety still report they have occasional thoughts of acting out. One of the gifts of recovery is learning to recognize the thoughts, emotions, and experiences that trigger cravings and then use the tools of recovery to counteract them. Since you are a sexual being, you will have sexual thoughts throughout your life. Recovery will help you make peace with your sexual thoughts so you can live in co-existence with them instead of returning to the chaos of addiction.

When am I at the greatest risk of acting out?

Your greatest risk occurs when you are triggered in ways that stimulate cravings or urges to act out. Triggers may be mental—related to your thoughts, emotions, or visuals—related to what you see. They may be tied to memories or to people, places, or things associated with your active sex addiction. Understanding your specific triggers is important so that you can be prepared, if and when you experience them. You may also be at great risk after using even a small amount of alcohol or other drugs. Even if you do not feel you have a drinking problem, alcohol lowers one's inhibitions and often clouds judgment. For this reason, many sex addicts who travel have an ironclad rule that they won't drink when they are out of town, or at any business function in town if their spouse is not present.

Twelve-step meetings talk about people being at particular risk when they are hungry, angry, lonely, or tired (HALT). Some have suggested replacing the H with an S for shame (SALT). For many people, feelings of boredom and anxiety are powerful triggers. Still others have suggested the acronym of SHED-F (shameful, hopeless, entitled, depressed, or fearful) as a way of identifying triggers.

Make a list of your triggers. Start by asking yourself, *when am I most at risk of acting out?* After you have made your list of triggers, come up with several healthy, recovery-supportive things you can do when faced with each of the triggers.

....

How do I stop lying?
....

Most likely, you learned to lie as a child. Perhaps you wanted to escape the wrath of an abusive parent, or simply the negative consequences of your behavior. As you grew older, you may have made up stories hoping to make yourself more popular. As addiction grows, lying is necessary to keep one's behavior hidden. When caught in the grip of your active sex addiction, you had to lie in order to keep others from finding out.

A good place to start is to spend some time journaling at the end of the day. Write down every lie that you can remember telling that day. Then see if you can write an explanation for why you told each lie. Did you lie at work to cover up laziness? Did you tell a lie to cover a lack of understanding about an assignment? Perhaps you told several lies simply because it was habit. Maybe you told a lie hoping to make someone think more highly of you.

Complete honesty is at the heart of recovery. Resolve that you are going to be scrupulously honest, beginning with the little things. If you are late for a meeting, rather than concocting a tale about traffic, why not say, "I didn't allow enough time for travel." If you do not complete an assignment on time, instead of excuses about workload, why not say, "I should have worked harder on the assignment."

The greatest area of dishonesty is with oneself. Make it your goal to be honest with yourself in everything. As you develop the habit of telling yourself the truth, it will be easier to tell others the truth.

How do I stop feeling shame about what I have done in the past?

This may be difficult at first. Shame comes from deep-seated feelings of being intrinsically damaged, broken, or not good enough. Such feelings do not go away easily or quickly. Or, you may have a subconscious desire to nurture the shame for fear that discounting it is an indication you are not properly remorseful for your past actions. The Big Book of AA captures the importance of not living in shame when it promises that in recovery a person will "not regret the past nor wish to shut the door on it."[42]

However, this may be more easily accomplished if one only struggles with alcoholism and is not a sex addict. Sex addicts leave a wide path of destruction behind them. There may be many people who have been harmed as a result of your acting out. That being said, with time in recovery people gradually heal from the shame of their actions during their active addiction. With work in recovery people learn self-acceptance, and self-acceptance is an antidote for shame.

As you work the Twelve Steps of recovery, you come to the Ninth Step in which you make amends to all persons you have harmed, except when to do so would further injure them or others. The amends process is one of the truly brilliant aspects of twelve-step work. Rather than fret over mistakes of the past, the recovery journey allows you to begin to right your wrongs.

If you are just beginning your recovery journey, take heart in knowing that your sponsor will guide you in your amends process in due course. If you have been in recovery for a while, perhaps you have neglected to work the Steps. This is the time to get started. Get a sponsor today and start working the Steps.

---

42 *Alcoholics Anonymous*, 4th ed. (New York, NY: Alcoholics Anonymous World Services, Inc., 2002), 83.

How can I truly learn to let go of the past and forgive myself for my lustful thoughts and actions?

Participating in an active program of recovery is the key. Although admitting one's wrongs and the harm sex addiction caused others is important, continually beating oneself up is counterproductive and keeps a person stuck in the past. The recovery process helps people learn how to accept their past and learn how to live differently. Forgiveness of oneself is a necessary part of this process. Whether or not others forgive you for what you have done, you need to be able to forgive yourself. Connecting with the spiritual side of life can help in this regard. For many people, forgiving themselves happens more easily as they accept God's forgiveness.

In recovery from sex addiction, people need to change how they think in addition to how they act. In sex addiction recovery, getting to a place where you can recognize that those you once objectified are human beings of worth and value, rather than merely objects for your fantasies, represents a significant change in thinking. Cultivating those types of healthy thoughts until they become habitual will give you that much more reason to forgive yourself.

Will I ever be normal?

Who is to say what normal is? Being normal can mean different things to different people. For some, being normal means there is nothing in their life they want to change. Thankfully, because of recovery, you will likely never be at that place. For the rest of your life, there will always be something you are working on to improve. Initially, the focus is on stopping all acting out and the belief that if you can accomplish that, you will feel more confident in your ability to make other healthy changes. Recovery changes the way you look at yourself. You will forever be in the process of becoming. Recovery will allow you to experience life to its fullest.

There may always be things you choose not to do in your recovery that others consider normal. For example, "normal" people may be able to watch movies that contain steamy sex scenes, but because you realize how those same movies impact your thinking and your moods, you choose not to watch them. You choose the tranquility of thoughts not dominated by sex. Many people consider drinking alcohol normal, but those in recovery from alcohol and other drug addiction choose not to drink because they know it's unhealthy for them. Your life will return to "normal" in many ways, but sex addiction will always be part of your life.

Does my sex addiction define me?

Although it may be a fact that you are a sex addict, your addiction does not define you any more than you are defined by your height, ethnicity, or eye color. Sex addiction is a factor in your life. As you embrace recovery, you will find that the many gifts that come from recovery will help redefine who you are and what is important to you.

You are not your sex addiction. Sex addiction is a condition you have. In twelve-step meetings you identify yourself by giving your name and acknowledging your addiction to sex. Yet, your identity is much more than your sex addiction. Sex addiction does not define you but the presence of sex addiction does dictate many things in your life. First and foremost, your sex addiction demands that you enter a program of recovery; otherwise life will continue to be unmanageable.

What will define you is your recovery. Through recovery you can get back much of what you lost as a result of your active addiction. Recovery will give back your self-respect. Through recovery, you can regain your reputation. Recovery may even allow you to rebuild the relationship with your partner.

How do I know which is the best way to get help for my sex addiction?

Although you are a unique individual, there are many fundamental qualities and experiences you have in common with other sex addicts. To get help, sex addicts ultimately must get to the point where they realize their lives are out of control, and they can't stop their destructive behaviors on their own. What has worked best for millions of people is engaging in a twelve-step program of recovery with meetings and sponsorship at its core. Looking across a room filled with those who suffer from sex addiction helps people recognize they are not alone. Listening to others share about their struggles and successes gives them hope.

Sex addiction is analogous to chronic illnesses such as diabetes. People with diabetes recognize that they need to remain aware of their illness, monitor it, and take care of themselves in relationship to it. If they want to stay as healthy as they can, they are careful about what they eat and are mindful to take their medication. Diabetics can often live lives that appear normal to others. But, if they abandon the measures that help them maintain a healthy lifestyle, diabetes could claim their life.

Some people tell me that twelve-step programs did not work for them. Closer examination usually reveals that they attended a meeting or two, did not like it, and stopped going. Or perhaps they attended meetings for a period of time but did not get a sponsor or work the Twelve Steps. Twelve-step-based recovery offers the greatest hope of restoring you to a place of health.

....

I just started attending twelve-step meetings and have been shocked by how many of the men are really telling my story when they tell their own story. Are sex addicts really that similar?

....

One of the most wonderful things about twelve-step meetings is how effective they are in helping sex addicts understand they are not alone. You are not the only one who has been supporting the multibillion-dollar pornography industry. You are not the only one who has paid for sex, carried on multiple relationships simultaneously, had affairs, and masturbated to the point where you rubbed the skin from your penis.

Until sex addicts walk into twelve-step meetings, they assume no other person could possibly be struggling with the same behaviors. They assume no one else could possibly understand them. You are not alone! There are many other men waiting in twelve-step meetings for you to arrive so that together you can share your experience, strength, and hope in the interest of your mutual recovery.

I live in an area that does not have any sex addiction-related twelve-step meetings. How do I do recovery without them?

Each of the major fellowships listed in Appendix D have telephone-based and/or online meetings. There are also many sponsors who will work with sex addicts long distance. Long distance sponsors are also helpful if no sponsors are available where you live. Although face-to-face meetings are preferred, it is possible to do quality recovery utilizing telephone-based or online meetings.

Perhaps you can arrange to travel to face-to-face meetings once a month or so. Pick a city that has an abundance of meetings. With careful planning, it is possible to attend as many as six meetings in a two-day period (morning through evening). You are responsible for supplying the motivation for recovery. If you are motivated, obstacles to recovery can be overcome.

If you are a non-believer, how can you turn to a higher power?

It would be interesting to know how you came to a place in life where you do not believe in anything bigger than or beyond yourself. Perhaps you were force-fed religious teachings. Perhaps so much has happened to you that it's difficult to believe in the existence of God in any form. A common belief of sex addicts is that if they depend on others or God to meet their needs, those needs will never be met. Instead, they believe in their own power and think they can pull themselves up from active addiction by their own bootstraps.

Some believe that in order to pursue the spiritual side of life, they need to completely abandon the beliefs that were instilled in childhood. They seek to find a new approach and leave anything that looks like organized religion. It's important to understand that the twelve-step programs are *spiritual* not *religious*. You may find that your current belief system is very far from the way you were raised. Nonetheless, a good starting place for some is to return to the faith of their childhood. Many people find that if they can get beyond the negative approach taken by caregivers who force-fed religion, some of the messages and practices have meaning and value.

If you didn't receive any spiritual training as a youth, it is time for you to begin the journey on your own. Start by writing down what you do believe. Is it possible that there is a power greater than yourself? How do you identify that power? Could God exist? Is it possible that God cares about you? Can you conceive of God as not only caring about you but also wanting to give you ongoing serenity and the strength to live a sexually sober life?

Your journey continues as you recognize that developing your spiritual life means taking the initiative to discover what path is right for you. Talk to others about their spiritual life and what works for them. Seek out those in recovery who are at peace with themselves and others and are living free from sexual acting out. Ask them to help guide you as you seek your own spiritual truth.

....

When someone has multiple forms of addiction (sex, alcohol and other drugs, and gambling), what should be addressed first and how is recovery different?

....

The answer is that these forms of addiction must all be dealt with at once. The very best option would be to go into inpatient treatment[43] for your addiction. Inpatient programs will give you the time and focus that you need to address all forms of addiction.

When you come out of treatment, your life will be consumed with recovery activities. You will likely be attending twelve-step meetings each day for many months. Your meetings will be a combination of several fellowships to address the various forms of addiction. You will also need a sponsor in each fellowship. You will work the Steps of recovery in each fellowship. In addition, you will want to learn all that you can by reading books that are focused on recovery from each form of addiction.

....

I never had wet dreams as a youngster but since entering recovery I have had several of them. Is this normal?

....

Many men have described having nocturnal emissions or "wet dreams" after entering recovery, especially those who have stopped

---

43 See Appendix D.

masturbating. Your body was most likely used to more frequent ejaculation before you entered recovery. Now in recovery, nocturnal emissions may happen occasionally as you readjust to a healthier sexual life.

I have been in recovery for two years and have remained sober but I still sometimes have sex dreams. I wake up in a cold sweat, fearful that I've acted out only to find it was a dream. When will this stop?

Such dreams are not unusual for people in recovery from sex addiction and may never stop. Moreover, because you are a sexual being, it is natural for you to have sexual thoughts, and when you are asleep, dreams put together random thoughts over which you have no control. It's extremely positive that your recovery is so important to you that the thought of losing control is that upsetting. This is a gift for which to be grateful.

If someone is doing well in recovery and has been sexually sober for a year, is it okay to take a break from recovery?

Sex addicts can take a break from their recovery only if they are not committed to remaining sexually sober. Recovery is not a bank that you can make deposits into for a while and then make periodic withdrawals when needed. One way of picturing recovery is to think of your life as a bucket with a hole in it. You continually add the "water" of recovery to keep the bucket full. But when you stop adding water the bucket immediately progresses toward empty. People in recovery from sex addiction need to keep filling their bucket!

How long does it take to regain your self-esteem?

Most sex addicts experience an increase in their self-esteem that correlates with their time in recovery and sexual sobriety. Rebuilding one's self-esteem may take several months to several years. In fact, it's not unusual for people in long-term recovery to achieve higher levels of self-esteem than they ever had before in their lives. Working the Steps of recovery, taking responsibility for one's behavior, and learning to live a life of honesty, integrity, and accountability promotes self-esteem.

Do I need to work with a therapist?

Therapy with a professional is of great value for many people. Sex addiction therapists can help you gain insight into the factors that contributed to the development of your sex addiction. They can help you process the many feelings that will arise as you work through the Steps with your sponsor. A skilled therapist will help you understand your triggers to act out and assist you in developing tools to counter them. When it comes to the work of restoring the relationship with your spouse and children, sex addiction therapists have the expertise needed to guide you.

How do I find a good therapist?

Since you are dealing with sex addiction, it is crucial that you get a skilled sex addiction therapist. Several websites offer listings of such therapists.[44] Most therapists do not have expertise in treating sex addiction. You have a right to inquire about their training and their philosophy of treating sex addiction. Ask what percentage of their practice is devoted to working with sex addicts and their partners. If they have sex addiction as one of many specialties, they may be more of a generalist than a specialist. For example, you may find a restaurant that specializes in Italian food, Mexican food, Chinese food, and steaks. But if you want a good steak, you will more than likely seek out a steakhouse. Treatment of your sex addiction deserves the same specialized focus.

My wife and I have had two previous therapists who said we just needed to have more sex with each other. Why don't they know better?

Unfortunately, there are still many therapists who do not fully

---

44 www.findachfp.com, www.sash.net, and www.sexhelp.com list therapists who specialize in working with sex addicts and their families.

understand sex addiction. They may reason that since the problem involves men engaging in sex outside the marriage, the solution is to have more sex inside the marriage. And sadly, some of the time the focus is placed unfairly on wives—suggesting that if they are more sexual their husbands will stop acting out. This is just another way of blaming wives for their husband's bad behavior. In the event you have a therapist (or a member of the clergy) who shows a lack of knowledge about sex addiction, give them your copy of this book. Then email us and we will replace your copy at no cost to you.

How can I integrate more of the spiritual aspects of recovery into therapy?

There are many sex addiction therapists who offer faith-based therapy. You can be intentional in seeking out a therapist who shares your faith perspective. I (Milton) have had many people ask if I am a "Christian therapist." I tell them that is not how I identify myself. Rather I am a psychotherapist who happens to be a Christian. By that I want to communicate to clients that I will not lead them to do something that will negatively impact their faith or belief system but our focus will be on psychotherapy, not Bible study, and it will not be a prayer meeting.

I know many Christian therapists who are knowledgeable, highly skilled, and do a fine job of blending faith aspects with therapy. They provide a fine service for their clients. At the same time, my guess is that you may already have a strong grounding in your faith. If that is the case, perhaps what you need is to seek out a spiritual advisor. This person may be your pastor, rabbi, or maybe even your sponsor. Then, you can find the very best therapist possible who can guide you through healing from your sex addiction.

Can medication help my sex addiction?

Remember, there are no shortcuts in recovery or to sexual sobriety. You cannot take a pill to cure sex addiction. Every sex addict must be willing to do the exacting work of recovery if they hope to live free from acting-out behaviors.

Naltrexone is a medication used mainly for help in managing cravings for alcohol and to block the effects of opioids. It is marketed under a couple of trade names but the generic form is called hydrochloride salt.

There is some growing evidence that naltrexone may be helpful in treating sex addiction. In 2010, there was a study of nineteen men who were being treated for compulsive sexual behavior at an outpatient clinic. They were treated with naltrexone for a period of two months to just over two years. Seventeen (89 percent) reported a reduction in their compulsive sexual behavior symptoms.[45] Another study at the Mayo Clinic found naltrexone useful in suppressing the euphoria associated with Internet sex addiction.[46]

The side effects of certain antidepressants, specifically selective serotonin reuptake inhibitors (SSRI), such as Prozac, Paxil, Zoloft, and Celexa, frequently include decreased sex drive. As such, these medications may be useful in intentionally lowering sex drive.[47] For sex addicts being treated for depression, it would be worthwhile to consider the use of an SSRI for both the mood disorder and the potentially beneficial sexual side effect. Other studies show a benefit of using naltrexone and SSRIs together for treating compulsive sexual behavior.[48]

....

What is the best blocking and tracking software for safer Internet use?

....

Blocking and tracking software certainly has its place. The greatest value comes in helping protect minor children. Such software can also be helpful for sex addicts who are in recovery to keep themselves from inadvertently going to websites that may be problematic.

However, I (Milton) no longer recommend any particular software due to the fact that they all have limitations and can easily be circumvented.

---

45 N. C. Raymond, J. E. Grant, and E. Coleman, "Augmentation with Naltrexone to Treat Compulsive Sexual Behavior: A Case Series," *Annals of Clinical Psychiatry* 22, no. 1 (2010): 56–62.

46 J. M. Bostwick and J. A. Bucci, "Internet Sex Addiction Treated with Naltrexone," *Mayo Clinic Proceedings* 83, no. 2 (2008): 226–230, doi: 10.4065/83.2.226.

47 D. Prabhakar and R. Balon, "How Do SSRIs Cause Sexual Dysfunction?" *Current Psychiatry* 9, no. 12 (2010): 30–34.

48 N. C. Raymond, J. E. Grant, S. W. Kim, and E. Coleman, "Treatment of Compulsive Sexual Behaviour with Naltrexone and Serotonin Reuptake Inhibitors: Two Case Studies," *International Clinical Psychopharmacology* 17, no. 4 (2002): 201–205.

It is inaccurate to think that blocking and tracking software can keep a sex addict sober, or to convince a wounded partner that he is not acting out because he has software that prevents it. Software will not keep a person sober. Internal motivation is more valuable than external restraints.

Think of blocking and tracking software as being similar to seatbelts on a car. They are helpful safety equipment but they must be used properly to provide protection. Filtering software has a benefit when used correctly. But remember, what keeps sex addicts from acting out on computers is not software that they or their spouse installs, but rather a program of rigorous recovery.

How do I remain sober in a culture inundated with sexual messages?

Sex addicts must develop an internal filter. If you formerly engaged in sexual humor with others at work, in recovery you recognize when someone starts sexual humor it is your cue to remove yourself. When something on television triggers you, either turn the channel or excuse yourself. You are not being prudish, but responsible for your sex addiction and for taking care of yourself.

It would be helpful if you develop a "neuro-net" for yourself. Envision a net around your brain with openings that expand and contract at will. If there is something healthy that you want to let in, the openings expand. When you encounter media unhelpful to your recovery, visualize contracting the openings to keep the offending content out.

Some of what you keep out with your neuro-net are the obvious things you want to avoid like movies or television programs with overtly sexual content. But there are also more subtle things you may want to avoid, like music that reminds you of an old acting-out partner or of a period in your life when your sex addiction was most out of control. Your neuro-net is also useful for helping to deal with fantasies. Calling up the mental image of your neuro-net constricting can be effective in helping to keep sexual fantasies at bay or even eliminate them.

I believe God has delivered me from sex addiction. Why do I still feel pressured to continue in recovery?

God can certainly heal. We have our own faith that is strong and includes many regular spiritual practices. We have seen truly amazing things happen as people progress in recovery. However, you are well advised not to let up on your recovery activities. Continue all of your spiritual practices and maintain the closeness that you feel to God. You can pray like it all depends on God, then get off your knees and do the work of recovery as though it all depends on you.

Sadly, we have had many clients who professed to have great faith that they were healed subsequently experience relapse. In the words of an ancient saying, "Let him that thinketh he standeth take heed lest he fall."[49]

---

49   1 Corinthians 10:12 (Bible, King James Version).

PART THREE

THE HIGHWAY TO HEALING—

THE PARTNER'S JOURNEY

FREEDOM

HOPE

CHAPTER 12

RECOVERY BASICS FOR PARTNERS

You probably never thought you would need to read a book like this. When you were a little girl dreaming about life to come, you never considered that you would end up in relationship with a sex addict. Never in your dreams could you contemplate the hurt and profound sadness you have come to know because of your partner's addiction.

Marie's Story

Marie had a feeling something was wrong with her relationship. Her husband Marvin seemed to be more distracted of late. Gradually they seemed to be drifting apart. She tried to rekindle the romance by getting new lingerie but felt rejected when he did not notice.

He used to love it when she would surprise him by joining him in the shower. Lately, Marvin locked the door when he took a shower. It had been four years since she found the text messages he was exchanging with an old high school girlfriend. He explained that he met up with her at his high school reunion but nothing physical happened between them. Marie pointed out that the text messages were overtly sexual. He assured her they were just friends, bantering the way they did in high school.

Now, Marvin was acting strange again. Some days, he was moody and withdrawn for no apparent reasons. On a whim, she looked at his cell phone when he was in the bathroom. To her horror, she found that he had many text messages from several women and they were all sexual in nature. How could the man she loved be unfaithful to her? What had she done to deserve it? Why hadn't she been enough to satisfy her husband sexually? Marie set out to find a way of attracting her husband's attention again. She thought she would have to put away her pain and compete with these other women for a place in her husband's heart.

It's Not Your Fault!

The hardest thing to accept early in recovery is that your partner's acting out is not your fault. He didn't do it because of some deficiency in you. This is especially hard to believe because often sex addicts who are confronted with their behavior are quick to blame their spouse. They may say things such as, "If you had been more willing to have sex with me, I wouldn't have been forced to look elsewhere," or "If you hadn't gained so much weight, I never would have strayed."

If there is even a tiny kernel of truth in the criticism and you may be inclined to accept all of the blame, his behavior is his responsibility— not yours. Looking back on your life together it will be easy to find things you could have done better. You can always find examples of when you could have exercised more patience with your partner, shown him more kindness, been more sexual, etc. Perhaps you can even remember times when you simply did not want to be sexual with him.

Regardless of the circumstances, nothing you did or did not do made your partner act out. He made the decision and took the action to be unfaithful. Your partner is the one who has engaged in behaviors that have harmed you and badly damaged your relationship. In virtually every disclosure I (Milton) facilitate with couples, I find that the sex addicts' acting out predated the relationship with their partners. You did not cause your spouse to become a sex addict and his acting out belongs to him and to him alone. It is his addiction and he is responsible for taking care of it.

Even still, it can be hard to refuse to take the blame for his behavior, especially if he continues to try to blame you. This is why it is crucial early in your recovery from the trauma his addiction has caused to build a support network of women who have been through similar circumstances.

You may be fortunate to have a friend in whom to confide who has been through something similar. However, many women find themselves isolated and unable to reach out to friends or family because they are so ashamed of what has happened. They may also fear that their friends will not understand or even blame them for the sex addicts' behavior.

In twelve-step meetings for the partners of sex addicts,[50] members talk about the three big C's associated with a partner's recovery:

- *Cause.* You did not cause his behavior.
- *Change.* You cannot change his behavior.
- *Control.* You cannot control his behavior.

It is natural for women to think that if they just change things about themselves, their partner's behavior will change. But even if you were able to remove ten years from your age, ten pounds from your weight, or add ten million dollars to your net worth, you cannot change your spouse's behavior.

Similarly, you cannot control his behavior. If Marie had declared that Marvin was no longer allowed to use his smartphone because of his texting other women, would that have stopped his acting out? That would be very unlikely. Even monitoring your partner's behavior 24/7 cannot prevent him from acting out. He can always act out mentally through fantasy and euphoric recall. And like it or not, you cannot control what goes on in his mind.

Twelve-Step Meetings for Partners

At the time of this writing, all of the major twelve-step fellowships for partners are based on the belief that partners of sex addicts are codependent. For this reason, many partners feel labeled and misunderstood at these meetings. We know most partners experience

---

50   See Appendix D.

trauma, and sometimes post-traumatic stress disorder, and that they desperately need understanding and help to heal. But currently, only a handful of more trauma-focused twelve-step meetings exist.

Unfortunately, in some meetings partners are encouraged to identify themselves as a "codependent of a sex addict," or worse, as a "co-addict." It is important to know that you do not have to take on such labels simply because you are in relationship with a sex addict.

Later in the recovery process, sex addicts and their partners will want to examine codependency and codependent behaviors. But initially, the focus should be on helping partners recover from the trauma induced by their spouse's betrayal.

In years to come we hope the major twelve-step fellowships for partners will acknowledge and embrace the need to address members' trauma, or new twelve-step fellowships will emerge to fill this void. Partners need more options to continue their healing in communities with like-minded, traumatized women in the not-to-distant future.

With the shortcomings noted here, partners can benefit from attending meetings in the twelve-step programs of COSA and S-Anon, but generally their trauma needs to be addressed first and early trauma recovery must be a priority. The most significant benefits these groups offer include: (a) the ability to join a community of women who, like you, have been wounded by a sex addicted partner and can provide mutual understanding, acceptance, and support; (b) a place to work on regaining your emotional balance post-discovery; and (c) an environment in which you can continue to grow and heal.

Being able to sit face-to-face with someone else who has been betrayed is very beneficial. The trauma partner's suffering is much harder to bear in isolation. Twelve-step meetings allow you to build relationships with other women who have had similar experiences and face similar challenges. For women who cannot find twelve-step meetings locally, there are telephone and online meetings.

When you attend these meetings, you do not have to identify yourself as a "co-sex addict" or "codependent of a sex addict." You can simply state your name and say, "I'm in relationship with a sex addict."

That may not be the norm in that meeting but it accurately describes your situation.

I (Milton) suggest you attend several meetings in a row before deciding if twelve-step meetings can be helpful for you. Even if you find the first couple of meetings unhelpful, continue going and try to be open to hearing at least one thing that is beneficial to you. At each meeting, look for other women who might become part of your informal support network. Exchange phone numbers with them and develop the practice of calling them between meetings for support. You need to have other women in whom you can confide who can help you make it through difficult days.

There is a relatively new twelve-step fellowship for partners called Infidelity Survivors Anonymous (ISA) that began in Houston, Texas, in 2011. ISA now has eight meetings in three cities in the US, as well as some meetings in Finland. The unique aspect of this fellowship is that it focuses on the trauma that accompanies being in relationship with a sex addict.

Those interested in starting an Infidelity Survivors Anonymous group can find more information at www.isurvivors.org. The organizers of this fellowship provide kits, direction, and ongoing support for women who would like to organize a meeting in their area. I (Milton) believe that in the near future other twelve-step fellowships for partners of sex addicts will embrace the need to focus on trauma rather than codependency. Either the existing fellowships will recognize this need or other organizations like ISA will form to fill this void.

Other Support Groups

A growing number of support groups have been organized by therapists, churches, and other organizations to give partners additional places to develop community. Journey to Healing and Joy[51] offers extremely effective telephone-based support groups for wounded partners. These groups are led by therapists and coaches who have been through this trauma themselves, and who have significant training and experience in dealing with traumatized spouses. In addition, training material is currently being written for partners of sex addicts to use in starting

---

51 www.acircleofjoy.com.

Journey to Healing and Joy support groups in their own area. Many of my (Milton) clients have participated in Journey to Healing and Joy groups. I believe they offer some of the most effective help available for traumatized spouses.

Often, strong bonds form among the women in these telephone support groups. Members connect between sessions, giving the daily support they desire and need. Some groups continue to stay in contact even years after their formal group time has ended. Some of these women even meet face-to-face in various locations.

Other Possible Options

Some sex addiction therapists offer group therapy for wounded partners. Some groups have set starting and end dates and last for ten to fifteen weeks or longer. Other groups are open-ended, with members joining at various times and staying in the group for as long as necessary, sometimes years. This can be a valuable resource in your healing if you live in an area where they are available.

Starting Your Own Recovery Journey

Why do you need to do anything just because your partner is a sex addict? After all, it's *his* addiction. He needs to get his addiction "fixed" so the two of you can move on with life. Obviously, there is a significant amount of work for him to do. But even if he gets into recovery and does the work he needs to, you have been deeply wounded; his acting out may have decimated your life.

Even if you think the relationship is over, there is still healing you need to do for yourself. You have been hurt, perhaps more profoundly than at any other time in your life. New trauma triggers residual pain from previous traumatic experiences. Your partner's acting out may well have reawakened pain from your past.

For that reason, you may be having thoughts, feelings, memories, or even flashbacks related to hurtful times during earlier periods in your life that you had forgotten about or thought you had left behind. Reactions to abuse you suffered at the hands of previous relationship partners or within your family of origin may emerge. You may find your thoughts dominated by past experiences of loss or trauma. For many people their current pain connects with past hurtful experiences, and all of this emotional tumult is brought into the present.

You may even find yourself looking at your partner and feeling like he is to blame for every past hurt you've experienced. That is the way trauma works. You are not trying to resurrect those previous hurts; they come without invitation. Even as you begin to heal, they may come up again unexpectedly and reawaken old traumatic events. Some partners report that it is as though their spouse is the face on every previous trauma—as if he caused every one of them.

Your job is not to get your partner into recovery, but to take care of yourself. This involves engaging in your own recovery process, separate from whatever your partner does or doesn't do. You must get healthy for what lies ahead, whether or not he does the work of recovery in his own life. Ultimately, whether or not your relationship is repaired, this experience has wounded and changed you. And, you need and deserve to heal.

FREEDOM

HOPE

CHAPTER 13

WHY DID HE DO IT?

We receive variations of this question from hundreds of wounded women. "Why did he do it?" is an especially difficult question in that the answers, while factual, rarely provide satisfaction. Unless you've struggled with addiction yourself and have a more personal understanding of how the cycle of obsessive thoughts and compulsive actions can drive decision-making and behavior, it can be extremely difficult to understand how a man (often a man of morals) who loves his wife and family can do what he has done.

With experience in your own recovery, it will make more sense. However, the potential for future understanding does little to diminish the great pain you may be in currently. In any event, part of why he did it is usually found somewhere in the sex addict's life story; most often in childhood. Please be advised that while the following information may partially explain a person's sex addiction, in no way does it serve as an excuse for it.

Many sex addicts were sexually abused as children. Every time I (Marsha) talk to a woman seeking help I ask her to tell me about her husband's childhood. Nearly always I hear about a seed that grew into his sexual addiction. Sometimes it's a tragic story, like one man, who as a young boy was kidnapped and raped by multiple men for several days. Other times, it's a more common violation like a needy mother who clung to her son as her emotional confidant or a raging father who berated him. Many boys found their father's porn stash and were mesmerized at an early age, and from that grew a life-long pattern of addiction. And recently I learned that two men got hooked by reading their mothers' romance novels when they were just eight and nine years old.

Many sex addicts were physically, emotionally, and/or verbally abused growing up. Perhaps your husband falls into this broad category, which leaves boys (and girls) starved for love and a sense of self-worth. When children grow up with abuse, they also grow up with deep emotional pain and unmet needs. And like all of us when we hurt, they look for ways to numb or escape from their pain. And since sexual feelings stimulate the pleasure center of the brain, sex provides a highly effective—and addictive—way to feel better—at least temporarily.

Many people who become sex addicts grew up starved for love and affirmation. Quite often the seeds of addiction show up even in the stories of addicts who grew up with their physical needs met. However, some of the essential emotional pieces were missing. Years ago, I worked with an older couple who had loved one another for more than four decades, but they had always struggled because of certain deficits in the husband's childhood.

As he shared his story with me, I learned that although he was the son of missionaries, he was never held, touched, verbally affirmed, or told he was loved. He described sitting on the floor of his parents' closet growing up, and rubbing the hem of his mother's dresses between his fingers in an effort to self-soothe and gain her comfort. Though it wasn't enough for his aching heart, it was his best effort to meet his own emotional needs. Decades later he sat in my office, a white haired gentleman, who, even after all those years, was still bonded to a fetish that sprouted from early childhood deficiencies. In spite of his wife's love and commitment to him, the connection in his brain held him captive.

Some males, especially boys and younger men, simply stumble onto sexually stimulating content, and they're hooked. In our highly connected technological world, no one can avoid the many sexually stimulating messages that bombard us every day. This includes our children and grandchildren. Because we're all sexual beings, it's easy to see how readily even a child can become preoccupied and ultimately addicted. One of my own grandchildren told me, "Grandma, we can't take our phones to Scouting events anymore because the leaders caught some of the boys looking at pictures of naked women on their phones." Increasingly, as I talk to newly heartbroken women about their recent discovery of their husband's addiction, they also tell me one or more of their children are already addicted to online porn.

Over the last few years one of the saddest things I hear in the stories of young women is even more troubling because it has become so common, especially in strong faith-based communities. These young brides tell me their husbands sought to remain celibate until marriage, but in their desire to be sexually pure until their wedding night, they masturbated to pornography. They assumed that once married, their wife would automatically become the object of their complete sexual attention. What they didn't understand until it was too late is that we bond sexually to our early sexual experiences. Without meaning to, they bonded with artificial intimacy and their own bodies. And now they were hooked. How heartbreaking that what began with such positive intentions went so drastically awry. But that's the way the brain works when coupled with the power of sexual stimulation.

Of course there are other reasons men become sex addicts, but these categories capture a huge percentage of the stories we hear. The most important takeaways for partners include:

1. Your husband's addiction has nothing to do with you.

2. The addiction button cannot be turned off easily or quickly. Relapse does not *have* to happen, but because the bonding that set the addict up for addiction takes place in the brain, most addicts have to work hard over time to change well-worn mental connections. They need other men on this journey for support, and they need the tools of a solid recovery program. In addition, because the seeds of the addiction are usually first planted during childhood, most addicts need the help of a skilled counselor to heal old wounds and replace the unhealthy coping mechanism of sex with new and healthier ways to respond to emotional pain and meet their needs.

What did I do wrong?

You didn't do anything to warrant your husband's sexually addictive behavior. Though none of us does everything "right," and we all make mistakes in life and our relationships, your behavior in your marriage is in no way connected to his sexual acting out. This is his issue, not yours, even though he may try to blame you for it. As we've said earlier, his addiction more than likely started long before he knew you, and would have continued if you had never met him and he married someone else.

However, now that you know you're living with this painful problem, I (Marsha) invite and encourage you to maximize the potential it brings for healing and growth in your life. And although partners do the healing work for themselves, their efforts sometimes cause their husbands to recognize they need to get to work and recover and grow too. Some even recognize they are at risk of losing the woman they love if they don't jump into a rigorous recovery process themselves.

There's a saying in twelve-step circles I often use on myself. It's short and helps me leap-frog trying to change things in life over which I have no control. With just five little words, it speaks volumes: *It is what it is*. And those five words represent one of the most important keys to our healing—that of acceptance. This is the acceptance referred to in the Serenity Prayer: *God, grant me the serenity to accept the things I cannot change, the courage to change the things I can, and the wisdom to know the difference*.

I hope that as you walk your own recovery pathway you too will use those five little words that can mean so much, and surrender to your own healing and growing process.

CHAPTER 14

WHOM DO I TELL?

I (Marsha) don't believe there is a "right" or a "wrong" answer to this question. Each of us is different, as are the people in our lives. You need to come to your own determination as to whom to tell about the presence of sex addiction in your relationship—based on whether or not you have safe people in your circle. In addition, like it or not, your history and story will factor into how you feel about sharing your heartache. If your feelings weren't allowed, or were labeled "bad" as you grew up, it will likely be more difficult for you to feel safe sharing your new reality.

However, I know from personal experience it is impossible to heal in isolation. We are wounded in the context of relationship, and we heal in the context of relationship. The God of our understanding did not design us to operate as lone islands in the huge sea of life. Rather, He designed us to live (and heal) in relationships. Some partners are blessed with a handful of safe women who can hear and hold their painful secret as a treasured gift and protect it. But for others, finding safe people with whom to share such pain can prove challenging. You may need to learn how to identify people you can truly trust. So let's talk about what makes someone safe enough to tell.

Safe people share and connect from their heart. As they come to know and trust you, they are able to be vulnerable with you about their own lives, their shortcomings, and their failures, rather than maintaining a false front of perfection and toughness. Do you already have people in your life who display this quality? If so, they may be safe enough to tell.

If you are testing new relationships for safety, observe how a friend or acquaintance responds when you share vulnerable feelings and information. In new relationships, it's wise to "test" the other person's safety by sharing a small piece of information about yourself—something that won't feel like the end of the world if your confidentiality is violated—and observe how she responds to your sharing. When she, in turn, shares something vulnerable about herself with you, it's usually a sign she considers you safe. Mutual vulnerability means both parties have an interest in maintaining a safe relationship where each other's sharing is held in confidence.

Psychologist Dr. Henry Cloud suggests considering these questions as you seek to find and create safe connections for your support system:

1. Can the other person listen and empathize with your feelings and vulnerabilities?

2. Can they share on an emotional level?

3. Do you go away from time with them feeling like you have connected, or do you feel alone in the relationship?

4. Is there a high level of assurance that your bond will be protected?

5. A healthy person will respect your wishes to be in control of yourself and what you want to do, or not do.[52]

I want to finish by sharing a poignant, real life story about two women that powerfully illustrates how fear can trap us in tombs of silence and prevent connection, even with those in our lives who are truly safe.

Let's call these women Amy and Candice. I've known Amy for almost a year; a year filled with mountains of hard work doing her part to heal her broken heart. But the one thing missing from Amy's recovery efforts was local women with whom she could share her story. Although she's had virtual confidants, she longed for face-to-face sharing. Even Amy's

---

52 H. Cloud, "Picking Good People," *The Compass* (Centerfield Productions, a division of CruPress, 2007), https://www.cru.org/content/dam/cru/legacy/2012/04/cloudpickinggoodpeople.pdf.

dearest friend of forty-five years didn't seem safe enough to tell. As a result, Amy stumbled toward healing pretty much alone in her day-to-day life, except for therapists and virtual support from other women.

As had often happened for these two women who've been intimate confidants since early childhood, life circumstances brought Amy and Candice together for a visit. Amy felt at home sitting at Candice's side as her friend faced overwhelming grief that could forever change her life. As Amy sat there in an effort to share her friend's heartache with her, Candice began to ask Amy probing questions, questions whose answers would reveal Amy's terrible secret.

Carefully, hesitantly, Amy answered her friend's questions, revealing as little as possible in each response. But each time she did, Candice followed Amy's answer with yet another probing question. And over the space of a few minutes, these two women, who are as close as sisters, discovered they were carrying the same secret. But what really blew Amy away was learning Candice had borne her secret totally alone for fifteen years—fifteen years that Amy would love to have been there for her if only she had known! And Amy could hardly believe that she'd been afraid to tell her closest friend, when she could have had Candice's support right from the beginning of her own devastating year.

Amy now says: "It is such a God story. So unplanned. So unknown. But so powerful. Friends for over four decades, our secret was too delicate to share even with each other, until God opened a door that made it possible."

Are there women like Candice in your life? Or perhaps more recent or less close friendships you can begin to test for safety? If you need support—and we all do—what proactive steps can you take to meet new women for potential supportive friendships? What plan can you develop to test the relationships already in your life for safety?

FREEDOM

HOPE

CHAPTER 15

MOVING FORWARD

....

What are the most helpful steps to take to move forward?

....

As described in the last chapter, the first thing every partner needs is at least one safe person; someone she can trust to not tell others. But where do you find these safe, helpful people if you don't already know them? Most women begin with an Internet search. However, to save you time, I (Marsha) suggest you begin with the resource directory provided in this book. But even there, know what you are looking for before you start.

The initial stage of discovery of the sex addiction is a time of chaos and confusion when it can be difficult to tell the real from the unreal. Wounded partners need the compassion and understanding that comes with the trauma model of treatment and healing. The trauma model not only provides the safety and empathy you need for your shattered heart, it also provides a road map for healing. It is a process that moves you through the early stages of grief, but also equips and empowers you for what lies ahead. After many years of working with partners of sex addicts, I personally believe this healing is done best in small groups with a few other women on the same journey, plus one-on-one counseling for those who need deeper healing for old wounds, or individual help for extreme triggers and anxiety in the present.

Groups provide emotionally corrective experiences that a therapist, no matter how skilled, cannot provide in individual counseling. These include:

- The knowledge you are no longer alone, and can safely share your story and pain

- The opportunity to hear and bond with others experiencing similar events and emotions

- Access to alternative ways of viewing and responding to the events in your life

- The opportunity to connect with other members outside of group, whether in person or via technology, both in the present and in the future after the group has ended

- The encouragement, support, and love of the other women in the group

- "Mirrors" to reflect back to you your value, your positive traits and gifts, and your innate worth

Listen as three women shared what the group meant to them after only one session:

"Yesterday, I felt so hopeless until the Skype call. I cannot thank you enough for your heart to heal hurting women. I am so grateful that I chose to trust God through the encouraging words you spoke to me. After speaking to all the women I went to sleep with a peace I have not experienced since the disclosure."

"Thank you for leading our group earlier this evening. I am finding it very helpful to be among other women where I can finally talk about the pain. It is so wonderful not to feel alone anymore."

"I'm thankful for the telephone group as I finally have an outlet to help process everything. Going it alone has not been easy."

As you look for a group to attend, seek out a guided process that provides the necessary content and structure to help you move forward in your healing. Some groups exist without that growth-producing foundation, and attendees often report little healing.

Is it okay (safe) for my husband to maintain friendships with other addicts?

I (Marsha) believe it is not only safe, but essential to his recovery if the addicts in his life are truly engaged in the process of recovery. Other addicts who are actually working a recovery program provide accountability, encouragement, support, camaraderie, and possibly sponsorship, which can be described as a sort of Big Brothers Big Sisters program within recovery circles. Sponsors help others in recovery begin to work the Twelve Steps and apply them in their lives, hold them accountable, and provide support for the challenges they encounter. As you can guess, all this can greatly increase progress and sobriety.

How do I know he's really stopped?

The only concrete, measurable way to know he has stopped acting out sexually is through a polygraph test. In some rare cases, even the polygraph can't determine the truth. A hard reality of life and love is that we all live with a certain level of uncertainty. Life comes with no absolute guarantees. For this reason, some couples choose to do an annual polygraph. It's valuable risk prevention for the addict, and offers a great sense of assurance for many partners.

Beyond polygraphs and their measurable results, you can expect quality recovery work to have a progressively positive effect on every aspect of an addict's being. Living a true recovery lifestyle changes people's approach to how they do relationships, the way they deal with money, follow through on commitments, their work ethic, and so forth. Often I hear women whose husbands are 100 percent into their sex addiction recovery say, "I've never been married to this man." That's their way of saying their husband is changing in every area of his life. That change is the best marker a partner has of how an addict is doing in his recovery.

If, after a season of living with a sexually sober husband, you see those positive changes begin dropping away, it could be a signal that something is wrong. If his new, healthy character changes begin to disappear, it could signal he's already started sliding down the slippery slope that often leads to relapse.

I frequently hear women rely in part on their God-given intuition, which they often refer to as their "gut" in assessing the status of their partner's recovery. That "women's intuition" may sense a gradual pulling away, a lack of interest, or the uneasy feeling that his mind is with someone else when he engages in physical intimacy with you. While it isn't scientific or 100 percent accurate, your gut is worth listening to.

....

How do I know if he is really in recovery or still lying and just faking it?

....

As skilled as they are at lying, faking authentic change over an extended period of time is beyond the ability of most sex addicts, especially in the bedroom. That notwithstanding, I've had clients who, looking back over years of marriage, can find absolutely no clues their husband was addicted, yet he was. There are addicts so skilled at deception that they can fake it. However, now that you *know* about his sex addiction, you are much less likely to be caught unaware—especially if you pursue your own recovery.

For most addicts, recovery is hard to fake because the "addict brain" leaks into their everyday life in numerous ways, betraying a lack of authentic recovery. Some typical signs include disinterest in you and/or family matters, selfishness, deceit, unexplained spending, unexplained loss of time, tardiness, financial irresponsibility, preoccupation, short temperedness, and any number of other character issues. It's most obvious if the addict has changed and grown through recovery, then slowly backslides as the healthy new behaviors begin to slip away and old attitudes and behaviors re-emerge.

Authentic recovery changes people. It spreads positive changes into the crevices of one's character and personality. When authentic recovery is happening in a man's life, that's when I hear women say, "I have a whole new husband!"

For other men who work hard at authentic recovery, change may be slower and it may take more time for you to see such encouraging signs. Each of us must decide for ourselves how long we can wait for the changes that let us know our marriages are safe places to spend the rest of our lives.

Is this marriage salvageable?

I (Marsha) have seen marriages so damaged by sex addiction that I thought all hope was gone, not only survive, but go on to thrive. So I know that virtually any situation is salvageable, *if* the addict wants his marriage badly enough to work harder than he's ever worked in his life, and, *if* the partner can focus on her healing and eventually find the grace to move toward a new beginning. Addiction to anything is extremely difficult to break, but freedom is possible—when you and your husband want it so badly you'll fight for it by embracing a recovery journey that has worked for millions of others.

Should I leave or should I stay?

This is another question everyone must answer for himself or herself, based on several factors. If a man is not willing to do the work to beat his addiction and heal his relationship, staying with him comes with many risks: risks to your physical, emotional, and spiritual health; risks to your finances; risks to negative influences on your children; and a host of others. Yet, if you give up and leave too early, you might risk losing a marriage that may have a chance to heal and be better than ever before. Again, each of us must determine how long we can wait for authentic change, and if it doesn't happen, decide if it's time to leave.

Now that I know, what should I do?

Educate Yourself about Sex Addiction

Books and websites provide a readily available library of educational resources for partners of sex addicts who want to understand what it means to be a sex addict, and what it means to love one. Coming to understand how events and situations in life—especially in childhood—can set one up for sex addiction proves helpful for most partners. From that awareness, they begin to see they are not the problem, and they can't fix it.

Until you recognize your inability to fix it, you may believe that if you try hard enough, you can keep your husband from his addiction. But by educating yourself, you learn an important, though dreadfully painful truth: you are powerless to control another person, especially an addict.

Do Your Own Healing and Recovery Work

In several places we've written about the important recovery elements that will help you heal. In addition to those, it's important your healing and recovery work includes two key pieces: (a) learning how to have healthy boundaries, and (b) creating a plan for how you can support yourself and start over alone, should your husband ultimately choose *not* to do recovery, or walk out on you, or you decide you've had enough. This plan needs to be written down and kept in a safe place so you know it's there if you have to use it. Just as we buy insurance coverage for events we hope will never take place, so too must one who loves an addict have an insurance policy—a written plan with the steps you'll need to follow should you ultimately need it. And for those without fresh, marketable workplace skills, a part of that plan needs to involve bringing old skills up to date, or learning a new career path and staying marketable, in case you ever have to go it alone.

Detach. Detach. Detach.

Most partners feel something close to stark terror when they recognize they are truly powerless to control their partner's acting out behavior. Without good detachment skills, much of what they think and do is in reaction to what their partner is doing. Detachment is a skill that will help you step out of that reactionary cycle with the addict in your life, and it can be learned.

Detaching from the addict is not withdrawing. It is not isolating, nor is it punishing. Rather, it is putting an emotional *buffer space* between you and your partner. Detaching is not negative or reactive; it is a positive, proactive step. It enables you to gain objectivity, face reality, deal with your emotions, and determine the best course of action for your life. And detaching helps free your partner to focus on *his* recovery because it calms the blame-cycles, anger, and tears, making time and space for recovery.

Determine What You Need If You Are Going to Stay

Staying with a sex addict presents a huge risk, and you are worth whatever hard work your husband needs to do to guarantee you it's safe for you to take that risk. If you read the sections of this book that pertain to the addict, you will begin to gain a better understanding of what you need to ask him to do to get sexually sober. Sex addiction recovery is a team sport. No matter what your husband says, he cannot do recovery alone.

So educate yourself and make a list of recovery actions you need to see in him if he wants you to stay and give him time to overcome his addiction and gain his freedom.

Develop a Plan for Asking for the Recovery Work You Need from Your Husband

Set aside some time to consider the best circumstances, timing, and place to share your requests for recovery with your husband. You know him well; think through what day of the week and hour of that day your husband is likely to be most open to heavy conversation. Avoid times that hold high potential to go awry, and try to choose a time when he is likely to be rested and less stressed. Although it can still go poorly, the goal is to do your best to help produce the results you're after: saving a marriage.

Follow Through and Have That Conversation

This confrontational conversation is discussed in more detail in the following chapter. But, in general, kind firmness, good boundaries, and respect need to be incorporated into this difficult conversation. Without those components, the outcome is often disastrous. Even when you do everything "right," it can still go poorly and not lead to the results you're after. Remember that you are talking to an addict, and you are asking him to give up his drug of choice, the one that has enabled him to cope with and medicate stress, perhaps for much of his life. You can expect that he won't be excited about that prospect. So pre-plan and take good care of yourself if indeed it does go poorly.

Step Back and Watch and Wait for a Pre-Determined Length of Time

The most agonizing part about loving a sex addict is living with their "No" if they don't want recovery. As hard as it is to face, some husbands make that choice. And though it can be devastating, it is what it is, so there is no choice but to face it. Many of those men would happily continue to live with the status quo. After all, if they can have you and their addiction, they have the best of both worlds.

If "No" is your husband's reaction, you are now faced with following through on your previously stated consequences. Without your follow-through, you render your words meaningless and teach him that you only cry wolf. In doing so, you set yourself up for many more years of emotional pain and increased loss of self respect, potential financial ruin, possibly devastating health effects, and potential damage to your children.

So, authentically search your heart in advance; gain certainty about what you are willing to do if he rejects your request that he enter recovery.

Signs He's Working to Gain Freedom and True Change

The number one rule of being in a relationship with a sex addict is: *Believe behavior, not words.* This advice is often given by former sex addicts who've worked hard for their own sobriety; men who understand the mind games addicts play, and who know what it takes to gain their freedom from addiction.

One woman put it well when she said, "His behaviors are the fruit of his recovery." If you see healthy behaviors indicative of strong recovery work, you are seeing the fruit that indicates it's safe to stay. However, if you see old behaviors and attitudes, more than likely he's not working a strong recovery program.

How do I deal with my grief?

Discovering your husband's emotional or physical unfaithfulness brings overwhelming loss into your life, much like the death of a loved one. And loss, no matter its source, requires time and a process to move you through the stages of grief. In addition, new loss often hooks into old grief and loss in your life, forming a tangled ball of pain. Much like two long, tangled chains, the old and the new grief must be carefully tweezed apart. Most people need help to take on this challenging task. Grief work is next to impossible to do alone.

The first step in dealing with your grief requires you to survey the available resources and choose one that looks promising, then check it out. Because both financial resources and the location in which you live shape your available options, the help available to each partner will look different. Yet, healing is available to everyone in one format or another, no matter where you may live. The Internet and other advances in communication technology have greatly expanded the possible resources. I suggest you re-read the answer to the question, "What steps are most helpful to take to move forward?" from earlier in this chapter. In addition, to help get you started in your search for help, I list ideas and options that will hopefully spark your creativity as you begin your own Internet search.

To learn what is available to you locally, combine search phrases such as "support groups for partners of sex addicts," along with the name of your town and state. If faith-based groups are a comfortable option for you, do the same kind of search, tweaking it a bit by including phrases such as "churches with support groups for partners of sex addicts in . . . ." Play with other combinations; you're on a treasure hunt.

Do a similar local search for counselors in your area who are trained in sex addiction. Again, use search parameters to find what you're looking for. As you search, you can also include acronyms that indicate a counselor has special training to help others heal from sex addiction. There are now a number of organizations that provide such training for counselors. The best known is the Certified Sexual Addiction Therapist (CSAT) program, but there are several others.

CSAT training is only now beginning to include the trauma model of helping partners of sex addicts heal. I (Marsha) have received reliable reports indicating that some therapists trained as CSATs still label partners of sex addicts as codependents. The key to healing requires that women be empowered to find the resources we need, and to advocate for ourselves, even if it means asking therapists hard questions. If we do that for ourselves, just as we would do it for someone we love, we can find professionals who will help us heal our trauma, then help us gain the skills we need to grow beyond our losses. That remains the goal for partners of sex addicts.

Do a search for twelve-step groups for partners of sex addicts in your area. In my experience twelve-step groups are not the best place for early grief work when our emotions are raw. However, they are free and often accessible—a place to meet other wounded partners and gain skills that can be incredibly helpful after early grief work is finished. There you can also connect with other partners of sex addicts in your area, and ask them about local resources they may have used or know about.

Do broader searches to look for helpful books for partners of sex addicts; for telephone or online support groups if you can't find in-person groups locally; and for other options for healing such as retreats, workshops, and conferences.

Once you know the options available to you that fit your time and financial parameters, you are ready to start your healing process. I strongly recommend you choose a group that provides a structure and process that will move you toward healing as you invest yourself in it. In addition, I recommend that, if at all possible, you seek out a group with a trained facilitator who understands your needs because she has been through the heartache herself, and has taken group facilitator or coaching training (if she is not trained as a therapist).

CHAPTER 16

QUESTIONS ABOUT RECOVERY FROM PARTNERS

With the discovery of your partner's acting out, your world has been rocked. Things that you once took for granted now may not look so certain. You may question your judgment, perception, even your sanity. In this chapter we want to answer many of the questions that you have been asking.

....

Did my spouse ever love me?
....

I (Marsha) can almost guarantee your spouse loved you on your wedding day, even though his addictive actions may now make that hard for your heart to believe. Because sex addicts compartmentalize—putting their spouses in one box and their addictive behavior in another—most sex addicts dupe themselves into believing that one has little to do with the other. Although such division seems illogical to you, it's the addict's reality.

Because as women we view each strand of our lives as interconnected with the others, we automatically assume his addiction is about us. Consequently, we assume the addict in our life must have never loved us. But in addiction, one has nothing to do with the other. As you have heard and will continue to hear, his addiction is not about you.

Like all forms of addiction, sex addiction is progressive; over time an addict can get so lost in his deluded thinking that he loses touch with reality and his ability to love. Entrenched sex addiction is so narcissistic and focused on the next high that an addict lost in deluded thinking may view his wife as little more than an obstacle between him and his "needs." At that point, he may be incapable of loving or caring about anyone except himself and his next "fix." Even then, if an addict learns he's about to lose something he's not prepared to live without (usually his wife, family, and half his wealth), change remains possible through authentic recovery and skilled therapeutic help—if he chooses that path.

....

How could he love me and carry on relationships with other women?

....

Virtually every woman who has learned her husband has been unfaithful has uttered this painful cry, seeking an answer that makes some kind of sense to her. Repeatedly, answers fail to satisfy. Educating yourself about sex addiction and how the brain works helps provide knowledge that, in time, your heart may be able to accept—especially if you see your husband working hard on his recovery.

Although difficult for most women to understand, men and women differ in their approach to the act of sex. Most women want and need to feel connected emotionally in order to engage sexually with their partner. But men are wired differently. They can more easily separate sex from love and emotion. I understand you don't like it. Neither do I (Marsha). But once again it is what it is, and there is nothing we can do about it. It is a fundamental difference in the brains of males and females.

Another key brain-based gender difference was mentioned earlier: that of how the brains of men and women organize the elements of their lives. For women, every area of her life is interconnected, and each part of her life affects the others, much like a plate of spaghetti. If she has a fight with her husband, she's not going to want physical intimacy until she once again feels emotionally connected to her husband. However, men tend to compartmentalize the areas of their lives, often keeping the compartments separate emotionally.

This truth is regularly shared by women in my groups. A woman reports asking her husband, "How could you have loved me but had sex with other women?" To her, one thing crosses out the other. And then she shares her husband's answer to her heart's question, and it's always the same: "It has absolutely nothing to do with you!"

His approach to dealing with different areas of life is like a waffle. Like the tiny squares on a waffle, each area is separated by little walls. In his mind, it's as if he used an eye-dropper to drip syrup into one little square, being careful that none runs over into the squares of his marriage. Nice and tidy, they remained separate in his mind. But not so for his wife.

Just recently when I asked a group member how she felt about this information, she quickly said: "I don't like it, but it is what it is so I need to accept it if I want to stay in my marriage." Fortunately, her husband is becoming a changed man because of his recovery journey, which makes acceptance much easier. But like it or not, if we can accept and adapt to this knowledge, love and life will become easier.

Does he really love me now?

If he is willing to "do" recovery work and make a real effort to overcome his addiction, I believe he almost certainly loves you. Rigorous recovery is far from easy. If he is not willing to work hard to gain freedom and sexual sobriety, there's a chance he's so lost in the self-focused narcissistic thinking of sex addiction that he's unable to really love anyone in a healthy way.

Active addiction is often considered a form of insanity for a reason: when we surrender ourselves to any addictive habit we lose our ability to think and act rationally. We can easily see that kind of insanity in the unkempt drug addict living on the street. With sex addicts it is usually much less obvious. But, the insanity is apparent when someone is willing to risk his or her life as he or she knows it—marriage, family, often his or her job, reputation, health, earthly wealth—all for another fix.

Nonetheless, the possibility remains that even if he's currently too lost in his addiction to love anyone, if you approach him with a planned, supported confrontation, he may respond positively. If he commits to recovery, brain scan research verifies that his brain can heal, enabling him to become a loving, caring human being.

Since our relationship was based on a lie and I really don't know who he is, why do I still really love my husband?

Everyone is a complex mix of positive and negative qualities, and we all struggle with what it means to be human and in need of ongoing grace, healing, and growth. No one, addict or otherwise, is all one way or another. No doubt, your husband's positive qualities drew you to him in the first place, and with his struggles and darker side, those positive qualities likely still exist beneath his ingrained addictive thinking and behavior. Those are the qualities that make him lovable and worth your effort—if he is willing to do the work required to gain freedom from addiction and establish long-term sexual sobriety.

If your husband is now being honest and seeking the help he needs to live free from the lies, there is hope that your love and commitment will be worth it in the not-too-distant future. This can only happen with hard work on his part along with your willingness to endure the pain of early recovery and to do your own recovery work.

How can I learn not to loathe my partner even though I love him?

Not all partners will identify with this dilemma, but for those who do, this is an important question. Recently, one of my clients went through a couple's intensive workshop that included a full sex addiction disclosure. As she listened to her husband read his list of sexual behaviors, she learned about something that repulsed her at a deep level. Later that day, she tried to process with me what she learned about the man she has loved for decades. She questioned whether or not she could love him again, knowing this new information. In the end, she talked with me about the fact that none of us is all good or all bad; that we're all a mix of characteristics, beliefs, and behaviors, formed by our experiences in life. And this man, like so many sex-addicted husbands, endured painful and damaging events during his boyhood, which fostered a grotesque sexual behavior. She eventually acknowledged the courage it took for her husband to risk this disclosure, knowing she may decide to leave him if she knew. But at the end of our two-hour phone conversation, it was his newfound commitment to honesty, as indicated by his willingness to tell all, that allowed her to look to the future and have hope.

I encourage you to remember that none of us is "finished" yet. With each new day, and each new challenge, we are being stretched and grown, refined by life's events and our responses to them. Like you, your husband is neither all good nor all bad. Rather, he's a broken human being who had the courage to risk letting you know everything about him, knowing full well you may leave. If his heart is soft toward you, and remains soft, if he continues to willingly focus on recovery, I'm guessing a stronger, more realistic love and respect for him will begin to emerge in your heart in the months and years ahead.

....

How do I confront my spouse about his sex addiction when he says he is not a sex addict?

....

This question gets asked again and again as women discover their husband's addiction, then learn that he doesn't think he has a problem. The answer is the same whether or not the addict admits his problem. Over the years I've come to believe that even if a therapist tells him he's not really a sex addict according to diagnostic criteria, the problem is not resolved. On a practical level, when one spouse is getting their emotional and/or sexual needs met outside the marriage, and the other spouse is deeply hurt by it, the relationship has serious problems that won't simply vanish because certain diagnostic criteria are not met. A confrontation is still needed, and change must take place if the relationship is going to heal.

However, unless we understand addiction and recovery well enough to remain calm and grounded, no matter how our spouse responds to confrontation, it won't produce the results we seek. Therefore, confrontation works best when we prepare for it. Including a support person in the process increases the potential for positive results. This support person might be a skilled counselor, or perhaps your minister or priest. Other women have included their adult children who know about the addiction and are ready to say "Enough" to their father. Some women have included another man who is in sex addiction recovery himself as their support person for confrontation. It can be helpful to have the presence of a man who has "been there and done that" and overcome it.

Whether you do it alone or with support, confrontation requires the following steps:

- A simple, clean, clear request for what you need the addict to do to get help. Give him a brief, stated period of time to take action, followed by a sentence stating what steps you will take if he chooses not to get into recovery.

- Then you need to take a step back and wait to see if he follows through. If he chooses to get help, it's time for you to detach enough to give up playing watchdog. Instead, focus on your own healing while observing his behavior from a detached point of view. This gives him time and space to dig into recovery. If, in the end, he does not choose help and recovery, you need to follow through with the pre-stated and predetermined consequences you gave him. Then your focus shifts to your own grieving, healing, and growth.

While this approach may seem extremely cut and dried—even harsh—when dealing with entrenched addictive behavior that's destructive to you and your marriage, it is the only path that will lead to help and healing. Even then, many addicts never follow through. In the end, many partners lose the man they loved.

Confrontation presents him with a clear fork in the road and requires him to make a definitive choice, so be certain you know what you need in order to remain in your marriage. And be advised, nothing will weaken your position—and his respect for you—more than not following through with your stated consequences.

I know my partner is a sex addict but he will not get help. What am I supposed to do?

Educate yourself about sex addiction so you gain enough understanding to know the challenges it presents in your marriage and in your own life. Get help for your own healing so you gain the strength you need to face your situation with grace, dignity, and confidence. And when you are ready, determine whether you want to confront the addiction in the way described above, or if you want to live with the addiction in your life. It's virtually impossible to live with active addiction without it changing us and our children in unhealthy ways, so my hope is you will refuse to settle for that. Although the fear of financial insecurity makes it incredibly difficult for some women to leave, if women take a long-range view and develop a plan, in time every partner can gain enough financial stability to leave an addict who is lost in his addiction. Yes, your life, and your children's lives, will change. But the change won't be nearly as catastrophic as living with unchecked addiction.

How do I get him to understand how he is killing our marriage?

Sadly, he may never have ears to hear your heartache, so all you can do is try. You've likely already tried to communicate this through a range of words and emotions with little effect. However, if you have not yet done a planned confrontation, I suggest taking that additional step when you're ready and have the support you need in place. It may be the first time he faces—clearly and directly—the reality that his addiction is about to cost him his marriage. Facing the magnitude of such a loss can be a powerful motivation for change.

Several women have shared in support groups that when their husbands failed to hear the magnitude of their pain, each asked her husband to read hand-picked pages from a book that describes the level of trauma and PTSD partners of sex addicts experience. And in each of those cases it worked to change their husbands' perspective, though there are no guarantees.

But, what if he never "gets it" or cares about your feelings? What happens to the marriage? I know there is no greater heartache than coming to grips with the reality that your husband is choosing his addictive lifestyle over you. The pain is so great it's nearly unbearable. Yet, it is what it is, and we're powerless to change it—or him. Recognizing our powerlessness over the addict we love, and proactively refocusing our energy on our own self-care and growth, requires huge effort. Yet, with it comes a new kind of freedom and power. Here's how one woman described the results: "I now realize I believed his sobriety was the key to my happiness. But seeing it that way kept me a victim. Now I am taking responsibility for my own happiness, and it's empowering."

If in the end he remains closed to understanding and change, you'll be faced with the heartbreaking decision of whether to detach and stay, or detach and leave. While neither of those choices are what your heart longs for, many, including the women quoted above, have survived the loss and gone on to live lives filled with love, joy, and purpose. And so can you.

....

How should I support his recovery?

....

Supporting a husband's recovery means making room for the time and emotional space his recovery will take. This is easier said than done. Taking this position, and holding it, usually requires enormous self-control, outside support, and your own recovery process.

Your husband's recovery means weekly meetings with other men; meeting with an accountability partner; reading recovery materials; perhaps meeting weekly with a counselor; and more. All this takes time—time he could be spending with you and your family. And counseling takes money, even though his addiction may already have caused debt or loss of savings for both of you.

Making space for his recovery can fuel mistrust because you now know he's lied to you for years, so it's only natural to wonder: *Is he really at his meeting?* And it can fuel resentment: resentment that he has support while you may struggle to find it for yourself; resentment that after all he's done to take from you, you must now give even more to him; resentment that the kids are without their father some nights each week because his recovery work takes time away from home.

Supporting his recovery by making space and time for it requires a certain amount of detachment. But detachment is usually hard to grasp, especially when we're reeling emotionally, so let's talk about it again. At the beginning of my own healing journey, railroad tracks helped me better understand how detachment looks and feels on a practical level.

Detachment is intentionally putting a bit of emotional space between you and your partner so you, for a time, can concentrate on your own individual recovery, and he on his. Detachment can prove challenging, especially when you're caught in early trauma emotions. But like a set of train tracks, you're still close enough to touch, you're headed in the same direction, and your love and commitment are the railroad ties that hold you together. Learning to detach is much like learning to walk on your own rail. If you're working with a counselor, he or she can help you develop your own set of marriage "railroad ties" by giving you intimacy exercises to do, along with other practices to keep you moving forward as a couple while helping each of you heal as individuals.

Without your own rail to keep you on course, trauma and anger commonly set off painful derailments that slow recovery, or bring it to a halt altogether. If you need additional support, find a support group and a counselor. With their help you can better learn to use the recovery skill of detachment. It's essential for your healing, as well as his recovery.

How does enabling differ from support?

Hopefully the explanation above helped you gain a clearer understanding of support. But how does support differ from enabling a sex addict?

When we enable an addict, we fail to ask for what we need because we fear we'll lose the relationship. Or we ask for what we need, and then get angry because he says no or does not follow through. Unfortunately, most addicts won't do the hard work recovery requires without boundaries placed in front of them and calmly held. In a very real way, *your* boundaries and recovery requests can hold the key to *his* freedom— if he doesn't want to lose you. Yet in the end, you are powerless over him if he says no. Your empowerment is birthed by focusing on your own journey.

We can also enable by trying to do his recovery work for him. We might do all the research to find meetings, groups, and therapists for him, then remind, nag, or coerce. Or we might "walk on eggshells" by tip-toeing around the issues, increasing our stress and our children's, rather than risk asking for the recovery work we need. We may make excuses or lie for him when he doesn't show up at home or events on time.

When we enable, we don't confront *in a healthy way*, and we don't follow through with consequences. We avoid our natural role in the addict's life: that of his partner and help mate. In addition, the probability our marriage will end increases exponentially when we enable because addiction continues unchecked.

....

How can I support my spouse when he goes through recovery without opening myself up for more hurt?

....

When you stay with your spouse and support him in his recovery, you are choosing to take the risk of further hurt. There simply are no guarantees he won't hurt you again. But there are things you can do to care for yourself and minimize destruction, should he relapse or give you further disclosures related to his previous acting out. Investing in your own recovery journey is the most important gift you can give yourself when you choose to stay and support an addict. Everything on the following list is essential:

1. Find support
2. Detach
3. Create safety for yourself
4. Grieve
5. Learn to manage your triggers
6. Practice self-care
7. Learn to self-soothe
8. Learn to intentionally build joy into your life
9. Learn how to communicate your needs in a healthy way
10. Develop healthy boundaries

11. Develop an exit plan. Hopefully you will never need it, but like insurance, it is good to know it's there

12. Rediscover yourself, and build on your talents and skills

These twelve elements are the resources and tools you need for your own healing and growth, whether your marriage makes it, or does not. So as you survey recovery options for your journey, make sure the options you choose contains these essential components.

How do I detach from the addict so I can recover?

Reread the earlier section titled "Detach. Detach. Detach." As you make your life more about you and your healing, and less about him, you will feel encouraged by a growing sense of empowerment to manage your own life and the confidence that you will be okay, no matter what he chooses to do with recovery.

After one wise group member internalized the value and mechanics of detaching from her addict husband, she shared this answer to a workbook question with her group: "In a lot of ways it's scary to take my focus off of him and put it on myself—my needs, my healing, my brokenness. But it's the best thing that I can do for myself and the situation. Making my brokenness about *him* keeps me locked inside his prison. I didn't choose infidelity . . . *he* did. But I can now choose what I'm going to do about how it affects me."

Generally, we fear another betrayal and living with the pain it will set off in our already traumatized lives. It's safety we seek. But when we finally surrender to acceptance we free ourselves to detach, refocus, and begin to heal just like the woman above.

He relapsed again. When should I think about leaving?

Relapse proves achingly painful for partners because it's a reminder that they continue to live with risk. Risk of more hurt, more loss, and more instability in their lives. And with each loss comes a new wave of trauma and stress. And once again, safety evaporates.

A dear friend of mine faced this question far too many times in her marriage with her husband who struggles with pornography addiction. Each time a relapse happens she agonizes and grieves, searching for her own answer to the question. But in the end she stays. "Why?" you might ask. My friend stays because she knows her husband's heart. It's tender, gentle, caring, and kind, and that deep down he's a good man.

"But how can you think he's a good man if he keeps relapsing?" I hear you asking. Because, he is more than his addiction. He is neither all black nor all white. And he sincerely wants more than anything in the world to be free from his addiction. Each time he relapses, old wounds, though previously grieved, are processed, and his commitment to recovery continues, one day at a time. And, for my friend, that's enough—as long as he remains committed to gaining progressive recovery, and his heart remains open and tender toward her.

If you are faced with the question of when to leave, I encourage you to look at the whole person, and remember he is more than his addiction. Ponder his heart. Is it tender toward you, or is he clinging to the addict brain's belief he is entitled to his addiction? Does he confess his failures with remorse and determination to try again? Or does he hold it secret, until you stumble upon it?

Each wounded partner must answer these questions, and more, as we sift and sort through the shattered parts of our lives. The answer rarely comes easily. Nor is it always correct. But no matter our answer, we can carry on.

....

How do you navigate finding a good therapist?

....

Finding the right therapist to work with can be challenging. It's complicated by the fact that few of us tell even close friends what kind of therapist we're looking for, and why. Fortunately, technology has made the process somewhat easier. I (Marsha) suggest you try the following steps in your search for a therapist; it may take some time, but once you find the right therapist for you, you'll know it was time well spent.

1. Do an Internet search with combinations of words such as "partners of sex addicts therapists" + the name of your town

or city. Study therapists' websites, looking for clues about their training, methods, and philosophy on trauma versus codependency, making notes about each. Then, call and ask if you can have fifteen minutes of their time to ask questions and learn whether or not he/she is a good fit for your needs. This has worked for me, and for some of my clients, though of course not all therapists will be this generous with their time. But whether you do it by email, phone, or fifteen minutes face-to-face, be brief and to the point in your questions to show you value their time. And even if you learn this is not the right person for you, you are likely to get referrals to other therapists more suited to your needs.

2. If, ultimately, you discover there are no therapists in your area specializing in helping partners heal, search for therapists who treat trauma and PTSD. It's best if your therapist understands that sex can become an addiction, since that perspective is necessary to understand your trauma. But even with little acknowledgment of the addiction, if he or she accepts that you are traumatized, and is willing to help you heal, that's a great start.

3. Your medical doctor, clergy, or a local women's resource center may also have referrals for you. Therapists who work with abuse/rape victims are trained in trauma, and could possibly help you heal. Once again, try your local crisis clinic.

4. If you still come up empty handed, many therapists provide counseling via Skype and/or phone, as well as in person. By expanding your search to include larger areas—other counties and states—you will find someone who can help you.

5. If you have friends or family members who have been through trauma or addiction and have found help through a local therapist, and you are comfortable asking them for a referral, do so. But use guidelines for identifying "safe people" discussed earlier; that's an important part of your self-care, too.

How long will it take me to heal from what he has done to me?

The time it takes to heal varies from person to person. It depends heavily on your support and your process for healing. Looking back over the years at the women I know on this journey, it usually takes somewhere between one and five years. In my own life, I could feel joy again after a year. But if you lose your marriage and all that goes with it, as many women do, creating a new life for yourself can take a number of years.

Having good support and a solid recovery process is an important key to healing, and a major factor in the length of time healing requires. But sadly, the financial resources available to invest in our healing often limits the professional help we can afford.

For those who can only afford limited professional help, Eye Movement Desensitization and Reprocessing (EMDR) therapy and Heart Centered Hypnotherapy often prove to be the two shortest routes to processing and resolving trauma and PTSD. They can accomplish more in a shorter amount of time than talk therapy. If you have limited financial resources to invest in counseling, I (Marsha) suggest you find a therapist trained in one of these modalities. With her help, you will be able to process and integrate the trauma caused by your partner's sex addiction. If—like many of us—you have unresolved childhood issues, these therapies can be invaluable in helping you process and integrate that part of your story as well.

Even if you lack the funds for professional help, that does not mean healing is beyond your reach. I've found that by participating in a small support group based on a guided healing process, facilitated by a therapist, coach, or even another partner of a sex addict who has gained healing in her own life and taken facilitation training, a great deal of healing can be accomplished. There is something almost magical in the sisterhood that develops between our hearts as we support and love one another on this journey. Some such groups are available at no cost and many are available at manageable cost.

If you struggle with childhood wounds, such as abuse, I encourage you to check with your local crisis clinic, area hospitals, and churches, as well as women's resource centers, to see if there are groups available that match the healing you need. These institutions often provide such services for free, or at very low cost.

I challenge you to pursue your own healing process and stay with it until you, too, can feel the light and joy returning to your life. It will be worth the effort.

When do I need to separate for my own health?

Because you're the only one who lives inside your body, only you can answer this question. Only you carry the stress and pain that lies behind the asking. However, I can reflect what I hear and see in women's lives, as well as my own, to discuss how your question is often answered.

We now know that a partner of an addict experiences relational trauma, and trauma is extreme stress. It's deadly if endured without relief, and ultimately, healing. The body's response to stress and trauma involves hormones and inflammatory chemicals which can foster effects from headaches to heart attacks.

As described by Christine Horner, MD, the ongoing stress reactions the body produces lead to chronic excess cortisol levels that cause high blood pressure, insomnia, anxiety, depression, and anger; they depress the immune system and increase the risk of stomach ulcers, diabetes, and heart disease.[53] Harvard neurologist Martin Samuels adds that "Norepinephrine [a hormone and neurotransmitter released during stress] is toxic to the tissues—probably all tissues, but in particular the heart."[54]

Living with extreme stress and trauma can destroy our physical and mental health. It also takes a toll on our children, even if they don't know what's going on. They can "feel" it in their parents' interactions, and in the home environment. Clients share numerous ways some children begin to act out, with a handful even becoming suicidal.

---

53 J. D. Bremner, "Hypotheses and Controversies Related to Effects of Stress on the Hippocampus: An Argument for Stress-Induced Damage to the Hippocampus in Patients with Posttraumatic Stress Disorder," *Hippocampus* 11, no. 2 (2001): 75–81.

54 G. Cowley, "Anxiety and Your Brain," *Newsweek*, February 24, 2003.

I (Marsha) encourage you to talk to your doctor, or a trusted friend or relative who knows you well and understands what's going on in your marriage, and ask for their honest reflection about impacts they may see on your health. Then, take some time to determine what course of action is needed to maintain your health and that of your children.

....

I just found out my husband has had affairs throughout our marriage. I want to leave him but I have four kids and never finished college because I supported him while he completed his education. What do I do?

....

So many dedicated wives and mothers find themselves in your difficult situation—with limited options. Although our inability to support ourselves and our children can leave us feeling powerless to make the changes we need to heal, by developing a plan and working it, we *can* make progress. Perspective is critical. It's imperative we recognize that we *do* have options. Otherwise, we feel trapped and cannot begin to heal.

I (Marsha) sit with women every week who find themselves in this confining predicament, hear the sense of helplessness they feel, and my heart aches for them. I know the impotence feeling helpless produces. It kills hope, energy, and joy. If you are in this situation, I encourage you to take a long view that leaves room for your preparation to be independent enough to leave if your husband does not choose recovery or you recognize you must leave your marriage so you can heal.

Seek help in your efforts to put together a long-range plan. See what help is available to you through the women's resource center at your closest college. Some women have been able to meet with school counselors for aptitude testing and help in identifying which career paths best fit them, and those that require the least amount of additional education. County or state offices may also have helpful resources for women. It's work, and it will take time, but gaining the information and skills you need to make your life work is empowering, as well as necessary.

I feel I need to separate from my husband but I have to stay in our house for the sake of our children. How do I set up an in-house separation?

In-house separations are generally used for one of two reasons. The first is temporary and often follows sex addiction disclosure when a wife feels enormous sorrow and loss, and needs time and space to process what she's learned. These situations usually include sexual abstinence and allow her safety in which to process and begin to heal. If you still have love and basic respect for one another, you can likely manage the in-house separation on your own without the help of a therapist.

However, if your relationship is marked by angry outbursts and tension prevails, I suggest you seek help from a therapist trained in sex addiction for the guidance you need to plan, implement, and monitor an in-house separation. A therapist's input can be especially helpful when the time comes to begin to move back toward each other in the home and bedroom. Moreover, professional assistance can be enormously beneficial if you have children in the home who don't understand what's going on. A therapist can offer input about what to tell them based on their ages and emotional development, and help you find resources for them if they need help talking about their feelings.

The second reason in-house separations are put in place is in lieu of actual separation or divorce. The motivation is usually financial, but sometimes it is to keep the family together for the sake of the children. Though some couples are able to live under the same roof while leading two completely separate lives, most find such an arrangement difficult at best, and impossible at worst. While the reasons for doing this may be noble, living this way proves impossible for most couples.

If you are contemplating an in-house separation for the second reason, find a good marriage and family therapist to guide you. Even then, don't be surprised if your arrangement is unsuccessful. For couples who remain angry with each other, where there is ongoing animosity, a clean break is often better for the entire family. If finances do not allow for a clean break, get the help you need to make yourself marketable in the workplace so you have access to more options.

Understanding the answer to this question requires that we accept two key things about addiction and the addict: One is that the sex addict has used his addiction to help him cope with the daily pressures and stressors in his life and/or past emotional wounds that have caused deep pain. The second is that sex addiction becomes a physiological condition as it takes root in someone's life and brain.

Because the sex addict's drug of choice (sex) causes a neurochemical release when he experiences sexual stimulation of some kind, sex helps him gain some relief from difficult situations, people, and things in his life. Like with caffeine, cigarettes, and even chocolate, people often use things to cope with life. And just like other coping mechanisms, whether it's alcohol, prescription painkillers, or hard drugs, sexual stimulation sets up an addictive pattern in the brain as the body grows used to needing the "high" the addiction brings.

We've all heard the term "dry drunk," but do you know what it means? A dry drunk is someone who has stopped drinking, but has not yet done the recovery work required for the whole person to get better. The alcoholic may have stopped drinking, but without lots of hard inner work, he remains an angry person who loses his cool over normal stressors in life, because now he is facing them with no help from the alcohol.

It's the same for the sex addict. In early recovery he may have stopped using his drug of choice, but he has not yet had sufficient time, or done sufficient work, to learn healthier coping mechanisms. If he's stopped acting out, he is living without the neurochemical relief sex addiction brought him. This often leads to grouchiness, a short temper, depression, anxiety, and the potential for a host of other difficult feeling states and behaviors.

For the partner, this is a particularly challenging time. Detachment, self-care, and support from others who understand can help you make it through early recovery as the man you love learns to live a different kind of life. And if he sticks with it, and works the steps with a good sponsor, given a year in recovery, these negative behaviors will begin to drop away. And hopefully, you will begin seeing in your husband the man you originally fell in love with. When that happens, it will be worth the wait.

....

What is "acting out" for wounded partners?

....

How one answers this question is colored in part by whether partners of sex addicts are viewed as codependent, or as victims of relational trauma. For people who see the partners of sex addicts as codependent, checking a sex addict's texts or phone log prior to disclosure or discovery is viewed as codependent acting out. However, those who subscribe to the trauma perspective believe a partner does this because she feels unsafe, and needs to learn the truth so she can protect herself. I hold the relational trauma view, so my answer is based on that perspective. But, even within the trauma model, there comes a time we know enough, and for our own sake, detachment and refocusing our efforts on our own healing and growth is what we need. Other acting-out behaviors can include (but are certainly not limited to):

- Acting out sexually to "pay him back"
- Uncontrolled raging
- Spending lots of money on "retail therapy"
- Staying in a toxic situation with an addict who's not interested in recovery, but raging because he won't change
- Giving him the silent treatment to punish him
- Engaging in reckless behavior such as driving at dangerous speeds to "let the anger out"
- Turning friends and family against him to intentionally punish him
- Using children as emotional confidants and/or turning them against him

These kinds of behaviors are often referred to as "offending from the victim position," and are based on the idea that because you are the victim you can do anything you want. These behaviors are evidence of a collapse of one's containment boundaries. Containment boundaries are just as important as protection boundaries that prevent others from hurting us. We must contain ourselves so we do not inflict harm on others, regardless of what they have done to us.

Some women go a different route and "act in" by punishing themselves in some way for their husband's transgressions. These behaviors can include putting on lots of weight; developing or returning to previous eating disorders; doing physical self-harm by cutting or similar behaviors; losing themselves to the trauma and becoming agoraphobic, sequestering themselves and their children in prisons of their own making.

In every case, what is missing is good self-care, support, and a way to process one's new reality so that over time the negative energy dissipates.

....

How can I help my therapist and others understand where I'm coming from regarding codependency vs. relational trauma?

....

Since we cannot change anyone but ourselves, you may not be able to help your therapist understand the trauma model and how that information can shift perception about partners' codependency. While some therapists become entrenched in their views, most are trained to acknowledge and examine new research and progress in their field. The trauma model regarding wounded partners is beginning to take hold in the therapeutic community, although broad change is going to take time. Even some clergy and medical professionals are coming to the realization that discovering one's partner is a sex addict produces trauma.

Most therapists want to continue to grow so they can do their best to help others heal. If you can share information from a book or research article written by one of their peers in addition to sharing your daily reality and need for emotional safety, you increase the likelihood of being heard. I often hear women say they gave their therapist a copy of *Your Sexually Addicted Spouse*[55] and that after reading it, their therapist's mind opened to change. I suggest you choose a section from a book or

---

55 Barbara Steffens and Marsha Means, *Your Sexually Addicted Spouse: How Partners Can Cope And Heal* (Liberty Corner, NJ: New Horizon Press, 2009).

article currently in print that was written by another mental health clinician; one that's based on clinical research supporting the trauma model of treating partners of sex addicts.

In the end, if your therapist remains closed-minded, you will need to find a therapist willing to work with your reality so you can heal. Advocating for yourself before you change therapists is good self-care, and provides one more step in your personal empowerment. With the individual efforts of many, in time the paradigm will change.

....

At what point does a woman extend her forgiveness?
....

While the idea of forgiveness may seem very far away for newly wounded women, at some point each of us needs to consider forgiving her partner for the pain and loss caused by his actions. Without forgiveness, the hurt in our hearts plants the destructive seed of resentment and bitterness. As resentment and bitterness sprout in our hearts, they not only wrap their roots around our marital relationship, they twist our very nature and interfere with all relationships. Over time, their grip reshapes us. In a real sense, forgiveness is something we do for ourselves, even though it touches everyone we meet.

Forgiveness is not denying, ignoring, or forgetting the past, nor does it equal trust, or necessarily mean reconciliation. Rather, it is a gift you give yourself so you can be free of the resentment and bitterness. It comes with a bonus: when we forgive, we create the opportunity for a happier future—whether we spend it with our present husband, alone, or with someone new.

Each of us must answer the "when" question for ourselves. Certainly, forgiveness should not be rushed or forced, even though many partners report their clergy pressed them to forgive right at the start. But artificial forgiveness isn't forgiveness at all. Moreover, it can impede the working-through process indicative of true forgiveness. When you're ready, you'll know it by sensing an inner letting go of the emotional debt your husband "owes" you. In its place will come the trademark peace that forgiveness imparts.

How can I ensure that this doesn't keep happening?

Unfortunately, there is no way to gain the assurance all wounded partners need. Love is a risk, and loving a sex addict is a greater risk. So hurt can happen again. But the risk can be greatly reduced with a proactive recovery plan in place for both the addict and the partner.

Part of gaining our empowerment is knowing what we need to see in his recovery if we choose to take the risk of staying in the marriage. And learning how to ask that those needs be met is one of the skills required for a successful outcome. So educate yourself until you understand what sexual sobriety involves, and embrace your own recovery journey so you gain the skills and empowerment needed to do your part to move forward.

Some couples choose to add an annual polygraph to help ensure it doesn't happen again. Many wives need that assurance, and many recovering sex addicts want it for themselves. They report feeling propelled to guard and grow their recovery, knowing that sometime in the next twelve months any secrets or lies will be revealed. Therapists who treat sex addiction are split on whether or not polygraphs are a good idea. However, as the former wife of a sex addict, and a woman who hears mountains of pain in other women's lives, I believe an annual polygraph is a gift every recovering addict should give to himself and his partner.

CHAPTER 17

COPING WITH TRAUMA

In our book, *Your Sexually Addicted Spouse*, Barbara Steffens and I (Marsha) present the case that many partners of sex addicts are not only traumatized, but their trauma rises to the level of post-traumatic stress disorder (PTSD). While this is gaining wider acceptance today, it was revolutionary in 2009 when the book was written.

While we cannot say whether or not you have PTSD, it is more than likely you have been psychologically traumatized by your partner's behavior. Trauma manifests with numerous symptoms. It is our hope this chapter will help guide your healing.

How do I deal with my triggers and flashbacks?

Among the most difficult aspects of discovering a partner's sex addiction are the debilitating, physiological reactions that take the form of intense anxiety, panic attacks, or flashbacks, and can leave you feeling crazy and totally helpless. These reactions are generated by triggers—thoughts, feelings, memories, and other experiences—that connect with and bring to mind traumatic events. Worse, as described earlier, this new trauma often hooks into earlier life traumas, creating a tangle of powerful emotional and physical reactions.

It helps to begin with gaining a good understanding of what's happening. You're not "going crazy," or in need of a mental ward, even though you may feel like it at times. Although there are specific internal differences between the anxiety produced by triggers, and the lack-of-knowing-where-it-came-from feeling when we suffer a flashback, both can, and often do, render us helpless to manage our daily lives.

Because flashbacks are intense episodes of re-experiencing something that happened in the past, we don't often hear partners of sex addicts talk about flashbacks unless they experienced trauma earlier in life. As we've said, new trauma often hooks into old trauma. Early life trauma generally overwhelms a child's coping mechanisms and the trauma memory is stored in the limbic system of the brain—not in the form of words or even pictures, but in the form of smells, emotions, or sensations that seem disconnected from anything real. It's that inability to verbalize what happened, along with the often overwhelming quality of flashback, that can leave people feeling crazy.

The good news is your brain is still trying to process the old traumatic event, but it still overwhelms your ability to cope and carry on your everyday life, especially when combined with the more recent discovery that the man you love is a sex addict. Learning to manage triggers, anxiety, panic attacks, and flashbacks while remaining committed to your own healing and recovery is key. Try the following coping skills, but I encourage you to get help from a trauma specialist as well.

1. Tell yourself aloud what's taking place. Say, "I'm having a flashback," or "I'm experiencing a panic attack."

2. Focus on breathing in and breathing out, slowly and deeply. Fear automatically changes your breathing, making it faster and shallower. This only intensifies anxiety, fear, and panic. By focusing on your breath, and breathing in slowly through your nose, then out, your physical responses can begin to calm.

3. If you live with someone you trust, and that person is home, seek her (or his) participation in moving through a flashback. She can help by saying in a calm voice, "You're having a flashback," and reminding you to breathe your way through it. That can help you stay, or become, grounded, which is essential.

4. Ground yourself. By reconnecting yourself to your surroundings and whatever you are standing on, you can reorient yourself back to the present. Stomp your feet on the floor or ground. Press your hands against the wall, and use all five of your senses to become aware of what's going on around you in the "now."

5. Use things that bring you comfort to help you self-soothe. Whether you pet your cat, hold a stuffed animal, or wrap yourself in a soft blanket, care for yourself by providing comfort in a way that works for you.

6. Recognize that it may take time to work your way through the memories that are pushing to the surface like molten lava. While it may only take an hour or two to fully reintegrate into your present after a flashback or panic attack, if they persist and come too close together, it may become necessary to consider inpatient treatment. By working regularly with a skilled trauma therapist, you can learn how to cope with and process the strong sensations and emotions that demand your attention.

7. Become aware of the people, places, and things that set off flashbacks, then remove, or limit, your exposure to them. Years ago, when old trauma broke into my present in the form of my first ever flashback, I was at a very large conference, seated in the front of the room. The conference was going to last for three more days. After a few minutes of trying to ground myself without being noticed, I knew I had to remove myself from the room to get back to the present. Although I didn't want to, I got up and walked down the long aisle and returned to my hotel room. I ended up spending the remainder of the conference in my room processing the things that were coming up. Gratefully, I had a fabulous therapist back home who worked with me over the phone to accomplish much healing during those three days. Though it wasn't my desire to isolate at an event in which I wanted to participate, I needed to set that boundary to take care of

myself, and to focus on using the experiences that came up to further my healing.

When does the underlying constant feeling of sadness lift?

I can say without a doubt that the constant feeling of sadness can lift for us all. But does that mean there will never be sadness over the losses we've experienced? Of course not. My own trauma, though indelible and real, long ago simply became a factual part of my story. There are moments when I miss what might have been; moments when I wish my own story had unfolded differently. But I also experience mild sadness at times over the other less-than-perfect pieces of my life, just like everyone else. Life is full of loss; it's part of the human experience. Whether it's our youth, special friends, the death of our parents, or something else, reflection on our losses can bring momentary pain when they come to mind.

Even in a marriage that is healing beautifully, sex addiction brings enormous loss that takes multiple forms: loss of trust, safety, our naive view of the world, innocence, our life as we knew it, and many, many more. But, as you work through the major losses that came with the discovery of your husband's sex addiction, moments of sadness no longer produce piercing pain. If we've been working to heal and grow from this experience, it's a softer, more short-lived sadness that crosses our radar from time to time, triggered by some event or memory. We can acknowledge its presence and move through it.

How do I get off the emotional roller coaster?

I (Marsha) have yet to meet a woman who has not been thrust onto the jolting roller coaster ride of wildly fluctuating emotions upon discovering the man she loves is a sex addict. No matter how strong we think we are, or how much emotional work we've done, if we believed our relationship was based on commitment, this discovery sends us careening. Our stability fluctuates wildly, leaving us feeling adrift, crazy, and undependable.

Once there, how do we get off? We feel powerless—and in fact we are powerless—over him, over his addiction, and over *his* outcome. That is our difficult reality. But does that mean we're powerless over everything in our lives? No, it does not. And therein lies the key to stopping the roller coaster of feelings. It won't happen overnight, and it will require hard work, but we can get off.

During those first days and weeks after the discovery of your husband's sex addiction, your emotions will continue to career as you begin to process and assimilate an alternate reality in your life. But if your healing moves forward with help from a trusted professional as your guide, before too long you will reach a place of acceptance, and when you do, the roller coaster of deep emotional plunges followed by sometimes strange highs will begin to smooth out.

As I (Marsha) work with women in groups, this smoothing out usually begins to happen by week five or six. By that time, women begin to understand that they are indeed powerless over their husband's behavior, and there is no guarantee that he won't do it all again. However, they *can* become empowered in their situations. There are specific skills traumatized women can learn; skills that provide tools and resources to cope, begin to adjust, and to recognize that while we're powerless over others, we can be empowered when it comes to ourselves.

Interestingly, when husbands see this change taking place in their wives, many of them sit up and take notice. Suddenly, they realize their wives are no longer helpless and totally dependent on them. With that knowledge many become afraid she may get strong and walk away because she's tired of living with the addiction. Most often, saving our marriages begins with saving ourselves.

Does the pain of betrayal ever completely heal?

Each of us is unique and comes with our own history of wounding across our life span. Those of us with traumatic wounding earlier in life usually need more time and work to relieve the pain of marital betrayal.

Most of the clients with whom I (Marsha) have worked whose husbands have done the necessary work to gain freedom from their addiction and grow do move out of the deep pain of betrayal, in time. It's vital to keep in mind that addiction recovery comes with no guarantees and many partners will bump up against triggers and painful memories, even when they think they have healed—and those can, at least temporarily, cause new pain. Nonetheless, I know women who no longer feel the pain of betrayal. Some report that now, on the other side of healing, their marriages are deeper and more intimate than they could ever have been without the work required to gain freedom and heal from the pain the addiction brought into their lives.

So, there is real hope that the pain can heal completely if your husband continues his fight for long-term sexual sobriety. So, too, there is genuine hope of complete healing for women who leave their relationship—if they do the recovery work to gain their own healing from this trauma, and any traumas that came before it. That does not mean the losses created by the trauma of sex addiction will be wiped from your memory, but the experience will soften and no longer cause pain.

How do I set healthy boundaries?

Many books have been written to answer this question because learning to set and maintain healthy boundaries is far from easy. This is especially true for those raised in family cultures without healthy boundaries. Healthy boundaries are essential in any important relationship; but even more so with an addict.

Boundaries are imaginary lines that separate us from other people. Learning how to develop and use them is one of the most important pieces of growth and healing as you strive to move beyond the pain of sexual betrayal.

Unfortunately, many women miss the spirit that *must* accompany boundaries. Yes, the one you love has wounded you. But trying to control him and calling it setting boundaries will not only fail to provide the emotional safety you seek; it will drive him farther away from you. One client reported to her support group that when she and her husband attended a couple's intensive with Milton (Magness), he advised her, "Don't tell him what to do (or not do). Call out the man in him by telling him how something makes you feel."

Boundaries are about learning to take care of yourself. A big part of taking care of yourself is the ability to know what you feel and need moment-by-moment, day-by-day. Being in touch with yourself is an important part of self-care, and a precursor to crafting healthy, helpful boundaries. If you need help identifying your feelings, seek out help to learn this skill.

How do we craft healthy boundaries? As Milton said to my group member, we begin with vulnerability. Though it feels risky, it is a key ingredient. Rather than playing cop to force your spouse to stop engaging in certain behaviors, a more effective strategy is to ask your spouse for what you need in order to feel safe within the relationship. This request comes from a position of vulnerability. As Nancy Groom puts it, "Her vulnerability softens him and he wants to help her feel safe."[56]

Though I also encourage you to read a book on this topic to learn how to use boundaries well, I'll include a tool counselors use to help clients learn how to create a boundary request. To use it correctly, you first need to learn to be able to tell the difference between a thought and a feeling. They are two very different things, though we often confuse them. It can be helpful to do an Internet search with the words, "feelings list"; it may surprise you to see the long list of feelings you may be dealing with.

Once you've identified what you are feeling, plug that feeling into the following formula:

When you (do this) _____, I feel _____.

Would you be willing to (do that)_____ to help me begin to heal, please?

Here's an example to help you gain the skill you need to use this formula well:

"When you take your phone into the bathroom, I feel afraid you will use it to act out like you used to. Would you be willing not to take it in there with you to help me begin to heal, please?"

---

56 Nancy Groom, *From Bondage to Bonding: Escaping Codependency, Embracing Biblical Love* (Colorado Springs, CO: NavPress, 1991).

Can you hear how the vulnerability about her fear softens this request? For tenderhearted husbands, this vulnerability is a game changer. Others will refuse to "hear" their partner's feelings and needs, even in the face of vulnerability. For that reason, once you've shared your boundary requests, the outcome is in the other person's hands. The possibility remains that your partner will say no; that he won't help meet your need. In those times, you have no recourse but to regroup, pray, and provide good self-care in other ways to take care of yourself and continue to heal.

Even if your husband says no, you've learned important information about what he is and isn't willing to do and where he is in his recovery. That is information that can help you determine what steps you must take if you want to heal and move beyond a life filled with the pain that comes from living with an active sex addict.

CHAPTER 18

LEGAL AND FINANCIAL PROTECTION FOR PARTNERS

Jocelyn's Story _____

"Shocked" was not a big enough word to describe how Jocelyn felt when she discovered that her husband of more than thirty years had been carrying on an affair with his secretary. She couldn't believe that the man she loved with all of her heart could be unfaithful to her. How could she not have known? She didn't see any signs that he was cheating. Nothing caused her to even question his fidelity until she walked in the open door of his office and saw him kissing this woman.

At Jocelyn's insistence, he agreed to go to counseling and even joined a twelve-step group for sex addicts. Over the next several months, he was a model husband. That is, until he came home one evening and said he was divorcing her.

Within days, Jocelyn found out that most of their money had been moved out of their savings account. Their portfolio of stocks and bonds had been liquidated. She was shocked to find out that several pieces of real estate they owned were only in her husband's name.

Jocelyn hired an attorney to protect her interests. With the help of a forensic accountant her attorney engaged, Jocelyn was able to locate some of the funds her husband had hidden. In retrospect, she wished she had taken a more active role in understanding the family finances. The unquestioning trust she placed in her husband resulted in her getting less of a financial settlement than she was entitled to.

As a woman who works with myriad other women who have few options for getting free from the chaos and destruction their life-partner has created, I am passionate about the question of how to protect oneself legally and financially. I run into this dilemma nearly every day, and oh, how I wish there were a simple answer.

Although each of our lives and our financial circumstances are unique, let's consider this question through two broad categories of partners of sex addicts: (a) Women whose financial reality sounds "typical" to western thinking. Their husband earns good wages, and these women often work and earn money of their own. (b) Women who have dedicated their lives to raising their children and have been out of the workplace for years.

If you are in the first category protecting yourself is a bit easier than if you fall into the second one. However, all women who love a sex addict—even one in recovery—need to engage in good self-care in the area of finances, and stay as informed as possible about protecting themselves and their children financially. The universal basics include:

1. Make duplicate copies of at least the last three years' tax returns, and keep them in a safe place outside of your home.

2. Make duplicate copies of any mortgages, all credit cards, bank, and other loans you may be obligated to, or carry in your name for someone else. Again, put all such documents together in a safe place away from your home.

3. Make sure your name is on all mortgages, car loans, and other loans for things you may need to support yourself. Too often, I talk to women whose husbands have found a way to keep her name off their mortgage, complicating her ability to remain

in the home if they part ways. Similarly, having legal title to a car is essential if you will need to go back to work.

4. Every woman in relationship with a sex addict should have her own, individual bank account at a bank other than the one where she and her husband bank together. I (Marsha) recommend you don't tell him about that account. It is like insurance money; if he doesn't stick with recovery, your life can become extremely difficult if you don't have access to at least some cash. While many husbands won't cut their wife off financially, some will. It's far better to be safe than sorry in this area, especially if you have dependent children. I strongly recommend you grow this account week-by-week, month-by-month. If all you can afford is to get a little cash back each time you're at the grocery store, do so, then deposit it into your account.

5. Every woman should have at least one credit card in her name only. This helps maintain a credit history under your name, so if you land in a desperate situation, you have access to funds as you transition from your marriage to singlehood.

6. Make sure you are "marketable" in terms of having up-to-date job skills so you can go back to work if you need to. If you married very young and did not go to college or work prior to the marriage, you will need to make yourself job-ready and keep your skills honed. For some women, this marketability begins at a women's resource center or similar place in your own community. As stated earlier, community colleges often have women's centers where you can take aptitude tests, and get consultation about career paths that require shorter amounts of training. If you have dependent children and are thrust into a dire situation, you may not be able to dedicate years to an education. On the other hand, if you don't have kids or if they are grown, life can take on a whole new meaning by pursuing your dreams, including education for a career path you may love.

7. Make extra copies of important keys, such as for your home, car, and anything else you need access to in the event your husband walks away.

None of this is intended as legal advice. Rather it's a list that has grown out of hearing thousands of painful stories over the years. To protect yourself legally, I highly recommend you see an attorney who is sympathetic to and knowledgeable about women in difficult marital situations. An attorney can help you understand the laws in your state regarding legal separation, divorce, custody of children, division of wealth, and much more. Take these steps so you are prepared—and feel empowered enough—to act on them in case you ever need to.

In a few extreme cases, surprises can come in spite of your best efforts to be prepared. It is not uncommon for a woman to learn her husband has spent in excess of $100,000 on his addiction behind her back. I've met women whose retirement accounts were drained by their husband's addiction, and others who learned about multiple credit card accounts they never knew existed, totaling more than $150,000 in debt. One woman's husband failed to pay the IRS year after year, choosing instead to use those funds for his addiction. Ultimately, she learned he/they owed the government $650,000. Removing her name from that debt took years in the courts.

Yes, we love our husbands. Yes, marriage requires huge amounts of grace, and taking the above approach may seem counter to both. But now that our naiveté has been stripped away, and we've faced the fact we're married to a sex addict, we must step into our empowerment and move forward with a well-thought out plan we can put in place quickly, should we ever need it.

PART FOUR

THE PATH TO RESTORING RELATIONSHIPS

Sex addicts have their recovery. Partners have their recovery. Now what about the relationship? Is there any hope that your relationship can be healed? Can it ever be restored?

Yes, relationships can be restored if both of you are willing to do the very demanding work necessary for that to take place. This may be the hardest part of the journey. With all of the work each of you need to do individually, restoring the relationship between you will demand even more work and patience— perhaps more patience than you may think you have.

Some couples give up. They determine that it is easier to end the relationship and start again with someone else. Those couples soon find that they still need to learn and practice new relationship skills if they ever hope to succeed in future relationships.

If your relationship was worth getting into in the first place, it is worth the effort to see it restored. One of you cannot make restoration a reality. If both of you are willing to do the hardest work of your lives, you can recapture what you believed to be lost and, for some, build what you never had.

CHAPTER 19

QUESTIONS ABOUT RESTORING RELATIONSHIPS

Alec and Mona's Story _____

Alec and Mona have been in recovery for ten years. They have worked hard at restoring their relationship, starting with a clinical disclosure backed up with a polygraph exam and continuing with annual follow-up polygraph exams.

Recently, Alec was contacted by a former co-worker to ask if he would write a recommendation for her. He agreed, and wrote the recommendation while sitting next to his wife on the couch. He then told his wife he was going to personally deliver the recommendation. Mona was shocked, having remembered that during his disclosure he admitted to having masturbated frequently to fantasies of this woman. He had agreed to not have any further contact with her. Alec told Mona he would just drop off the recommendation and not talk to her.

When he went to the woman's workplace the next day, she happened to be standing near the receptionist as he dropped off the recommendation. She thanked him and hugged him when he gave it to her. That evening, when he told Mona exactly what took place, she was crushed. He minimized her feelings, saying he didn't do anything wrong.

Although Alec did not act out or break his sobriety, he did not realize how dangerous it was to have contact with someone who had been the object of his past fantasies. The other critical mistake he made was not recognizing how painful his actions were for his wife. By minimizing his behavior, he invalidated Mona's feelings. He was basically placing the other woman's needs ahead of his wife's feelings.

....

How can I begin to better understand and empathize with my wife's feelings?

....

You need to understand that your wife is angry because you have betrayed her by engaging in sex outside of your relationship. You promised when you married that you would be true, loyal, and faithful to her. Your wife wrongly assumed that you were not engaging in any sexual behavior that did not involve her.

On top of your betrayal, you have lied to her and led her to believe that the difficulties in the relationship were her fault. At home, you have often not been mentally or emotionally present. She asks you how your day has been. Sometimes you just say "fine" and other times you can talk endlessly—so long as it is all about *you*. How frequently do you show any real interest in her day and how *she* is doing?

If things do not go well at work, perhaps you have a tendency to take it out on your wife. You may rarely help around the house, and consider it her job to do the cooking, clear and clean the dishes, do the laundry, clean the house, and raise the children. Perhaps you gripe when she makes occasional requests of you.

When was the last time you took the initiative to try to improve the relationship? When your wife first suggested that you see a therapist about your relationship, did you derisively dismiss the request? Is your idea of a date with your wife dinner where you want to eat and a movie that you want to see? How much interest do you demonstrate in what she truly wants to do—in what is important to her?

How much of this describes your relationship? To what extent can you recognize and sit with the truth about how you have harmed your wife? The more you can place yourself in her position, spending some time "in her shoes" and really considering what her experience within the relationship is like, the better you will be able to understand and empathize with your wife's feelings.

....

What am I supposed to do if I've been working really hard on my recovery, but my wife still doesn't trust me?

....

Many men seem to think their wives should be impressed by their recovery efforts and accept their word that they will never be unfaithful again. They often think she should be willing to just turn the page and let go of the past. Your wife's trauma is not something that will go away easily or quickly, and not just because some time has passed and you are working a recovery program.

As I (Milton) write this, my wife and I just completed climbing a mountain behind our house in the Canadian Rockies. I would like for you to imagine that you and your wife are climbing a mountain together. At one point she is climbing a sheer rock face and you are holding a rope, belaying her so she will not be injured if she slips. However, rather than pay attention to the rope you should be holding, you take a break to eat a snack because you're hungry. Your wife slips and falls, and is badly injured in the process. She is taken to the emergency room with multiple serious injuries.

As you look at her broken body, you have no trouble understanding that she is badly injured. You can see the extent of her injuries and you know you are responsible for her trauma. In this situation, you would not expect her to just "get over" her injuries. You would understand that she will take a long time to heal and that even when she has healed as well as possible, she may never be the same again.

In the same way, your sexual acting out has severely wounded your wife psychologically. The wounds she has may not be visible, however, they are just as real as any physical wounds. It will take your wife a long time to heal. The fact that you are in recovery and you are trying hard will not make her pain go away.

Are you willing to be there for your wife and allow her the time she needs to heal? Are you willing to be patient as she continues the healing process? Can you wrap your mind around the possibility that even five years from now, some of her wounds may still be present? Nothing in her life has prepared your wife for what you have done to her. She tries to tend her wounds by talking about her feelings and by asking questions. She may ask the same questions again and again, trying to make sense of what defies explanation.

You can either assist or hinder your wife's healing. On the one hand, if you can commit to recovery and learn how to be supportive of her as she works through her trauma, you will help facilitate her healing. On the other hand, if you are less than totally committed to recovery or you expect her to just "get over it," you effectively obstruct her healing.

....

When should I start marriage counseling with my wife?

....

Most sex addiction therapists encourage couples to wait six to nine months before beginning couples work. The idea is to focus on individual work first. That being said, we feel it is crucial to do a clinical disclosure followed by a polygraph exam as soon as possible after discovery of the sex addiction. Following the disclosure, the focus will be on individual work, but there are important couples' communication and intimacy-building exercises that are helpful to start immediately. We have found that couples who began these sooner rather than later do better in the long term.

....

What are the chances of our marriage truly recovering?

....

Obviously, the chance of any marriage recovering depends on the two people who comprise the couple, their priorities, and the work they are willing to do individually and together. It certainly can happen, and we see it happen with many couples. However, there are also plenty of couples who are not successful. In those cases, we usually see one or more of the following:

- One or both partners refuse to do the individual work necessary for recovery

- The sex addict begins to act out again

- The sex addict is less than 100 percent committed to recovery

- The sex addict procrastinates and can't seem to get around to doing what he needs to for solid recovery

- The sex addict does not prioritize rebuilding intimacy

- The partner has experienced so many traumas in her life that she simply cannot endure the additional trauma brought by the sex addiction

- The sex addict has a deep spiritual experience he believes makes it unnecessary to do any additional recovery work and so discontinues twelve-step program participation

- There is an unwillingness on the part of the partner to move forward in her healing journey so she stays stuck in her trauma

- The sex addict continues to be dishonest even if he stops all acting out

- The sex addict expects his wife to "just get over it"

- The sex addict does not change his attitude toward his wife and continues treating her disrespectfully

- The sex addict continues to be defensive, to be impatient, to minimize his past behavior, to argue, to rage, and to withdraw from his wife

....

When are major life changes (relocating geographically, new job, new church, a totally new start) necessary?

....

As a rule of thumb, it is good to delay major life changes until both of you have a year of solid recovery. The purpose of this delay is to help protect people from making impulsive, ill-advised decisions in the midst of a crisis. With few exceptions, this continues to be the best advice. Cases where change may be needed sooner include when a person has lost his or her job, where an acting-out partner lives next door or very close by, or is a co-worker, or a member of the same church.

Often couples may be so committed to supporting early recovery that they want to move away from their current city or even out of state. They reason that what is needed most is a new atmosphere; a clean slate. In recovery this is called seeking a *geographical cure*. Often, this is much less effective than people believe it will be—the change needed most is not a change in geography, but rather a change in the sex addict.

How involved should a spouse be in defining what a sex addict must do to recover?

One of the boundaries for both partners is that each must focus on his or her own recovery. Neither partner can do recovery for the other. When the focus is on the partner's recovery program, attention is diverted from one's own individual work.

At the same time, the spouse of a sex addict has the right to demand that, if they are going to have a future together, the sex addict must have a robust program of recovery. This doesn't mean the partner defines what that recovery looks like, but if the sex addict is just making a show of recovery without really doing the work, it will become obvious and the future of the relationship will be at great risk.

What boundaries are recommended for couples to put in place after discovery?

The following are some of the basic boundaries that are necessary for the relationship to survive. You will work out additional boundaries together. In establishing couples' boundaries, it would be helpful to work with a sex addiction therapist.

- Each partner must do his or her own recovery work

- All sexual acting out must stop—immediately

- Verbal, emotional, or physical abuse (including blaming and shaming) is not allowed from either partner

- Children cannot be used as pawns to strengthen either partner's position
- Both partners agree not to abandon one another and to stay in the relationship and work through recovery from sex addiction and healing from the resultant trauma

How do you counsel a man who sees no benefit in pursuing recovery since his significant other is deeply affected by her own issues (PTSD, anxiety, depression, etc.) and refuses to see a counselor or get other help for herself?

Whatever gets a person into recovery is a true gift. Many men get into recovery to save their relationships. Others get into recovery to minimize the negative consequences of their addiction. The only motivation that makes recovery work long-term is doing it for the sake of becoming a healthy and whole human being and a person of integrity. If the only motivation for recovery is to save a marriage, sex addicts will waver in their commitment to recovery whenever their partners express ambivalence or struggle.

Marriages that survive typically do so because both partners are at a similar level of health or dysfunction. As one partner gets healthier, the other partner will also need to get healthier. Otherwise, there will be an ever-widening gap between partners that will make it increasingly difficult for the relationship to continue.

What can partners realistically expect from the recovering addict during the first year?

Partners should be able to expect all acting out to stop. Sex addicts' attitude and behavior toward their partners should improve significantly. Blaming, shaming, and raging need to come to an end.

The first year of recovery serves as the foundation for recovery throughout the rest of life. During the first year, recovery should be so important that it becomes a lifestyle. Multiple recovery activities need to become routine: daily, weekly, and monthly. A sex addict in solid recovery will establish a habit of attending multiple twelve-step meetings each week. One of the first tasks is enlisting a sponsor to serve as a mentor in recovery.

Many sex addicts complete working through the Twelve Steps during the first year. Although there is not one right speed for working the Steps, it is important that sex addicts not drag their feet in recovery. As they work through the Steps, they will be engaged in reading and writing assignments each week given by their sponsor. The sex addict will have multiple contacts each week with other men who are in recovery. Sex addicts in recovery may change their friends and will certainly change the way they spend their time. Recovery needs to be a high priority.

....

The walls between us are up and I can't imagine how they can come down anytime soon. Is there any real hope that we can learn to love each other again?

....

Yes, there is real hope, but you will both need significant help to make the changes that are necessary to restore your relationship. At the end of this book, you can read the stories of couples who have rebuilt their relationships. This can happen for you if both of you are committed to the tasks ahead.

CHAPTER 20

DISCLOSURE: WHY? HOW? WHEN?

We firmly believe that for your relationship to thrive in the future, it must be based on truth. Sex addiction is about deception and secrecy. Recovery is about transparency and integrity. Relationships that survive sex addiction are built on a foundation of trust. Often this foundation begins with a formal disclosure that details the specifics of the sexual acting out read to the partner in front of a therapist.

Why?

When you and your spouse first decided to embark on a committed relationship, you likely assumed that you could fully trust the other based on many experiences you shared during your time dating. When that trust is shattered by multiple acts and the many lies that cover it up, in order for a relationship to be restored, trust must be rebuilt—often from the ground up. Disclosure represents the ground on which trust can begin to be rebuilt.

Disclosure may be the scariest and most misunderstood part of couples' sex addiction recovery. This is not a do-it-yourself event where a sex addict dumps the particulars about his sexual past on his partner. To be clear, disclosure is a clinical process that needs to be carefully facilitated by a skilled sex addiction therapist. It is not to be confused with various incidents of telling about select episodes of past acting out. Often when caught in acting out, sex addicts will finally admit to what was discovered (after many denials), then reveal a bit more and deny there is anything else. There may be many such occurrences through the years—each starting with denials before the revelation of some additional details.

Most sex addicts want to opt for simply forgetting about their past, promising never to repeat it, and moving forward without ever looking back. They often claim they are thinking of their partner; not wanting to hurt her with the details of their past. In reality, they are selfishly thinking of themselves, wanting to avoid facing their past.

Partners have a right to know to whom they are married and what their sex-addicted spouse has done. They can deal with the truth. What is crazy-making are the various versions of a sanitized past that sex addicts offer as they try to conjure up a history that sounds believable and does not make them look too bad.

How?

Disclosure involves the sex addict following detailed instructions developed by his therapist. Since the goal of a disclosure is to establish a foundation upon which trust can be reconstructed, the completed disclosure should cover *every* sexual event in the sex addict's life. Additionally, the disclosure should include all of the ways the addict has deceived the spouse as well as any other secrets kept from the spouse outside of the sexual arena.

We cannot stress enough that you should not attempt to do a disclosure on your own. There are many potential pitfalls that require the skilled guidance of a trained sex addiction therapist to avoid.[57] Whether or not you choose to do additional work with a therapist, this is an occasion when it is critical to engage the skills of a professional.

When disclosure is complete, the partner should know everything related to the sex addict's acting out. Perhaps for the first time in the relationship, there should be no secrets. From a place of total honesty, couples have a chance to create a future together marked by

---

57 You will find specialized sex addiction therapists listed at the following websites: www.findachfp.com, www.sash.net, and www.sexhelp.com.

transparency. For trust to be reestablished, the partner must know that she finally has the truth—the whole truth!

Partners must prepare to hear new information. Regardless of what they already know, disclosures always bring out new information. Sometimes there is just a little new information but most of the time there is a great deal the partner did not know. Occasionally, when I (Milton) am working with a sex addict preparing to give a formal disclosure, I will ask how much his partner knows. The answer is usually that they know most of it, sometimes giving percentages like, "She knows 90 percent" or "She knows 98 percent." After the disclosure is read to the partner, I may ask her how much of it she already knew. I frequently hear answers such as, "I knew less than half of it," or "I didn't know most of it."

Once the disclosure has been read, the partner needs to be able to verify that she now has the truth. We utilize polygraph examinations to validate the sex addict has been truthful. Polygraphs are a useful tool but should only be used as part of the total disclosure process, and when they are integrated into therapy.

When I first began using polygraph exams with disclosures about fifteen years ago, I knew of only one therapist who used them as a tool for restoring trust, though they were not part of a clinical disclosure. Since my first book[58] was published in 2009, in which I advocated for the strategic use of polygraphs, hundreds of therapists have begun to use polygraph exams to assist couples in rebuilding their relationships after the devastation of sex addiction. Clinical disclosures backed up by polygraphs are becoming widely accepted as the norm, especially with more couples requesting this from their therapists.

For a more thorough explanation of the process of disclosure and the use of polygraph exams, refer to *Stop Sex Addiction*.[59] That book provides details of the process followed at Hope & Freedom and by Certified Hope & Freedom Practitioners (CHFP). *Stop Sex Addiction* also describes the ongoing use of polygraphs in relationship rebuilding and includes an in-depth interview with my lead polygraph examiner.

---

58 Milton Magness, *Hope & Freedom for Sexual Addicts and Their Partners* (Carefree, AZ: Gentle Path Press, 2009).

59 Milton Magness, *Stop Sex Addiction: Real Hope, True Freedom for Sex Addicts and Partners* (Las Vegas, NV: Central Recovery Press, 2013).

When?

When should a disclosure take place? I believe it should take place as soon as possible after the partner's initial discovery of acting-out behavior. Other sex addiction therapists advocate for taking up to a year or even two to prepare the disclosure, as well as the relationship partner. Such therapists take the position that the couple should basically put any relationship rebuilding on hold during that time and concentrate on individual recovery. The problem with this approach is that many relationships do not survive this interim period. When the disclosure finally takes place, the partner may believe she already knows about most of the acting out. Then, the delayed disclosure rips open wounds that may have started to heal and the partner is re-traumatized, necessitating starting the healing process all over again.

It does not take a year or more to prepare a disclosure. We have many clients who come to our Three-Day Intensive program[60] after as little as a month of preparation—and several just a few days after discovery. Find a sex addiction therapist willing to help you prepare and facilitate a disclosure, and do it as soon as possible.

Post-Disclosure

Knowledge is power, and partners are empowered by the knowledge they receive from disclosures. Sex addicts are often set back on their heels as the façade they have built and carefully maintained comes crumbling down. But from a place of complete honesty, the relationship has a chance of being rebuilt stronger than ever.

Sex addicts get impatient and wonder how long it will be until their partners get to a place where they are willing to rebuild the relationship. They may even think that their partners' inability to move into relationship rebuilding is an attempt at payback for their bad behavior. As described earlier, due to their trauma, wounded partners may be unable to move toward restoration for some time.

How sex addicts respond to the wounds they've inflicted on their partners can either help or hinder the healing process. Taking responsibility for the pain and trauma the sex addict's acting out has caused helps partners

---

60 See Appendix B for a complete listing of Three-Day Intensives offered at Hope & Freedom Counseling Services and by CHFPs.

heal. This is not a one-time event. Taking responsibility means that years into the future, when his partner's trauma is triggered by some event or thought, the sex addict responds with love, caring, patience, and kindness, just as he would if she were physically injured.

Sex addicts can do many things that will impede the healing of wounded partners. These include but are not limited to

- Minimize past behavior. Sex addicts must continue to take full responsibility for what they did in the past that caused trauma. It is not helpful to point out that acting out has stopped. Partners typically do not feel better when sex addicts seek affirmation of their recovery efforts or for achieving sexual sobriety milestones.

- Get defensive. Defensiveness on the part of sex addicts sends partners back to a dark place. Defensiveness communicates to partners that the sex addict really does not appreciate how much damage his behavior has done.

- Become angry/rageful. Anger toward wounded partners not only shows insensitivity but a complete disregard of the sex addict's own unacceptable behavior.

- Lose patience. Wounded partners will need to talk about their trauma over and over. They will ask the same questions repeatedly. They are simply trying to make sense of what does not make sense to them. When sex addicts sigh or roll their eyes or say, "You asked that question before," they are communicating to wounded partners that even in recovery they continue to be fundamentally self-centered.

- Argue. Sex addicts tend to insist that partners view things from their perspective. However, sex addicts must be willing to see things from their partners' perspective if they want healing to take place.

- Correct. As a way of attempting to get wounded partners to see things from their perspective, sex addicts often try to correct partners' versions of the past by amending the order of events, correcting dates, or just telling partners they are wrong. Partners must be respected enough to be able to relate the events the way they see them. Trauma will often cause events to be jumbled in memory.

- Withdraw or abandon. Sex addicts may be so focused on not getting angry that they withdraw when their partners try to talk about and process their trauma. As a result, partners may become more demonstrative, hoping to see sex addicts respond with recognition of how their actions have been traumatizing. Worse than withdrawing mentally and emotionally from partners is to physically abandon them, walking out on a conversation or leaving the room when things become uncomfortable. For partners to heal, sex addicts need to be present physically and emotionally.

- Make it all about themselves. Turning conversations around so that it is always about the sex addict only increases the trauma of partners. This is just another expression of the narcissism of sex addiction. Sex addicts need to resist the urge to make themselves the focus.

- Try to fix their partner by giving her advice about how she can heal. Leave this to her, her support group, and her therapist. Men generally want to take action and "fix" things. But for this part of the journey, sex addicts need to accept their own powerlessness and respect the healing and recovery journey of their partners.

After disclosure, the couple's relationship will never be the same. The deception and duplicity of the past has been brought out into the open, bringing rawness and a freshness to the relationship. Sex addicts and wounded partners now need to get to know each other all over again.

CHAPTER 21

QUESTIONS ABOUT DISCLOSURE

Murray and Cindy's Story _____

Initially, Murray was adamantly opposed to the idea of a formal disclosure. He wanted to do what was necessary to rebuild the relationship with his wife Cindy, but could not understand how disclosure would help. He wanted to promise that he would never act out again, forget about the past, and just move forward.

Cindy was tired of his lies and did not think she could move forward unless she knew specifically what he had been doing. She got to the point where unless she knew the whole truth about Murray's behavior, she did not think they could have a future together.

Immediately after the disclosure and polygraph, Murray felt a huge weight lift off his shoulders. He realized that he had just been completely honest with her for the first time in their relationship, and that, in fact, this was the first time he had been completely honest with anyone.

Cindy worked with her therapist closely for several months following the disclosure. She would vacillate between anger and sadness. She was disgusted with the things she had heard, but for the first time, she did not have to worry that there was still more. She also realized that as bad as the acting out was, the continual lies she had been hearing from Murray were even more damaging for her.

Following the disclosure she noticed a difference in the way Murray treated her and talked to her. He no longer became defensive when she talked about what he had done. Instead, he listened to her and responded with statements like, "You didn't deserve what I did to you." How healing it was for her to hear him say those words.

Six months after the disclosure, Murray could not believe how well he and Cindy were getting along. He learned to validate Cindy rather than blame her for his addiction. Murray also realized how much closer he felt to Cindy now that she knew everything about him.

They have a lot more work ahead of them. There will continue to be ups and downs, but Murray and Cindy know they can have a completely restored relationship so long as they are willing to continue their recovery work.

....

Why do I need a therapist to do a disclosure? Why can't I just pick a night when my wife would be most receptive and tell her myself?

....

As described earlier, this is not a do-it-yourself project. Disclosure requires a skilled therapist to facilitate the process. When a couple attempts disclosure by themselves, serious problems can occur that only make the situation worse. You may think you are disclosing everything but without the help of a sex addiction therapist to guide you through the process, you are likely to leave out some behaviors. It is much more harmful to your wife to have to come back later, perhaps more than once, and tell her about acting out that you left out, didn't think of, didn't think was necessary to include, or forgot about. This would be significantly re-traumatizing for her.

Further, without the presence of a sex addiction therapist, your wife does not have the support that she needs to be able to make sense of what she has heard. Your therapist will work with your wife, preparing her to hear new and difficult information, then support her through and beyond the disclosure.

Moreover, you need a skilled therapist to help you move forward after the disclosure. You need help to put your relationship on a healing trajectory. Without professional guidance, you are simply dumping on your wife, causing additional unnecessary damage that can make it much more difficult to restore your relationship.

....

I am working on my disclosure to my wife. I'm willing to disclose everything but I don't want to tell her I have given oral sex to prostitutes. Is that okay as long she knows everything else?

....

By planning to tell her you have disclosed everything when you know this to be untrue you are conspiring to deceive your wife. Disclosures must be complete; otherwise you should tell her you are going to give her a *deception* instead of a *disclosure*. One of the two main reasons for doing a disclosure is to have the opportunity to rebuild your relationship with your wife on a foundation of having been totally truthful about all of your past actions. That includes telling her about the things you most want to keep secret. She has a right to know to whom she is married.

The second reason for doing a disclosure is for you to come face-to-face with your behavior—getting totally honest with yourself. Secrets have shame attached to them. As long as you hold on to your secrets, the discomfort of the accompanying shame will obstruct your recovery and draw you back toward sexual acting out. It is time for you to get free. Find the courage necessary for you to disclose *everything* to your wife.

....

When should a disclosure be done immediately?

....

I (Milton) believe disclosures should take place as soon as possible. I do not agree with delaying them for one to two years. However, there are times when disclosures must take place very quickly. In cases where children are at risk, disclosures must be fast-tracked so that children can be appropriately protected.

When sex addicts have contracted STDs, their partners must have that knowledge immediately so they can seek treatment.

Military personnel facing deployment may want to hurry a disclosure so it is completed beforehand. However, I have not seen as positive results in regard to the rebuilding of relationships when couples are separated for long periods of time immediately following disclosure.

Ideally, couples will move back into the same residence after disclosure and begin the long and important journey of rebuilding their relationship in multiple dimensions.

Is it ever a good idea to wait before doing a disclosure?

The main reason I (Milton) delay disclosures is when sex addicts are not ready to stop their acting out. It is harmful to the partner to hear all of the details of past acting out if a sex addict is not ready to discontinue that behavior. However, I do not require that a sex addict has a certain period of sexual sobriety before agreeing to facilitate his disclosure.

There may also be times when pending legal action dictates that disclosure should wait. Even though therapists will do everything within their power to keep their records and session notes confidential, courts have successfully subpoenaed them in the past.

Because disclosures need to be facilitated face-to-face, the process should wait if a sex addict is in the military and on deployment. Disclosures may also need to be delayed if one of the couple becomes seriously ill.

Are there ever cases when it is inadvisable to do a disclosure?

It is inadvisable to do a disclosure when I get the sense that a sex addict may be looking forward to the process as a way of hurting his partner. Some sex addicts are so narcissistic that they revel in detailing their sexual exploits. These are cases where sex addicts are engaging in exhibitionism under the guise of doing a disclosure.

It may not be advisable to do a disclosure if one of the parties has a terminal illness. However, there are many cases where such couples opt to do disclosure so that their remaining time will be based on truth.

I will not facilitate disclosures when one or both parties are not committed to staying in the relationship. We (Milton and CHFPs) require wounded partners to sign a contract committing to stay in the relationship for at least twelve months after the disclosure, regardless of what comes out and regardless of what happens during that year. Understandably, many partners are not able to make that commitment. However, our process is focused on seeing relationships and marriages restored so we require the contract to give the couple time to rebuild their relationship and see the positive impact of recovery.

We also require sex addicts to commit to staying in the relationship for a minimum of two years after the disclosure. It is longer for the sex addict because his actions have brought the couple to this place, and it provides assurance to partners who wish to stay in the relationship. This is also another way of acknowledging that it will most likely take the partner longer to heal than it will for him to get on a solid path in recovery. Therefore, we want him to be prepared for the fact that his partner will not be completely healed when her year-long commitment is up. He continues giving his best support through the additional year, even though she has fulfilled her commitment.

Few partners are completely healed even after two years. Both partners need to be committed to recovery over the long haul. Full restoration of the relationship can come, but it will take time.

Couples who cannot make this commitment are not accepted for our treatment program. There are some cases where couples say they are committed to staying in the relationship, but it becomes obvious that one or both are more interested in improving their legal position as they head toward a divorce. If they are not willing to do everything within their power to make the relationship work, they are not accepted into our Intensive program.

Other therapists may take a different approach. Some believe even if the wounded partner is intending to divorce she needs to hear a disclosure. Although I can understand the reasoning of this approach, at Hope & Freedom our stance is that we not only want to see marriages restored but that we will do everything within our power to keep from being forced to release therapy records to a court.

....

My husband is going to do his disclosure to me very soon. I know I can ask questions afterward. What things should I ask about?
....

Your questions should focus on anything about which you are still unclear. To the extent that you can, prepare your questions ahead of time. You can ask as many questions as you desire. You will want to include questions that you have already asked him. It is important to cover previously asked questions, particularly if he is going to take a polygraph exam following the disclosure. Beyond questions related directly to sexual acting out, you will want to ask questions about other deceptive behaviors including any secret or hidden financial transactions. We have had many cases where sex addicts had started moving or hiding their financial assets in anticipation of ending their marriage.

You will also come up with additional questions as you hear the disclosure. These questions may be related to dates that were mentioned, people who were involved, and behaviors that were revealed. You have a right to know about the particulars of all of his hidden behaviors.

Your therapist may also ask questions on your behalf, helping to make sure you have a clear understanding of all of your husband's acting out. If your husband will be taking a polygraph exam afterward, your therapist will assist with writing the specific questions for the exam. Basically the questions for the polygraph will focus broadly on the entire disclosure. Was he completely truthful? Did he intentionally leave anything out?

....

In his disclosure, will my husband reveal to me the names of the people he has had sex with?
....

The guidelines we follow at Hope & Freedom include naming the sex partners in all cases where the husband worked with them, the wife knows them or has ever had contact with them, if the relationship covered a significant amount of time, or if there was an emotional attachment. You certainly have a right to know every name—even of anonymous or one time encounters.

We have found that names of previous partners have the potential to be trauma triggers. Not having to hear a litany of other names may ultimately spare the wounded partner some future trauma triggers. However, if you would like to know the name of every person with whom he has had sex, that is certainly your right.

....

The Ninth Step talks about making amends to people unless it would injure them or others. Does doing a disclosure go against Step Nine if I think it will injure someone else?

....

Disclosure is not making an amends; it is part of sex addiction treatment. Twelve-step work and treatment are separate and different. The reason to disclose to your partner is that your actions have betrayed her trust and hurt her in profound ways. She has a right to know about your actions, many of which may have put her at risk medically and financially. The only hope you have of being able to restore trust with your partner is to give her the complete truth about your past behavior and continue to be honest with her.

....

Should disclosures include sexual thoughts and fantasies, in addition to actual incidents of sexual acting out?

....

Disclosures should detail every behavior, leaving nothing out. The focus is not on thoughts and fantasies. Many active sex addicts have fantasized about virtually every person they have met. It is not helpful to list all fantasies or the objects of fantasies. However, having masturbated to fantasies of particular people is relevant. Wives often ask if their partners have masturbated to fantasies of their friends or of their children's friends, and this is fair game.

Though perhaps understandable given a wounded partner's hurt and trauma, an insistence on attempting to monitor her husband's thoughts and dreams post-disclosure will not be helpful or healthy for either of them. The wounded partner needs to concentrate on her own healing rather than trying to control her husband's thoughts.

How many marriages end after disclosure?

I (Milton) assume that you are wondering how many end as the result of disclosure. Some of the marriages that end do so some time after disclosure. They may or may not directly be the result of disclosure. For example, there are marriages that end sometime after disclosure because of a relapse or even repeated relapses. In those cases, it would be more proper to say that the marriage ended after relapse.

In all of the years I have conducted disclosures, there have been only a very few times the partner moved toward a divorce after hearing a disclosure. Other therapists may have a different experience. Certainly disclosures are very hard for partners to hear. And, some of them have told me that it was a good thing they signed the contract to stay in the marriage for a minimum of a year after disclosure. Partners of sex addicts, for the most part, can handle the truth. What they have greater difficulty handling is not knowing what the sex addict was involved in and how his behavior impacts her.

Jennifer Schneider, MD, PhD, conducted some of the earliest research on disclosures and continues to write extensively on the subject. When I posed the question as to the frequency with which marriages end as the result of a disclosure, her response was as follows:

> "The problem with obtaining such data is that you need a careful study design and the very specific question (in order) to answer. First, how do you define 'disclosure'? Is it limited to situations where a couple, as part of ongoing therapy, does a formal disclosure with a therapist? Does it include when an addict discloses the behavior to the partner when confronted by the partner at home? Most of the early studies asked addicts and partners about disclosure without specifying the circumstances. When you recruit subjects through their therapists or through twelve-step programs, you're going to miss couples who split up after the behavior came to light, and couples who never ended up with couples counseling or twelve-step recovery."[61]

---

61 Personal conversation with Dr. Schneider on August 28, 2016. Additional research and information about disclosures are available at www.jenniferschneider.com.

Do I need to do a disclosure to my children?

The primary reason to do a disclosure to your children is to break the cycle of addiction so it is not passed on to the next generation. Two factors are important: first is the timing and the second is making sure the disclosure is age appropriate.

As far as timing, it is important that you are able to speak of a past problem you have had rather than a current problem. Although disclosure to your spouse comes as soon as possible, disclosure to your children should wait for several months after that. I (Milton) typically encourage couples to wait until at least three to nine months after the disclosure to the spouse to do a disclosure to children.

It is important that the couple form a united front when doing a disclosure to children. This is not a time for mom to "tell on" dad. Rather, it is a time for both parents to talk directly about a problem they have faced together. I even encourage couples to hold hands while doing the disclosure to demonstrate solidarity.

Terms like "sex addict" and "sex addiction" are not helpful to children. Behaviors are important to report without labeling them. For very young children perhaps the disclosure is something along the lines of "I hurt mom by being special friends with other women. That is why I am sleeping in the guest room for now." For older children, "In the past, I was unfaithful to mom and that hurt her a lot. When I hurt her, I also hurt you. I have been working hard to make sure this never happens again. I see a therapist each week and also attend meetings with other men who are committed to not hurting others anymore."

The big question children want to know is how this is going to affect their lives. If you are married, they will want to know if that means you and your wife are getting a divorce. Giving this disclosure together helps them understand that you are both committed to working through the difficulties and remaining a family.

Older children may have questions, but often they are simply silent, not knowing what to ask. For those who ask if you had an affair, answer factually. If they ask with whom, tell them that is information that is reserved for you and their mom.

Follow the same general guidelines for adult children. Some men prepare a letter they can read to their children. In some cases, couples arrange to have all adult children attend a family therapy session where a therapist will facilitate the process.

....

Should I do a disclosure to my parents? What about my in-laws?

....

Several variables need to be taken into account with parents. If they are elderly, disclosure may not be appropriate. Also, sex addicts need to consider the timing of such a disclosure. It is important that you have enough recovery to have a solid understanding of not only your behavior, but of how your addiction developed.

It is important to get to a place in your recovery where you can talk about your life, your addiction, and where you are headed now without coming across as blaming your parents. However, it may be therapeutically valuable for you to confront your parents matter-of-factly about egregious errors they made that helped your sex addiction to develop. For example, if you found a stash of pornography that belonged to your parents, you may have a need to tell them it was unhealthy to allow you to be exposed to it. If they sexualized you or other members of the family or they raised you in a sexually charged environment, you may need to tell them the impact that had on your life.

You have a right to say the things that need to be said but keep your expectations low—do not expect your parents to be ready to accept any ownership for their deficiencies in parenting or not protecting you as a child. A useful definition of success is to be able to say what you need to say for yourself, regardless of their response.

I (Milton) view a disclosure to in-laws as being a natural part of the twelve-step amends process. When working your Ninth Step, you will likely want to make amends to your wife's parents, taking responsibility for your unfaithfulness and how you hurt their daughter, and by extension, how you hurt them. Doing this demands that you will have already done significant work in recovery so you will be able to tell them with conviction that you have changed the way you live and want to make sure that you never hurt their daughter again.

CHAPTER 22

QUESTIONS ABOUT POLYGRAPH EXAMS

Owen's Story

When Owen's wife first mentioned that she wanted him to take a polygraph exam, he was terrified. He was certain whether he passed or failed their marriage would soon be over. Owen found a polygraph examiner who told him that he could help him pass the exam. The examiner carefully avoided certain areas and asked questions intended to deceive Owen's wife, and he passed his exam. Later his wife learned there were a great number of additional acting-out behaviors that the polygraph exam did not reveal.

Unfortunately, there are unethical people in every profession, including polygraph examiners and even therapists. Although the behavior of Owen's polygraph examiner is more extreme, often polygraph exams do not prove to be helpful. Sometimes, the polygraph exam is too narrowly focused. In other instances, the polygraph was not used to back up a clinical disclosure. The biggest mistake partners make is to insist on a polygraph after their discovery of some acting out that focuses only on certain events, people, or time periods.

Polygraphs that ask narrowly defined questions may leave partners with the impression they know everything. However, without a clinical disclosure, all they really know is related to the exam's specific areas of focus. By themselves, polygraphs are not designed to restore trust in a relationship. However, if they are integrated into therapy and used to verify a clinical disclosure, as well as ongoing sexual sobriety, they can be very helpful.

How reliable are polygraph exams?

Depending on what research is cited, the reliability of polygraphs is reported to be 90 percent or higher. Are they absolutely foolproof? No. As with any test, there is a margin of error. We have honed our process through the years, and have found polygraph exams to be highly reliable.

Polygraph is useful for sex addicts who want to stop their acting out and for couples who want to rebuild their relationships. Sex addicts who do not have a desire to stop their acting out will try to pervert the polygraph process to their own ends, whereas those who are committed to recovery find polygraph a useful tool to keep them on track and provide objective evidence of their progress.

Is there a better gauge of truthfulness than a polygraph exam? Currently, research is being conducted using Magnetic Resonance Imaging (MRI) to pinpoint deception, although as of yet, there are no definitive standards that verify truthfulness or deception. Even if it is validated as a lie detection tool in the future, the cost and availability of MRIs make this technology less than ideal for use in sex addiction treatment. There are some who tout the use of voice stress analysis to detect deception. However, research has shown that the results are so mixed that they are no more effective than a coin flip.

Can a sex addict be trusted to tell the truth about anything, including his recovery and sexual sobriety, without a polygraph?

Sex addicts lie to cover their acting-out behaviors, to avoid the consequences of those behaviors, and often, because they believe they will not be loved or accepted if others knew about their behavior. Can sex addicts learn to tell the truth? Of course, they can. Utilizing polygraphs in recovery can help them develop the habit of living honestly. We believe that sex addicts in sustained recovery can be trusted. That trust grows through the years as partners are able to verify that their actions match their talk. Polygraph exams are a resource through which this can be accomplished.

Why is it so important to use polygraph exams in conjunction with a sex addiction therapist?

Clinical disclosures that are verified to be complete by a passed polygraph exam provide a foundation upon which trust can begin to be rebuilt. Skilled sex addiction therapists[62] know how to phrase polygraph questions appropriately, so as to validate the disclosure as complete. In the event a sex addict fails a polygraph exam, sex addiction therapists know how to guide clients to release the secrets that may be the key for them to get honest and begin to get free from their addiction.

Polygraph examiners working directly for the spouse of a sex addict are charged with finding out if the addict is being truthful or deceptive. When working only with a polygraph examiner, if the sex addict fails the exam there is no way forward. Where would you go from there? In contrast, when an examiner is engaged by a therapist to validate a disclosure, his or her job includes finding out additional information. Examiners that we use following disclosures are skilled at helping sex addicts examine their lives at a much deeper level so that they can get all of their secrets out in the open.

Why should I do polygraph exams subsequent to the disclosure?

Polygraph following a disclosure gives you a baseline, verifying that a sex addict has disclosed to his partner every sexual behavior he can recall. Since disclosures take many hours to prepare, sex addicts need to thoroughly search their memory to make sure they are being completely truthful.

We encourage couples to engage in an Intensive Aftercare program[63] after disclosure to keep the relationship on track. As part of this program,

---

62 www.findachfp.com

63 See Appendix B.

we give sex addicts the opportunity to take follow-up polygraph exams at prescribed intervals, as a way of verifying that they are still actively pursuing recovery and have not acted out since their last polygraph exam.

How long follow-up polygraph exams should continue is up to the couple and based on the sex addiction therapist's recommendations. Sometimes polygraphs continue every six months for three years or more. In cases where there was a long-standing pattern of unfaithfulness, couples may opt to continue having follow-up polygraph exams annually.

How do we make arrangements to get polygraph exams?

The best thing to do is to contact sex addiction therapists in your area and ask if they utilize polygraph exams to validate clinical disclosures. An increasing number of therapists are doing this so the availability of polygraph examiners who work with therapists is growing. If you do not have sex addiction therapists near you, it would be worthwhile to make the time and financial commitment to locate a therapist outside of your area that has broad experience in integrating polygraph exams into the clinical process.

Is there training available for sex addiction polygraph examiners?

The only training I (Milton) know of is that which we do as part of the Certified Hope & Freedom Practitioner training program.[64] We train therapists to become proficient in working with our polygraph examiner Stephen Cabler,[65] and then we, in turn, give them guidelines for training their polygraph examiners to follow our treatment model.

Many polygraph examiners believe they do not need assistance with this because they have broad experience in testing for infidelities or in testing sex offenders. Those processes are often adversarial. In working with sex addicts, we utilize polygraph exams very differently—as a tool to help sex addicts get honest with themselves and their partners and to help them reestablish trust.

---

64 www.hopeandfreedom.net
65 www.cablerpolygraph.net

CHAPTER 23

REBUILDING INTIMACY

Theo and Kit's Story_____

Theo and Kit had been married for 17 years when Kit found out about Theo's acting out. She was devastated. Although she didn't think their marriage was perfect, she thought her husband was happy and had no clue that he had been having sex with other people.

Together, they sought the help of a sex addiction therapist who led them through a disclosure. The disclosure revealed many more behaviors that shocked Kit. She did not see how it was possible for her ever to trust Theo again. After the disclosure Theo was relieved to not have to continue to carry his secrets. He recognized how much he had hurt his wife. His goal was to do whatever it took to regain her love and trust.

Kit saw Theo diligently working his recovery. He did a 90/90 (90 twelve-step meetings in 90 days) and then continued attending three meetings every week. He got a sponsor immediately and did Step work each week. She was surprised how Theo changed in his behavior toward her and their children. His moodiness lessened significantly and there was a new softness about him. Each evening Theo would sit and talk with Kit, and show genuine interest in her day.

To her surprise, Kit realized that her trust in Theo was growing daily. She also realized that her love for Theo was even deeper than it was before the disclosure. She still had some difficult days in dealing with memories of what her husband had done, but she believes they can continue to grow together and their relationship can thrive.

Making Amends

I am working on my Ninth Step. How do I make a proper amends to my wife?

In twelve-step meetings there is often talk of making a "living amends" to partners. But some men's interpretation of a living amends is "I just won't act out any more." That is part of it—an important part to be sure—but stopping your acting out is simply being faithful, which is something you promised when the two of you got together. You also need to take responsibility for changing your behavior and attitude in other ways, and treat her the way she deserves to be treated.

When it comes to making your Ninth Step amends to your wife, it is important to work closely with your sponsor. However, I think there is also wisdom in asking her if she has given any thought as to what she hopes and/or expects from you. Assuming she has been doing her own recovery work and attending twelve-step meetings herself, she may have some definite ideas. For example, one man recently did this and his wife was very clear that she wanted him to get her a particular piece of jewelry so that as she looked at it and wore it, it would remind her of his recovery. Other women request a letter that details how they have been mistreated and wounded by the addict's behavior, and what the sex addict will continue to do to ensure it doesn't happen again.

What amends do you make for your wife? Talk with your sponsor and ask your wife. Take their direction. Then make sure that in addition to whatever your wife says you make a living amends to her daily. Treat her daily as the special child of God that she is.

In making amends to my wife, is it possible to have the wrong motive?

Making amends is about taking ownership of the way you have harmed your wife. A wrong motive for an amends would be to do it with the specific hope your wife will forgive your acting out. Similarly, it would be wrong to make an amends with the selfish thought that she may treat you differently afterward. The proper motive for an amends is to do it because it is the right thing to do, both for her *and* for you. Regardless of how she responds to your amends, you have harmed her and you owe her your best efforts in recognizing that harm, expressing appropriate regret, taking responsibility for it, and doing what you can to make things right.

....

My husband wants his amends to me to include renewing our vows. He wants to do this publicly, and it seems to me he is interested in putting on a show for others. Am I wrong for not wanting to do this?

....

If you have reason to believe your husband's desire for a vow renewal ceremony is more a display for others than an amends to you, it is important to respect your intuition. Would renewing your vows in private be more to your preference, or are you not yet ready to consider renewing your vows? Perhaps you feel that repeating vows he has broken in the past is an inadequate amends. Be willing to talk this through with your husband and your therapist. Hopefully, your husband is getting healthy direction from his sponsor on how to make amends. You are certainly within your rights to request that he come up with an amends that feels more genuine to you.

....

How do I make amends to my children?

....

This is an area where it is important to consult closely with your sponsor, but the recommended approach to making amends to one's children follows closely that of doing a disclosure to them. An age-appropriate amends for younger children would be to tell them that you have hurt their mommy by liking other women and you are not going to do that any more. You can express to them that their mom did not deserve what you did and that you are going to spend your life making it up to her. For older children, it is proper to add that you broke your wedding vows and were unfaithful to your wife. You also make a living amends to your children by making sure that you remain sexually sober and always treat your wife with respect.

The other aspect of amends to your children is that your addiction made you much less physically and emotionally available to them. In the self-centeredness of your active addiction you may also have treated them harshly. It is time to own that behavior and commit to showing up differently for them in the future.

Emotional Intimacy

Emotional intimacy begins with the disclosure. It continues with couples being able to talk about things more honestly and on a deeper level. Set a time aside each evening to talk about the highlights and lowlights of the day, with all electronics off. Reinvent the way you spend your evenings. Instead of letting television and Internet surfing dominate, give your relationship priority so that you have a chance to reestablish closeness.

Show curiosity about your partner. It is not enough to simply ask, "How was your day?" Be interested in what interests your partner. Think of this part of your relationship as a time to get reacquainted.

We encourage couples to seek out books about relationship rebuilding that they can read together. There are many good books on couples' communication that can be helpful. Spend half an hour each evening reading from one of these books aloud and talking about what you have learned together.

Play a game together. Take a walk after dinner together. Find a hobby that you can enjoy together. You have a chance to rewrite the script of your relationship—do not waste the opportunity.

Many sex addicts realize that they need to win back the love of their partners. Rather than immediately jumping back into a sexual relationship, wounded partners need to be treated gently. They need their spouse to care enough to get to know them emotionally before pressing for a more normal sex life. Sex addicts need to be patient because wounded partners may need some time to pass before they are willing to engage in *any* emotional intimacy. Courting is an old fashioned word but it aptly describes what needs to happen in rebuilding the relationship. If they want to reestablish the relationship, sex addicts must care enough about their wounded partner to take whatever steps are necessary. If these steps are not taken, the relationship will likely not heal.

There has to be a willingness on the part of both partners to reestablish emotional intimacy. As part of this process, most couples we work with schedule a regular date night. Wounded partners may not be ready for this initially but, as they begin to heal, most will long to have a regular time each week to enjoy each other's company. Sex addicts need to take the lead and exercise the same creativity they would if they were trying to win the attention and affection of their partner for the very first time.

Spiritual Intimacy

Couples can strengthen their spiritual intimacy by sharing a time of worship, prayer, or meditation. Let this be a quest that you undertake together. Be relentless in your search for multiple spiritual outlets. Find a place of worship that is meaningful for both of you. Add daily spiritual practices to your life. Think of your spiritual life as needing to be exercised and kept in shape much like your body. An added benefit is that as you pursue your spiritual life you will likely meet other couples who may become part of your social life.

Sexual Intimacy

Sexual intimacy may be the last aspect of your relationship to be rebuilt. Sex addicts must be patient as their partners heal. Often partners have mixed feelings and may send conflicting signals. Even if your partner would like to be sexually intimate with you, for a time she may be repulsed at the thought of being touched by someone who has been unfaithful to her.

Many couples find a period of celibacy helpful. This allows partners time to feel safe without feeling as though they have to perform sexually. They may need time for some of the intensity of their emotions to dissipate.

A period of celibacy can also give time for sex addicts' brain chemistry to settle down and begin to reset. Since sex addicts engaging in a formal period of celibacy are also agreeing not to have sex with themselves, they can build greater sexual desire for their partner. For more information on establishing a formal celibacy contract, see *Stop Sex Addiction: Real Hope, True Freedom for Sex Addicts and Partners* (Central Recovery Press, 2013). We will spend more time discussing healthy sexuality in the next chapter.

CHAPTER 24

HEALTHY SEXUALITY

Guy Talk

For you to successfully rebuild the relationship with your spouse, you must be willing to enter lifelong sexual sobriety. There may be a sense of loss that comes with this new mindset in that sexual acting out has been a way to medicate your emotional discomfort and cope with life.

One man looked back at his masturbation and said, "From the time I learned to masturbate, getting high sexually has been my friend. If I was lonely, sex relieved my fear of being by myself. If I was anxious, sex would act as a tranquilizer, taking away my stress. When I was mad, sex helped me escape my anger."

As with any loss, there are feelings of grief. Sexual acting out has been a long-time companion for you. As a result, it may be important to work with a skilled sex addiction therapist in coping with the grief accompanying your loss.

Grieving the loss means coming to terms with the fact that you will never have sex with anyone other than your spouse. It means permanently sealing your habitual escape hatch. This means changing your mindset to remove thinking about seeking out other sexual partners. The sooner you can come to terms with giving up your fantasy of being with someone else, the sooner you can begin repairing the breach in your relationship caused by your sexual acting out.

A healthy sexual relationship is not the basis of a good marriage. Rather, it is the result of a good marriage. Sex starts well before the bedroom. It is not an act but rather a natural expression of a couple that enjoys being together and sharing time with one another.

What is missing from the majority of relationships that have been rocked by sex addiction is romance. Romance is intangible but we know it when it is present. It encompasses the mystery and excitement that comes from a blossoming relationship. Genuine romance is much more than gift giving. It includes routine, as well as unexpected, acts of kindness and surprising ways of expressing deep emotion.

If you were single now and just met your partner and wanted to win her love and affection, my guess is that you would be very creative in the area of romancing her. The interesting thing is that being romantic costs nothing. The act of picking a flower for that special someone may be more meaningful than an expensive bouquet of several dozen roses.

Courtship has become a lost art. Yet, I have heard many women say that they longed for their husbands to court them. One couple had been through a painful disclosure backed by a polygraph exam. Both were committed to making the marriage work, and after six months were doing exceptionally well in their individual recovery processes. The man very much wanted to show his wife he cared for her and to prove he was trustworthy. He would kiss her whenever he saw her and hold her hand when they were sitting beside each other. From his perspective he was doing the best he knew to do to express his love for her.

An important clue about what she needed came when she told him that she wanted him to court her. She wanted him to *work up to* a place where she would welcome him to hold her hand. Her desire was for him to pursue her to the point where he would win her affection and *ask* for a kiss rather than assume she was open to him kissing her.

The message for men is that this is a time to decide whether you will do whatever it takes to be romantic through a process of courtship to win back your wife's trust and heart *or* stick with what you have done in the past with its questionable results. If you make the effort, you can develop new skills in romance and your relationship will benefit.

It's important to be aware that your wife may not be ready for you to romance her. This is especially true if you have yet to do a formal disclosure or if you have only recently done your disclosure. If you make efforts and she does not respond, time and patience are required. You need to understand that she may not yet be at a place where she can respond because of the trauma that your behavior has caused. It is essential to appreciate that your wife may be so hurt by you that all she feels is pain—perhaps even hatred for you. Park your ego and resist the urge to react with anger or to pout. Get over yourself, do your own recovery work, and give her the time she needs to heal. Rebuilding the relationship is your responsibility, not hers.

Work on establishing a dating and courting routine, but resist the urge to do a full court press in your courting rituals. Allow the time and space to get to know each other again. Gradually increase your acts of love toward her. A single flower or a homemade card may be better than something more extravagant.

At times, when I (Milton) am working with couples who have completed their Three-Day Intensive and are working through our Aftercare program, I ask the husband to make a list of things that his wife enjoys doing. It speaks loudly when someone who has been in a relationship for many years and is unable to identify what his wife enjoys. What it says is that such men have been so focused on themselves and what they like that they have little knowledge of their partner's wishes and desires.

Why not spend some time right now making a list of things that your wife enjoys? Think back to when you first met and try to recall the things she enjoyed prior to your relationship. Chances are you paid much closer attention to her preferences then. How did she spend her time? What were the things that gave her energy or joy? What did she do to relax? How did she have fun before she met you? What did the two of you do together to have fun when you first began to see one another?

When you complete the list, sit down with your wife and ask her what you have forgotten. Ask her to help you include all the things that bring her joy. This list can form the basis for future dating ideas.

One man's wife really enjoyed going to museums but he couldn't remember the last time she had gone to one. He decided to purchase a museum membership for them with the thought of being able to take her to the special opening day receptions that were often held for members only at the beginning of new exhibits. This was so meaningful to her that she remarked, "It was the best gift I have ever received!"

Beau's and Lena's Story

Lena and her husband Beau had been in recovery for six weeks. They worked through a clinical disclosure with a therapist followed by a polygraph to verify that she knew everything. She thought she would be ready to restart their sexual relationship, but their first attempts were so emotionally painful for her that she had to stop. In tears she told her husband that her mind was flooded with images of him being sexual with other women. Beau listened while he gently held her hand. He let her talk about the pain of her intrusive thoughts. To her surprise, Beau didn't press her to move forward and he didn't minimize any of his behavior. He simply said, "I understand."

Over the next month, they attempted to be sexual several more times but each time ended with her in tears thinking about his sexual behavior with others. Each time, Beau held Lena's hand and listened to her. He told her he would wait as long as necessary for her to feel safe with him and reassured her that he was not going anywhere.

They agreed that they were going to wait for intercourse but that they would cuddle in bed each evening. After a couple of nights cuddling while wearing their bed clothes, Lena suggested that it would be fine for them to cuddle skin to skin. Lena was surprised that in the following week she initiated intercourse and did not have her intrusive thoughts.

Lena said Beau's patience with her and his willingness to listen to her concerns without defending himself were the main factors in her being able to move forward. She knows she may have intrusive thoughts from time to time and that there may be ongoing challenges as they reestablish their sexual relationship, but she also is confident that as she continues to heal, their relationship will continue to improve.

For Partners

Ladies, you will be a key to helping your partner understand how you want to be courted and romanced. It is all right to be mysterious but many men are a bit thick when it comes to understanding their wives. You can help him by telling him the things that you would like to do. Help him understand how you want to be treated and what is romantic *to you.*

You may or may not be ready to restart your sexual relationship. Be true to yourself. Do not feel pressured that you have to be sexual to keep him from looking elsewhere. He made the mess that you are in. It is time for him to put your needs and desires first.

Often women feel pulled in two directions. On the one hand, they may be disgusted with the thought of even touching their husbands. On the other, they may also wonder if their husbands still find them attractive. Be willing to take whatever time is necessary to feel safe being sexual again. Talk to your partner and tell him you need some time and ask that he be patient with you as you heal.

Restarting Your Sexual Relationship

As noted earlier, your sexual relationship does not begin in the bedroom. Unless you have established or reestablished emotional intimacy, it is probably too early to think about physical intimacy. Sex addicts must be willing to postpone sexual activity until their partners are ready, taking care not to pull back emotionally. Give her time to feel safe again in your arms.

A common error in thinking is to believe that the present situation will continue forever. If their partners are so wounded that they are not able to be sexual now, sex addicts may conclude they will never be sexual again. The greatest gift you can give your partner is to be patient and willing to wait as long as necessary for her to be ready to be sexual with you again.

It's okay to talk about sex. Communicate with each other about likes and dislikes, turn-ons and turn-offs. Ideally, each of you will have healthy-enough boundaries to listen to what the other person says without becoming defensive or shaming. Even with the best boundaries in place, a discussion about sex may leave one or both of you feeling a bit raw and vulnerable. The last thing on your mind after this discussion may be being sexual. Spend the rest of the evening enjoying each other's company. Watch a movie together. Play a board game together. Talk about your next vacation. Read a book together. Just be together.

Touch and Oxytocin

When you are both ready to restart your sexual relationship, begin with non-sexual touch. When is the last time you held hands? Taking a walk together while holding hands may be very pleasurable for both of you.

The largest organ in the body is our skin. Touching skin to skin feels good for a reason. The hormone oxytocin is released into the blood stream when you touch skin to skin.[66] Among other things, oxytocin plays a part in sexual motivation, bonding, and the formation of trust.

Oxytocin is the hormone responsible for the strong bond that comes when a mother breastfeeds her infant. The hand massage and sucking by the infant triggers the release of oxytocin.[67] Similarly, oxytocin is released when you and your partner hold hands, hug each other, and cuddle skin to skin.

Agree to take intercourse off the table for now. Try mutual touching without focusing on genitalia and just concentrate on hugging and holding each other. Plan to have several evenings where you sleep without clothes and hold each other in bed. Enjoy the warmth of each other's body. As you touch each other, more oxytocin will be released.[68]

Foreplay

The next time you want to move toward physical intimacy, remember what your partner said about likes and dislikes. Forget your old patterns of sexuality and be willing to start slowly in getting to know each other sexually.

---

66 Department of Physiology and Pharmacology, Karolinska Institute. (1994). Oxytocin and behaviour. *Kerstin Uvnäs-moberg*, 26(5), 315-317.

67 Matthiesen, AS, Ransjö-Arvidson, AB, Nissen, E, and and Uvnäs-Moberg, K. (2001). Postpartum maternal oxytocin release by newborns: effects of infant hand massage and sucking. *Birth: Issues in Perinatal Care*, 28(1), 13-19.

68 Stock, S, and Uvnäs-Moberg, K. (1988). Increased plasma levels of oxytocin in response to afferent electrical stimulation of the sciatic and vagal nerves and in response to touch and pinch in anaesthetized rats. *Acta Physiologica Scandinavica*, 132(1), 29-34.

Your goal is intimacy, not intensity. Rather than trying to have the highest high possible, focus on developing emotional closeness and integrating that into your physical relationship.

Your focus is on each other. Rather than selfishly working toward what you want, what does your partner want? What would make this experience better for your partner? That does not mean that your focus is on orgasm (for either of you). You are expressing love.

Foreplay is not just physical—it involves the emotions. It is not merely a prelude to the main event. Foreplay can often be satisfying by itself.

Things that may be turn-ons include:

- Talking together
- Love letters
- Reading poetry
- Telling your partner how happy you are that you found each other
- Kissing
- Cuddling
- Undressing each other
- Sharing a bath together
- Conversation in a candlelit room

Notice that nothing on this list is focused on genitalia. Foreplay that is unhurried and gentle can be very pleasurable for both people.

Things that may be turn-offs might include:

- Always depending on your partner to initiate sex
- Confining tenderness to the bedroom
- Foregoing kissing
- Rushing or hurrying
- Course language
- Moving too quickly to genital touch
- Grabbing, pinching, or other aggressive behaviors
- Alcohol or other drug use

If you have already asked your partner about likes and dislikes, have you made use of this knowledge or are you relying on what you have always done? Be willing to expand your range of sexual behaviors with your spouse.

Questions About Healthy Sexuality

What sexual behaviors are healthy?

Think of your sexual relationship as an orchestra. Orchestras come in many sizes, from a small chamber group with a few instruments to the New York Philharmonic with over 100 musicians. What you and your partner deem to be healthy or unhealthy is up to you so long as you agree on a few guidelines. Anything is allowed so long as:

- No other people are involved
- None of the acts are hurtful or degrading
- No pornography is involved

Beyond that, you and your partner decide what will be included in your sexual orchestra. You each get a vote. Two *yes* votes means you add that instrument to the orchestra. A *yes* vote and a *no* vote means that instrument does not get added. As your relationship progresses through the years, you may add some instruments to your sexual orchestra and remove others. A helpful option when considering a new sexual behavior is to vote *not now* instead of immediately voting *no*, so that it can be reconsidered at some later time.

How will I know if he is still thinking about someone else when he is having sex with me?

You have a right to know. *Ask him.* A better way to phrase the question would be to ask if he fantasizes about other people or about pornography when he is being sexual with you. If you can see his eyes while you are having sex, you get a good sense of whether or not he is mentally and emotionally present. The next question and its answer expand on this critical issue.

What boundaries can a wife set with her husband to feel safe about trying sex again?

The first boundary is sex addicts must be mentally and emotionally present during sex. We would go so far as to even suggest that, at least for the first year of recovery, wives only have sex in enough light to see their husband's eyes. A lamp or candle or the bathroom light will provide enough illumination. It is important to look at each other during sex. And for the first year, only be sexual in positions where you can see each other's eyes. This is not meant to limit couples sexually but rather to help sex addicts stay present and their partners to feel safe.

We often get some opposition from men on this guideline. Those who are most vocal are still thinking that their goal when being sexual is to aim for the maximum neurochemical high. Again, the goal of sex together is not intensity but intimacy. When the focus is on intensity, sexual behavior frequently becomes selfish. When the focus is on intimacy, sex is about mutual connection and enjoyment.

When being sexual together, we suggest that you talk to each other. The talk is not coarse language or so called *dirty talk*. That focuses on intensity. Rather, the talk we encourage is comprised of loving words and affirming words.

Finally, wives have a right to stop their sexual behavior at any time, even if they are in the middle of intercourse. Sex addicts need to understand that their wives can be triggered during sex and may need to stop in order to feel safe. If this happens, this is not a time for guys to pout, but rather to be gentle and loving. When that happens some wives will request that their husbands just hold them. Others may need to not be touched at all.

What am I to do if we have been in recovery for over two years but my wife still will not engage in sex because of her anger toward me?

We suggest that you and your wife begin working with a sex addiction therapist. Things may be exactly as you present them—that you have remained sexually sober and are doing your part in recovery. However, it is possible that your wife sees you as being unsupportive of her. Have you been a true partner in her healing? Do you make sexual demands of her and then pout if you do not get your way? Are you engaging in other activities with your wife to develop both emotional and spiritual intimacy?

A sex addiction therapist can objectively evaluate your situation and guide you in rebuilding physical intimacy. Depending on your situation, your therapist may see the need to refer you for more specialized assistance.

....

My husband blames me for our lack of a sex life because I am not patient when he fails to get an erection. Before I knew about his sex addiction, his erections seemed to be instantaneous and now nothing works. My mind automatically goes to: I no longer excite him; I am unattractive and undesirable; I am less than his previous sexual experiences. What are we supposed to do?

....

After a few months of solid recovery with absolutely no acting out, if your husband still has erectile dysfunction (ED), it would be helpful for him to consult a urologist. Even sex addicts in their 20s and 30s may have temporary erectile difficulties after entering recovery. Medication for ED can be very effective.

....

Is there still room for "play" that includes sexy lingerie and marital aids in our sex life or will that hurt a sex addict's recovery?

....

For at least the first year or so, the focus should be on getting reacquainted and developing true emotional intimacy that leads to sexual intimacy. Although sexy lingerie, toys, and marital aids are not inherently harmful for sex addicts, until sex addict's neurochemistry settles down and their arousal response has a chance to normalize, these things may be more associated with intensity than intimacy. This is especially true if these items were part of his sexual acting out. When you do introduce anything you characterize as "play" into your sex life, it is crucial that you and your partner talk about how he is feeling and what he is thinking. If he is having difficulty staying mentally present with you, then it would be advisable to delay making any significant changes in your sexual relationship for a while.

....

Does "no" ever mean "well maybe" or "yes?"
....

Coercion has no place in a consensual sexual relationship. Healthy sex and emotional safety demands that a person never be coerced—directly or indirectly—into being sexual against her will. You always have a right to decline to have sex. He has the same right. If you are not feeling sexual, or not feeling safe, you have a right to say no.

....

My husband has not wanted to be sexual with me for more than three years. He used to find me attractive. I am in good shape and I take care of myself. Why doesn't he find me appealing now?
....

Everyone has an arousal template such that some things are sexually stimulating and other things are not. The husband in this question has warped his arousal template by his sexual acting out that likely included pornography. Pornography is focused on extremes in behavior and on getting the most intense sexual pleasure possible. Once pornography has become part of a person's sexual template, things that once satisfied sexually no longer bring as much pleasure. Sex addicts use of pornography and activities that continually increase their level of stimulation develop a tolerance for certain forms of sex—much the same way someone addicted to alcohol or other drugs needs an increasing amount in order to get the same effect.

As a sex addict engages in other sexual behaviors and gets hooked on pornography that is base, degrading, and violent, sexual activities that once stimulated him no longer have that effect.

You cannot turn back the clock. The problem is your husband. The good news is that if he enters recovery and maintains sexual sobriety, his arousal template will eventually normalize. It may take more time than either of you prefer, but if he stays in recovery it will happen.

Over the past few years, I have developed a significant problem with premature ejaculation. Where can I go for help with this?

There are several potential causes of premature ejaculation. Both biological and psychological factors may be involved. A visit to a urologist will be necessary to address the biological side. Here, we'll address the psychological side.

For sex addicts struggling with premature ejaculation, an obvious first step but one that is often overlooked is that all other sexual outlets must be closed. That is, there must be an absolute end to pornography, as well as any other sexually oriented media, including books with sexual themes.

Additionally, masturbation will need to be eliminated. Masturbation drains the sexual energy that would otherwise go toward the marriage. A related problem is that the partner in a committed relationship cannot compete with the sexual fantasies likely present during masturbation.

Finally, sex addicts struggling with premature ejaculation may also want to consult a certified sex therapist and, if possible, one who is also a sex addiction therapist. A sex therapist without an understanding of sex addiction may suggest things that could be detrimental to your recovery.

PART FIVE

DETOUR INTO RELAPSE

Dylan's and Rena's Story_____

Dylan was a regular at his twelve-step meetings. He found that Rena drew comfort from his recovery efforts. For a while he stopped all of his acting out. Dylan enjoyed the friendships he developed in his twelve-step fellowship and quickly began to be viewed as someone of wisdom by other members.

He recalled the accolades he received when he got his one-month sobriety chip. Each month he would change the way he introduced himself in the meetings to include his newest sobriety milestone. Yet, within six months he began to slip back into some of his old behaviors.

Rena told members of her support group about how hard Dylan was working and how she increasingly trusted him. Dylan knew he was drifting further into his old behaviors and had even started some new acting-out behaviors, but still rationalized that since they were not as bad as things he used to do he did not have to reset his sobriety clock.

Two years after entering recovery, Rena caught Dylan looking at pornography. At first, he lied and told her it had just happened that one time. Later, he admitted that his pornography use started back up two months into his recovery. He opposed the idea of starting his sobriety clock over again since in his thinking he had never really had a problem with pornography previously and that he was not acting out with people.

At Rena's insistence, Dylan sought out the help of a sex addiction therapist. He was shocked to hear the therapist say that he had been in relapse since his pornography use started again after two months of recovery. Gradually, Dylan returned to solid sexual sobriety. He reviewed his recovery plan with his therapist and realized it had multiple holes that needed to be fixed for him to reestablish and maintain sexual sobriety.

It is important to be aware of the difference between a slip and a relapse. A slip is a one-time occurrence (return to sexual acting out) that is not premeditated. A slip happens because a sex addict is not adequately prepared for a situation or he has let his guard down, or allowed his recovery to deteriorate. The sex addict then engages in a forbidden behavior—one of the things on his sobriety contract that indicates he has broken sobriety.

A relapse occurs when the sexual acting out happens more than once, or the behavior happens over a longer period of time, or has been premeditated. For example, someone knows he has an upcoming business conference in another state. Prior to recovery, every time he was out of town alone, he would act out with prostitutes he engaged in strip clubs. As he plans the current trip, he also plans to go to a strip club and act out. When the trip takes place, he goes to a strip club with the intent of paying for sex. After being inside the club for only 10 minutes, he comes to his senses and leaves the club. Did he have a slip or a relapse? He had a relapse because he had premeditated the behavior and going to strip clubs is a behavior he clearly indicated was a breach in his sobriety.

FREEDOM

HOPE

CHAPTER 25

GENERAL QUESTIONS ABOUT SLIPS AND RELAPSE

Drake's and Fran's Story _____

When Drake and Fran first married, he told her he was a sex addict and that he had been in recovery for several years. Now married for thirty years, Drake admitted to her he still had a bit of a problem with pornography but he was continuing in recovery and attending meetings.

Drake's wake up call came when he returned from a business trip and found that Fran had moved while he was gone. She left him a letter explaining that she put up with being second place to his pornography for years because she did not want to get divorced and subject their children to the pain of that. Now that the children were grown, she was filing for divorce and her decision was final.

As Drake read the letter, his world began to collapse. He realized he had taken Fran for granted and that although he did attend meetings, his twelve-step friends had become more of a social outlet for him. Drake admitted to himself that he had never worked the Twelve Steps. The few times he had a sponsor he only communicated with him at meetings and then realized what he was looking for was not a guide for his recovery, but a friend.

Drake now has three months of sexual sobriety. He is working on his First Step with his sponsor. Fran will still not take Drake's phone calls. He does not know if she is going to follow through with the divorce or not. What he is sure of is that regardless of the future of the relationship, he is going to stay committed to recovery—real recovery rather than the social club recovery he was doing previously.

Why do I repeatedly slip despite my resolve not to?

Recovery is much more than having a firm resolve to not act out. Do you have a well-defined recovery program? Are you attending multiple meetings each week? Do you have a sponsor? Are you diligently working the Twelve Steps of recovery?

What is missing from your recovery? If you can identify the deficiencies in your recovery program you have a chance to eliminate them. What can you add to your recovery today to help you remain sexually sober? Rather than regretting the past or dreading the future, live in recovery in the present. At least for today, you know you can live soberly. Tomorrow, you can do it again.

Is there still hope if my husband has a relapse?

So long as someone wants to get better, recovery is possible. Many sex addicts who suffer a relapse use the experience to help them become more firmly grounded in recovery. They learn from their relapse experience and use that learning to build a stronger recovery program to achieve lasting sobriety.

Sadly, after a relapse, sometimes the partner is too wounded to be able to move forward in the relationship. Importantly, there is still hope for the sex addict even if there is not hope for the relationship. However, I (Milton) have worked with many couples who stubbornly refused to give up on their relationship after a relapse and now enjoy a closeness they never experienced before.

What are the signs that my husband may have had a relapse?

Changes in the sex addict's attitude and behavior toward you are common warning signs of relapse. That does not mean he has acted out but you may rightly associate what you observe with his attitude and behavior prior to recovery. Lying to you or to others is another danger sign of impending relapse. If recovery activities become less important, if he finds excuses not to attend meetings or has stopped talking to his sponsor, or abruptly stops therapy, you should be concerned.

If I think my husband has had a relapse, what do I do?

Rather than make an accusation, it is helpful to express your concern. You might say, "I noticed you stopped attending your twelve-step meetings the past several weeks. I get frightened you will go back to acting out." Or you might say, "I have noticed you seem to be short-tempered more often lately. I remember that seemed to happen a lot before you got into recovery. I get afraid that you may be headed back toward acting out."

Talking about your feelings rather than suspicions is easier for him to hear and less likely to evoke defensiveness (which will only obstruct communication). Hopefully, your husband will listen to your concerns. If he cares enough about you and your feelings he will want you to feel emotionally safe within the relationship, and one of the things that provides a sense of safety is seeing him make recovery a priority.

My husband has just told me that he relapsed. What should I do?

Even though your husband has relapsed, his recovery is apparently strong enough that he has the courage to face it rather than hide it. That is a very hopeful sign. That makes it more likely he will take the steps necessary to return to sexual sobriety and hopefully prevent future relapses.

Regardless of what he does moving forward, you still have to deal with the new trauma of his revelation. You need time and space to consider what next steps are important for you to take. At such an emotionally charged time, it is inadvisable to act impulsively. This is not a time to declare that the relationship is over or that you are filing for divorce.

Instead, tell him to get with his sponsor or therapist and they can figure out what he needs to do. Request that he leave you alone and not communicate with you unless you initiate it. You need to be able to work on yourself without pressure from him. Many women request that their husbands move out of the house or at least out of the bedroom long enough for them to be able to process some of their feelings. This is not punishment for the sex addict but rather an arrangement that gives the partner the time and space needed to make sense of the situation and determine healthy direction.

It would be beneficial for you to engage the services of a therapist. Most sex addiction therapists have expertise working with the partners of sex addicts. Be sure to ask prospective therapists about their training and experience in working with partners of sex addicts.

Hopefully, you have built a support network of other partners of sex addicts. Their support will be crucial to you during this time. Some women find it helpful to take a few days away from home. They may stay with friends and spend time journaling and engaging in self-care activities like physical exercise, meditation, and taking walks.

Ultimately, you may find that you cannot endure the pain of continuing in the relationship. However, do not assume a relapse automatically means the relationship is over. We have seen many relationships restored, even after multiple relapses.

....

My husband has had yet another relapse. How many relapses before enough is enough?

....

Only the partner involved can answer this question, but if all you see from your husband is regret over his behavior but no real effort to change, then maybe it is time for you to move on. On the other hand, he may finally be at a turning point in his recovery to take the steps necessary to end his serial relapsing.

Unfortunately, some sex addicts seem to believe they have an endless number of second chances; that as long as they can tough it out through their wife's anger she will eventually get over it and they can go back to business as usual. If you do decide to stay and work on your marriage, it is imperative that your husband understand your willingness to stay in the relationship is not another second chance for him, but his last chance. You have to love yourself enough to set a boundary that his acting out must end permanently.

What is the relapse rate for sex addicts?

We need to start with the relapse rates for other forms of addiction. The US National Institute on Drug Abuse has found that the relapse rate for drug addiction is similar to the relapse rates for other chronic illnesses like diabetes, hypertension, and asthma.[69] The rate of relapse is between 40 and 60 percent.[70] The relapse rate of sex addicts is believed to be similar; however, as of yet there have been no studies that confirm it.

Is it worth it to continue to work on a marriage with a sex addict given the risk of relapse?

Although relapse is always a possibility, life is full of uncertainty and there are many other unforeseen difficulties that could also adversely impact your marriage. One or both of you could become seriously ill—this is a risk you judge to be worthwhile. Intuitively, you know that sooner or later one of you will die before the other. The death of a spouse brings tremendous grief, yet you determine that the happiness you can have in your marriage is worth the risk of this pain.

If your marriage was worth getting into in the first place, then it is worth doing the work necessary to see it restored. While the journey to restoration is a difficult one, couples willing to take this journey

---

69 National Institute on Drug Abuse, (2008). *Addiction science: From molecules to managed care*. Retrieved January 6, 2015, from NIH: National Institute on Drug Abuse: http://www.drugabuse.gov/publications/addiction-science/relapse/relapse-rates-drug-addiction-are-similar-to-those-other-well-characterized-chronic-ill

70 National Institute on Drug Abuse, (2012). *Media guide: How to find what you need to know about drug abuse and addiction*. Retrieved January 6, 2014, from http://www.drugabuse.gov/sites/default/files/mediaguide_web_1.pdf

together can create a future that is not only meaningful, but potentially marked with happiness they once thought impossible to achieve.

....

When I have a relapse, I tend to binge for a few days. How can I pull myself out of that spiral?

....

Mindfulness (which we discuss further in an upcoming chapter) is one of the most promising ways to stop binging. Spend time noticing and observing your thoughts and feelings behind the binge. What are you trying to medicate with your acting out?

If you feel the need to binge, make a deal with yourself that you will postpone it for 30 minutes. Spend that time journaling about your feelings. Notice what you are feeling in your body. Try to identify each of your emotions. Are you feeling stressed, anxious, guilty, ashamed, or depressed? Concentrate on your breathing and visualize yourself in warm, peaceful surroundings.

Several forms of psychotherapy incorporate mindfulness practices, including Mindfulness-Based Stress Reduction, Dialectical Behavior Therapy, Acceptance and Commitment Therapy, and others. These approaches can be very helpful in understanding and modifying binging behavior. Contact a therapist and ask if they use one of these modalities. If they do not, ask for a recommendation to a therapist who uses them.

....

How do I deal with relapse without giving up on recovery?

....

Having a relapse means you have lost your sexual sobriety, but it does not mean that you have lost what you have learned in recovery. You have experienced something that happens to many sex addicts. The important question is what can you learn from your relapse? If you learn from your mistakes, your relapse can be very instructive and even helpful. What were the things that led to your relapse? How had your recovery slacked off before your relapse? If you accumulated time in recovery, you are capable of living a sexually sober life.

Affirm yourself as a human being who has flaws but is capable of living a sexually sober life. Give yourself the grace that you would want others to give you. Whether others can ever forgive or get beyond the hurt you have caused by your acting out, you can forgive yourself.

Forgiving yourself begins with accepting your humanity. You may be expecting yourself to live a perfect life or to do perfect recovery. That will never happen. What you can do is learn from your relapse and make the changes necessary to keep from relapsing in the future.

FREEDOM

HOPE

CHAPTER 26

RECOVERY FROM SLIPS AND RELAPSES

When a person experiences a slip, it is essential that he take immediate steps to get back into solid sobriety. A helpful first step is to do a 90 in 90; attending ninety twelve-step meetings over a 90-day period. During that time, it is valuable to start one's Step work over, beginning with Step One. He also needs to consult with his sponsor for suggestions and guidance on building a stronger foundation of recovery.

A relapse is much more serious. Recovery strategies would include all of the same things as for a slip, but we also strongly recommend doing a Relapse Recovery Intensive with a Certified Hope & Freedom Practitioner CHFP,[71] a longer intensive outpatient program (IOP), or an inpatient program for a month or longer.[72] Rather than punishment for being bad, this additional treatment is necessary to get recovery back on track and prevent additional relapses. If multiple forms of addiction are involved, inpatient treatment is indicated.

Recovery activities must be significantly increased after a slip, and especially so after a relapse, otherwise sex addicts have an extremely high probability of returning to active addiction. Going back to the same recovery routines that were not sufficient before and expecting different results is the very definition of insanity.

---

71 www.findachfp.com

72 Appendix D has a list of IOP and inpatient programs.

Harley's and Casey's Story_____

Harley and Casey had been married for three years when Casey discovered his pornography use. He used sophisticated Internet trolling programs that located and downloaded thousands of pornographic videos. Harley would watch these at work and also when Casey was away from the house or he was out of town. The many hours he spent looking at pornography severely impacted his job performance. It also caused him to lose sexual desire for Casey and instead look for the type of sexual partner he saw in porn videos.

Together Harley and Casey entered a brief intensive program where he did a disclosure followed by passing a polygraph exam. In that program, they learned a number of techniques for rebuilding intimacy. He committed to an active program of recovery that included attending four twelve-step meetings every week and working with a sponsor.

Three years later, Harley had a relapse. His wife threatened to leave him if he did not get his recovery back on track. He went back to his therapist and initially reported that he did not know why he relapsed because everything was going so well, but upon exploration Harley revealed he had actually stopped attending meetings about eighteen months before. Additionally, he had not talked to his sponsor in over a year and during that time had not had contact with any of the men who used to hold him accountable.

Harley admitted that he thought he had beaten his addiction through his diligent work in recovery. He reasoned that since he was no longer struggling to stay sexually sober, he did not need the same level of commitment to recovery. His relapse helped change his mind.

Harley returned to the recovery routines that had served him well and expanded upon them. He did not know if Casey would stay with him or not. What he did know was that whether or not their marriage survived, he had to stay in recovery and stay sober—for himself.

If you have experienced a relapse, there are some serious questions you need to ask yourself. What is missing from my recovery? What set me up for a relapse? Relapses do not just happen. There is always a cause. Go back to your personal recovery plan and see what is missing, what you didn't do or discontinued doing, and/or what you have changed since entering recovery.

After a slip or relapse it is important that you return to recovery as soon as possible. Relapses are often so discouraging and fraught with so much guilt and shame that when they occur, many people want to give up on recovery—and some do. When there is a slip or a relapse, the person has broken their sexual sobriety, but has not lost recovery.

It is helpful to do an in-depth review of a relapse to identify specifically how the relapse occurred. It did not happen by accident. It happened because you did or did not do specific things. The autopsy begins with the changes that took place immediately prior to the relapse. The next layer involves identifying what happened just before that. Layer by layer, a person can dig into the details of changes—actions he took or did not take—that (usually) gradually took him away from recovery and led up to relapse. A number of questions may be helpful in uncovering the reasons the relapse occurred:

- When was the last time you attended a twelve-step meeting?
- Has the number of meetings you attend each week changed recently?
- When is the last time you shared at a meeting?
- If you have been working with a therapist, when is the last time you had a session?
- When is the last time you spoke to your sponsor?
- Have you isolated yourself from other people?
- When is the last time you did any Step work?
- Have you worked through all Twelve Steps? If you have, did you then stop Step work or did you continue to work through the Steps again?
- Have you recently celebrated a recovery milestone? If so, did you then think you could let up on recovery activities?
- How long has it been since you talked to your Circle of Five?

- When did you first start engaging in yellow light or dangerous behaviors?

- Have you lied to your spouse, sponsor, or therapist about anything (e.g., meeting attendance, struggles, etc.)?

- Have you made changes in your sobriety contract without consulting your sponsor or therapist? (For example, have you decided that something that had been a red light or forbidden behavior could be reclassified as a yellow light or dangerous behavior?)

- Have you noticed changes in your mood?

- Have you engaged in any high-risk behaviors that you have minimized?

- What changes have you noticed in your attitude?

- Have you gotten angry with someone recently?

- Do you have resentments toward someone?

- Are you blaming someone for some personal setback or failure?

- Have you entertained thoughts that it might be all right to go back to some of your old acting-out behaviors?

- Have you stopped taking medications or changed the dosage without medical direction?

- What changes have taken place most recently in your spiritual life?

- When is the last time you read a book about sex addiction or recovery?

- When is the last time you made an entry in your journal?

- Are you still using the tools you have learned to combat intrusive thoughts?[73]

- Have you started engaging in other activities that have gotten out-of-control (e.g., drinking, gambling, video game playing, watching television, etc.)?

---

73 Magness, M., *Thirty Days to Hope & Freedom From Sexual Addiction: the Essential Guide to Beginning Recovery and Preventing Relapse*, Carefree, AZ: Gentle Path Press (2010), contains two chapters filled with tools for countering intrusive thoughts.

- Have there been any changes in your exercise routine?

- What changes have taken place in your sleep schedule?

- How many days did you engage in healthy eating this past week?

- What changes have taken place in your work schedule?

These questions will help you pinpoint the changes in your life, attitude, and actions that contributed to a relapse. It might be helpful to enlist the aid of your sponsor or someone else in recovery to help you honestly address these questions. Give this person permission to dig deeper, asking you additional questions to follow up on each of your answers. If a person learns necessary lessons from a slip or relapse, it can be one of the most powerful events in his or her recovery process. We have worked with many people who have relapsed and learned invaluable information about recovery and how to stay sober as the result of their relapse.

FREEDOM

HOPE

CHAPTER 27

PREVENTING RELAPSE

Relapse is the end result of a gradual process that usually begins weeks or even months before you act out. If you can spot the potential warning signs of a coming relapse, you have time to correct your course.

What are the early warning signs of relapse?

They include:

- Having just completed a treatment program (a significant number of people relapse right after completing treatment)
- Isolating
- Not sharing your feelings
- Changes in mood, becoming irritable
- More frequent arguments with your partner
- Increased stress at work
- Slacking on recovery activities
- Reducing/discontinuing attending meetings or sharing at meetings
- Feeling spiritually disconnected
- Poor sleeping or eating
- Stopping exercise
- Not asking for help

- Romanticizing past acting out experiences

- Entertaining thoughts of past acting out partners

- Discontinuing using tools to deal with triggers

- Minimizing the consequences of past acting out

- Lying to yourself or others

- Having contact with former acting-out partners

You may have additional early warning signs of relapse. Spend a few minutes listing the places, occasions, circumstances, situations, and people that trigger you. Are you able to identify when you are at risk of relapse?

The most basic way of preventing relapse is sticking to your personal recovery plan. You have already identified many things that you do daily, weekly, monthly, and annually for your recovery. Stick to that plan with consistency and persistence. When a person loses focus on his or her recovery plan, he or she is taking the first step toward relapse. Whenever someone believes he has conquered his addiction and can let up in his recovery efforts, he is moving toward relapse.

Relapse may begin with selective recall, as sex addicts mentally caress some past acting-out behavior. They think of what they enjoyed about their acting out. Perhaps they think of an acting-out partner who they romanticize "really understood" them.

When you find your thoughts going there, play the tape all the way to the end. Rather than focusing on the things you liked about acting out, remember the negative consequences of it. What do you have to lose if you act out again? Make a list of things you lost previously because of your acting out and what you stand to lose if you return to active addiction.

Practice the skill of disciplining yourself so that anytime you begin to embrace your addictive thinking, you go back to mentally reviewing how low your addiction took you and all the pain it caused. Reaching out to your recovery support network and sharing about your thoughts of acting out will help you see it more accurately and give people who care about you the chance to provide feedback and guidance.

This is not the time to be by yourself. You may want to believe, "I've got this," but the majority of sex addicts who succumb to this belief end up relapsing. Fight the desire to isolate. Increase the time you spend with other recovering sex addicts. Go to a meeting. Talk openly in the meeting about your desire to act out. Addictive thinking loses its power when you reach out to others and talk about it.

No one can stay sexually sober alone. You need the experience, strength, and hope that comes from others who are on the same path. Their knowledge and their experience can help you to stay on the recovery path—even when you don't feel like it.

When your sex addiction was running your life, you were disconnected from others. Loneliness marked your days, even when you were around other people. Your acting out was an attempt to be connected, to feel less empty, to feel less lonely. Now, with recovery in your life, you connect with people in meetings. You talk about your feelings and are honest with others when you are triggered to act out. Your recovery connections give you a sense of belonging.

Develop your awareness of situations that may compromise your sobriety. Be careful to avoid the situations that put you at risk, and do not hesitate to remove yourself from people, places, or things that trigger for you.

Stress is a powerful relapse trigger. When you are feeling stressed, use exercise or relaxation techniques to help you ease it. Listen to calming and soothing music and concentrate on taking slow, steady breaths. Get some meditation recordings and listen to them as you close your eyes and envision a peaceful setting.

What are things I can do if I recognize I am on the road to a relapse?

Immediately attend a twelve-step meeting and talk openly about your triggers and your impulses/desire to act out. Contact your sponsor and strengthen your recovery plan as appropriate. Make an appointment with a sex addiction therapist to process your thoughts of acting out.

Additional things you can do include:

- Engage in a hobby
- Change your scenery by taking a walk
- Make a list of the negative consequences of your past acting out
- Make a list of the likely negative consequences if you act out now
- Challenge your thinking by looking for thinking errors or cognitive distortions, such as thinking in the extremes of all black or all white, jumping to conclusions, catastrophizing that things will be horrible, thinking that things must be a certain way, or "should" be that way, thinking about the negative but ignoring the positive aspects of a person or situation—or the opposite— thinking about the positive but ignoring the negative aspects, and thinking that something is better or worse than it really is.

Additional Relapse Prevention Tools

Journaling is a powerful tool for preventing relapse. It is helpful to make a journal entry every day, even if it's a short one. With each journal entry, address the following questions: What happened today? What am I thinking? What am I feeling? If you are journaling daily and reading the journal entries once a week, you will have a good barometer of your recovery. You will be able to spot changes and signs of trouble before a relapse takes place. If you take stock of what you record in your journal and then make the course corrections and other changes indicated to get back into solid recovery, you will minimize the chances of a relapse.

Another important tool for preventing relapse is the Recovery Points System.[74] This system assigns recovery points to various recovery activities and lets sex addicts track their recovery progress week to week. If a person sees his or her recovery points slacking off each week and does not make changes, chances are that a relapse is lurking ahead.

Recovery must be a lifestyle that permeates every part of life. Every decision a person makes should be with an awareness of its effect on recovery. Does this decision enhance or hinder recovery? If a behavior is not helpful to recovery it needs to be reconsidered. Do your behaviors

---

74 See the iPhone app, iRecovery in the App Store or go to www.recoveryapp.com. A PDF version of the Recovery Points System can be found at www.30daysthebook.com.

enhance your recovery activities, your spiritual life, your psychological health, or your physical health? If they do not, it is time to consider eliminating them from your life.

Do the friends you keep enhance your recovery? Do your spending habits support a recovery lifestyle? Does a study of how you spend your time indicate recovery is a top priority in your life?

Anything less than 100 percent commitment to recovery sets sex addicts up for relapse. There is no middle ground, no gray area. Sex addicts are either moving toward recovery or they are moving away from recovery and toward relapse.

A useful analogy is that of being in a motorboat with the drain plug pulled out. If the boat is stationary, water immediately starts to fill the boat and, if enough accumulates, the boat will sink. The amazing thing about the sinking boat is how quickly the situation can be remedied. Crank the motor and take off across the water and water will stop leaking into the boat. Moreover, the water already in the boat will run out of the drain hole. Sex addicts can get their lives back on track again by engaging in those activities that propel them forward.

The motor that pushes a person forward is recovery. Recovery is what keeps a sex addict's life afloat. Without a complete commitment to recovery, the person has effectively stopped the engine and is allowing water to fill the boat—allowing addictive thinking and behavior to put him or her at risk. Decide today that you are going to begin every day with a renewed commitment to spend each day fully engaged in your recovery process.

Adjust Your Expectations

Although it is true that many sex addicts relapse, relapse is not inevitable. When you hear someone say, "Everyone relapses" or "Relapse is part of recovery," they are often speaking from the perspective of the pain of their own relapse. Since those who relapse often experience a degree of shame and feelings of failure, sometimes such statements are intended to provide support. Partners of sex addicts are sometimes advised by other partners to prepare for their husbands to relapse because it happened to their own husband.

If you expect to relapse, you likely will. If you expect that you will live a healthy and sexually sober life, you will look for the help necessary to make that happen. Reframe your thoughts. Expect that you will do well—as long as you stick to the recovery basics, follow your recovery plan, continue consistent involvement in recovery activities, and remain committed to recovery.

Mindfulness in Relapse Prevention

Mindfulness is a set of practices and a way of approaching life that emphasizes being aware of one's thoughts and feelings without judging them as right or wrong. When people practice mindfulness, their attention is tuned into what they are sensing in that present moment, internally and externally, rather than going back over the past or imagining the future. The practice of mindfulness has its origins in Buddhism, but the secular practice of mindfulness is increasingly used in therapy.

Mindfulness is helpful in recovery because it focuses on what is happening in the present. Sex addicts tend to spend a great deal of time and thought reliving the past, either wanting to repeat past acting out, or after entering recovery, regretting the pain acting out caused themselves and others. Sex addicts also anticipate the future, looking toward better times, thinking about how different life will be when their acting out stops or when their relationship heals or when they complete working the Steps. They frequently look forward to an imagined perfect time in the future. Yet, even if it comes, the "perfect" time is never as perfect as we want it to be.

Mindfulness is about paying attention to your present experience, and accepting that experience, whether it is positive or negative. After all, the present is all that you have in which to do your recovery, to take care of yourself, and to cultivate healthy relationships. The past is over and the future hasn't yet arrived, and who knows what it holds?

In addiction, certain emotional cues are tied to acting out. For example, when a person is feeling lonely he or she may be more susceptible to acting out. The acting out fills the void of loneliness and becomes linked to the experience of (temporarily) alleviating feeling lonely. Other people may act out when feeling stressed, bored, angry, or self-pitying. In such cases, these feelings get connected to sexually acting out, and so become triggers.

Mindfulness helps sex addicts develop the ability to notice and feel those emotions without judging them to be good or bad. It helps people learn how to better accept and tolerate these uncomfortable feelings. In this way, mindfulness helps uncouple emotions from sexual acting out, reducing the strength of the emotions as triggers. Mindfulness also helps a person detach from automatic thoughts that frequently lead to relapse. When sex addicts can be aware of their triggers and learn how to respond to them consciously, they can interrupt what may have become almost automatic behaviors and make new, different, and healthier choices.

The practice of mindfulness meditation helps people increase their tolerance for uncomfortable emotions. This alleviates the need to act out in order to medicate or avoid those uncomfortable emotions. Mindfulness-based relapse prevention[75] has been used successfully in alcohol and other drug treatment, and is now being used with sex addicts. Developed by the Addictive Behaviors Research Center at the University of Washington, one of the tools that mindfulness-based relapse prevention uses involves breathing exercises centered around the acronym SOBER. When a triggering emotion or thought takes place, sex addicts can:

- S: Stop. Pause wherever and whatever you are doing.
- O: Observe what is happening in your mind and your body.
- B: Breathe. Focus on your breathing as a way of staying anchored in the present.
- E: Expand awareness to your whole body and to your surroundings.
- R: Respond mindfully rather than automatically.

Another mindfulness tool used in relapse prevention is *urge surfing*, a term coined by G. Alan Marlatt, PhD. The powerful cravings/urges to use alcohol and other drugs that are so common to addicts in early

---

75 Witkiewitz, K., Marlatt, GA, & Walker, D., Mindfulness-based relapse prevention for alcohol and substance use disorders, *Journal of Cognitive Psychotherapy*, 19(3)(2005), 211-228.

recovery actually do not last very long. If people can be mindful of this reality and tolerate or surf the urges that arise, they can effectively ride them out. Just like waves in the ocean, cravings and urges fade. In adapting this technique for sex addicts, sex addicts would notice the urge to act out. Then, they would practice mindfulness to get in touch with their feelings and thoughts. For each emotion related to wanting to act out, they notice the thoughts that are related to it. For example, they may think, *This desire to act out is driving me crazy.* In response they can say to themselves calmly, something along the lines of, "This too shall pass."

This is continued with every emotion and thought connected to urges to act out. Sex addicts can remind themselves that their thoughts are just thoughts, and give attention to their breathing to get in touch with body sensations and center themselves. Each time a person resists the urge to act out, their recovery gets stronger, and so will yours.

PART SIX

THE JOURNEY HOME

In the aftermath of sex addiction, more relationships fail than succeed. Yet, many relationships survive and go on to thrive. In this section of the book we share some of those stories as told by the couples themselves. While many couples shared their success stories with us, due to space constraints we were only able to include a few of them here. We found that couples were eager to share their stories to help others who are on this difficult journey. Our deep gratitude goes out to each of these couples for their contribution to this book. As you read these stories, you will see the common themes of pain, setbacks, determination, and a willingness to move forward in spite of the pain.

SUCCESS STORIES

Rob and Ginny's Story

"After learning of another episode of my husband's acting out, I was convinced he was a sex addict. I believed strongly that we needed a program that treated us both. I knew I was traumatized and that the only hope for the survival of our marriage was treatment for my trauma and treatment for his addiction. Our three-day intensive was the beginning of our survival. It was the first time I saw my husband's addiction addressed directly in therapy. I am convinced that it took complete disclosure for him to realize the extent of the damage he had caused to me, to himself, and to our marriage. I call the lie detector test 'the bone scan' for this disease. He has done the test three times and each time it reassures me that we are on the right path.

"He attends his twelve-step meetings and has been in individual and group therapy. We attend a couple's twelve-step meeting twice a month when possible. I have had EMDR [Eye Movement Desensitization and Reprocessing, recognized as an effective therapy for trauma resolution] treatment for my trauma.

"The triggers were brutal in the beginning. The disclosure information would suddenly get triggered by the most innocent situations—TV shows, conversations with friends, innocent mentioning of a name, etc. For the first six months, triggers felt like drive-by shootings; out of nowhere I would fall to my knees in pain. Thoughts of what had occurred were constantly in my mind and in my dreams.

"We are very grateful to have the gifts of recovery. We are closer than we have ever been. I have a strong sense of trust in him now that I never had before. Even though I was shocked and devastated each time I learned that he had acted out and believed that his remorse was sincere, I never believed that he truly got to the bottom of what caused the acting out in the first place.

"We have a level of intimacy that is remarkable. I have never been happier! My husband is more calm and joyful than I have ever seen him. We are solid. We have been through hell and stood by each other. We have each other's back—I feel certain of that. He is the man I fell in love with. That man is around all the time now.

"If you are suffering from addiction, the message is that with hard work and commitment, your marriage can recover. Actually, it can more than recover—it can deepen and grow. I feel so grateful for what we have now. I know that I love deeply and am loved deeply. The road is difficult—but just like recovery from any other life threatening illness, it requires good care, patience, and hard work. In the long run, it is worth it."

Rob and Ginny, Pennsylvania

Chuck and Laura's Story

"At the time we began recovery I had no thought that we could actually recover. I was there to try to get through this process and see how we could work through his recovery. I just wanted to have an amicable divorce without ruining his life and mine. We remained in the same home and went to a Christian counselor until we were able to attend an intensive three-day session.

"Although the disclosure was painful, it was in some way completely freeing. No longer did I have to judge stories to be true or false. It was all out there. It also showed me that it was not just me—this would have happened to anyone he was with. I think the combination of him finally being willing to be completely truthful and the polygraph test gave me a chance to catch my breath and stop my mind from dreaming up more craziness. The knowledge that he would take a polygraph again in three months gave me the ability to stop checking emails, phones, where he was, etc. I could actually rest and focus on my own recovery, which of course was a complete surprise to me because until this point I had blamed this crazy relationship completely on him. I learned to own my willingness to accept this kind of relationship and to make personal changes a goal. Why had I thought so little of myself that I continued to deal with this treatment?

"I was able to start reading, doing phone meetings, having recovery meetings with my husband, and focusing on our relationship with each other and with God, as a couple—actually working together as opposed to against each other. Daily readings and connection helped me to feel that there was not only a chance to work through our problems, but to have a relationship that exceeded anything I had ever dreamed of. My husband became a person who could actually say and show how he really felt. Although the pain I went through in the past was real and horrible, I have learned to treasure the changes we have both made in our individual lives and our lives as a couple. I thank God every day that we are able to show our children what a truly healthy relationship looks like.

"It is not all one big romantic life—but it is a real life with two people who have differences of opinions but also have enough respect and love to work through that in a healthy way, with God at the forefront of our relationship. It is now not words that tell me my husband truly respects and loves me but his everyday actions.

"We not only have a great love for each other but a deep respect and our faith in God has grown so much. We are now at a point where we can help others to see that there is hope for the future if they do the work. This is an ongoing life change that must be guarded every day. Sobriety is not to be taken lightly. Often we have people ask why in the world we go to marriage counseling in Houston and why we go on retreats as we seem to have a great marriage and true friendship. We always try to explain the deep dark hole where we were and that we must work on our relationship every day.

"I was at a point where I just wanted my husband to literally no longer exist. Now I can't imagine my life without him. I have a respect and love for him that I didn't have before our recovery, even in times that I thought we were happy."

Chuck and Laura, Louisiana

Shimon and Marcia's Story _____

"Immediately after discovery we separated for about ten days. During that time I got on the Internet, looking for some indication that it would be possible to recover our relationship. Mostly, what I found was hopelessness and despair until I learned about three-day intensives. I suggested to my husband that this was a chance to recover if he was committed to making it right. Three weeks later we did an intensive in North Carolina during which my husband disclosed everything, including lies he had told me completely unrelated to his addiction. It was shocking and left me in a daze.

"We came back from North Carolina and both of us went to work. I found a support group that I went to every week. He found three SAA meetings nearby and went to two every week. My husband started to work seriously on the Twelve Steps. We started working with a terrific therapist. For nearly a year he went, I went, and we went to therapy. And, perhaps most important, we began meditating together every morning and found a spiritual foundation for our lives and relationship. This work, together, allowed us to create an entirely different dynamic than the one that had gotten us where we were.

"The intensive and the polygraph were critical, early on. The fact that we did it so quickly after discovery, and didn't have to go through the slow and painful period of lies, broken promises, and discovery leaking out over months and months, allowed us to begin healing without the opening and reopening of wounds. The lies were in many ways more painful to me than the sex. Once the truth, in all its ugliness, was told, we could move forward. There is no way he would have come clean without the polygraph, and I would have continued seeking out the truth and uncovering more lies. I doubt we could have survived without the bright-line of truth that the polygraph allowed.

"The fact that my husband immediately recognized his addiction and embraced his recovery was critical. I would not be in a relationship with an addict who was not in recovery. He didn't defend, justify, deflect, or explain his behavior. He apologized for the damage he did, he promised never to lie to me again, and I believe he has kept that promise. He has lived a life of 'walking amends' ever since the intensive.

"Confronting my own delusion was the hardest part. Really seeing that our relationship had followed the pattern of his addictive rituals. Getting that the 'sweet nothings' I thought he had reserved for me had been spoken to total strangers. Realizing that he had put my life in danger by having unprotected sex with multiple strangers who were themselves having unprotected sex with multiple strangers. Looking at the way I had disregarded warning signs and even disregarded my own feelings and values during the years leading up to discovery. Finding that the 'perfect marriage' I thought I had was a scam and that my 'perfect man' was a con artist. Once I fully told the truth to myself (which was several months after he told the truth to me), I could begin to see the possibility of forgiveness and start to heal.

"In many ways we now have the relationship I had deluded myself that we had before. We are still in couples' therapy twice per month. He still goes to SAA meetings and is now a sponsor. I continue to go to my support group, but mostly as a support to other women. We still meditate together. But now we are also taking dance classes and having fun together. We are facing retirement now with a sense of excitement and adventure rather than a sense of dread.

"We are both, in many ways, grateful for what we went through. It has allowed us to be closer than we ever would have been given the shame he felt. We both believe we learned important lessons during this experience and that we have both matured in the process. At some point while driving in my car I realized that, knowing everything that was going to happen, I would still choose to be married to him. That was when I was sure we were going to make it."

Shimon and Marcia, California

Amy and Jesse's Story_____

"*The most important part of our success story is that it 100 percent belongs to turning our marriage over to God. First, we had to open our hearts to Him individually and then turn toward each other. We each had support groups and we found free marriage counseling at a local parish. We both read recovery books. We communicated daily on our issues. I was free to mourn and cry and be angry.*

"*We have twelve children and one income so we could not afford pricey counseling or intensives. We had to lean on God and be resourceful in how we found healing. We did and still do weekly check-ins. Jesse had to humble himself completely in order to break free of the chains of addiction, lying, and fear of intimacy. I had to humble myself completely to put aside the pain and embarrassment of a husband who had kept me in the dark, pushed me away sexually, and lied to me for so long.*

"*We had gotten rid of cable television long before and had Internet security but Jesse made other provisions on his phone and at work to encourage the healing process and rebuild trust. Humility, charity, and forgiveness have contributed to our success, along with not giving in to the world's idea that happiness is all that matters and realizing that there will still be hard days ahead, and being OK with taking those days as they come.*

"*Don't give up. Believe actions and not words. We were told that in order for us to really succeed we had to start marriage number two, but first we had to work through the trauma of marriage number one. For the spouse who is an addict, patience and understanding are key. I prayed daily to see my husband as Jesus did and act accordingly. There is no 'quick fix.' This is a long process but in the end, I believe it will be worth it.*"

Amy and Jesse, Michigan

Woody and Betty's Story _____

"*I wasn't caught acting out, I just reached a point where I couldn't live with myself anymore. I didn't want to be a liar anymore and*

I didn't want to be lonely in my marriage. I was also a pastor of a small country church. On May 18, 1991, I came clean to my wife. I was still having an affair at the time, and just couldn't seem to end it, and this led my wife to seek counsel from a trusted friend. She left me and that was a wake up call—but it wasn't enough. I said what I needed to say to smooth things over and we got back together again, but I was still seeing the other woman. Finally, I resigned my position and we set off to go camping to see if we could heal our marriage. Along the way, I began telling her even more about what I had been doing and she became frightened of me. So, the next day, I called a treatment center where I stayed for three weeks.

"After getting out, my wife and I went to some after-care groups, read a lot of recovery-themed books, and we sought out friendships among fellow addicts in recovery and their spouses. The churches where we have been members have also been a source of strength and hope, providing an atmosphere of hopefulness, encouragement, and service. In each church we began support groups, led marriage classes, and helped couples privately.

"Today, we are deeply in love, committed to each other, have no secrets, trust each other—and now, I have the kind of marriage I used to see in other people and wish I had. None of this has been possible without God's power and our trusting Him for strength.

"We both realized we had problems that needed professional help. We both sought counseling. We walked this path together and were determined to learn how to communicate. We have used the Twelve Steps as our framework for working our own recoveries. In short, recovery became our new lifestyle.

"She needed to know she could trust me and I needed to earn back her shattered trust. I proved to her by my former actions that I was untrustworthy, so I took extra measures to earn back her trust a little at a time. I got into accountability groups with men seeking recovery. Initially, I never went anywhere alone and made sure she always knew where I was, where I was going, whom I was with, why I was with them, and when I was going to be home. I had no secrets and practiced rigorous honesty. I did all this willingly *and without resentment. As the years went by, and the Internet and smart phones became a reality—I got filtering software on my devices and gave her complete access to all email, social media accounts, computers, etc. This is all second nature to me now, but initially, it felt mechanical and uncomfortable.*

"*At first, we simply did not know how to talk to each other. I can remember us sitting at opposite corners of our bed, looking at each other, and not even knowing what word to start with to begin a conversation. So, I began by telling her what my day was like and my struggles with sexual purity that day. That was hard for her to hear at first, but eventually, she began to tell me about her day. From there, we built a pattern of sharing, listening, and not trying to 'interpret' what the other person was saying, but actually hearing each other. We learned to ask questions without getting defensive and express feelings, hopes, and expectations. All this was gradual—very gradual—but today we can talk about everything.*

"*We are in-tune with each other. We each know what's going on in our lives and we trust each other, but mostly we are deeply in love. We were separated, headed for divorce (which I deserved), and today, by God's power, strength, and love and our submission to Him and His will, we will be celebrating our thirty-seventh wedding anniversary. We flirt with each other, we say loving things to each other, and we have very passionate love-making. We are each other's best friend.*"

Woody and Betty, Texas

Lee and June's Story _____

"*Success comes only one way: hard. I started my recovery thinking I could handle it and all was under control. After two years, I acted out again and found myself at rock bottom. Shame and guilt drove me to do the right thing. My wife, who is my inspiration, was there for me and never gave up even after all the pain I had caused her. From there I admitted all that I had done and went over all questions she had, as hard as it was. My wife found a great therapist, who had us participate in psychodrama. This event really opened me up and helped us both see my pain from childhood.*

"My success came from a loving wife, and my determination to change my path and the way I was raised. I had chosen to become a horrible person and forced it onto everyone around me. I have become a caring, loving, responsible human being that my wife and family want to be around. And I give back to them: my time, my love, and anything they need. It is a great feeling; a feeling that acting out never gave me.

"The most difficult part of this journey was admitting the wrong I had done, realizing the way I had carried on for all these years was incorrect, and letting go of my need to control. My wife and I have lived and worked together since 1995 and have never been as close and connected as we are now. Being a caring and loving husband shows her that she is the most important person in my life. We grow closer every day.

"If you truly love one another and you want to continue in your relationship, you need to realize what you are on the verge of losing. You are making a choice to be a sex addict, based on events that you may or may not have had control over and are heading down a dead-end road. It is a hard obstacle to overcome, but it can be done. You have to quit taking and start giving.

"The only way to recover is to make a choice to yourself that you want to become a better person. You can read and participate in all types of recovery programs, but don't limit yourself to only one path. Learn all you can about your past, your childhood, and see how it is all connected. Find a spiritual path."

Lee and June, Alabama

Joe and Nicole's Story_____

"My marriage was rocked by my behavior. After years of excuses and rationalizations, my acting out was revealed to my wife after I had used a laptop of her employer to access online pornography. Her boss confronted my wife who then confronted me.

"I was ashamed and crushed. I had hurt my wife and her relationship with her boss, who in turn was traumatized by finding the pornography on her laptop. I was ashamed that I could do something like that. But the pain I felt provided the motivation to do whatever it took to not feel that way again. Now that my secret life was out, I had nothing left to lose. I determined to take whatever steps were necessary to deal with my problems before they consumed me.

"I entered therapy and began attending a twelve-step group for sexual addiction. I got just about every book I could on the topic and devoured them all, reading them several times in some cases. My wife and I both attended a separate twelve-step group for couples. Once I had made some progress in my own recovery, we began seeing a marriage counselor. The work that we did paid off, and allowed us to deal with our individual problems and the dysfunction in our relationship.

"We knew this problem was one we could not handle alone. We needed to reach out to a community that would accept us despite our problems and to which we could be accountable. We were blessed to find this community in our church and in twelve-step groups.

"A second factor in our success was utilizing the available tools of recovery. Picking up the phone and calling someone in my twelve-step group, digging into recovery literature, daily prayer and meditation are all practices that help with recovery. But like any muscle or skill, they only develop when they are used regularly.

"Finally, we were determined to do whatever it took to fix our relationship. We both came from broken homes, and didn't want to perpetuate the cycle of divorce and relationship failure that we grew up with. Although we didn't have children at the time, we wanted to prove to our future children that imperfect people can still have a healthy and loving relationship.

"The hardest thing is to rebuild trust, and it was painful to learn about how my actions led my wife to lose trust in me. That trust was not lost overnight, so it could not be rebuilt overnight. Instead, it takes faithful and persistent action to prove that I can be a man worthy of her trust.

"Dealing with my addictive behavior was actually only the first step. My addiction was a source of distraction from an often unwelcome and uncomfortable reality, such as stress at work, stress from debt, uncertainty about the future, and so on. Stopping the addictive behaviors meant that I had to deal with the fears, habits, and negative thought cycles that perpetuated those behaviors. Without the addiction as a shield, I was forced to confront the parts of my life I was running from.

"One of those pieces of reality I had to confront was that I have a problem with anger. I do not scream, swear, or shout, like my father did, and so I never thought of myself as an angry person. Yet, I can be coldly distant, harsh, critical, and abrupt with my wife, all of which stemmed from an underlying and unacknowledged anger. I was more like my father than I realized.

"My wife is my best friend. She has stuck with me through my deepest lows, and has seen me at my best. She has loved me through all of it. I have learned that my marriage will only work if I work at it. In order to have the home life I want I must be proactive to help bring it about.

"For example, we hold financial meetings once a month. Instead of dreading those times and dragging my feet, we work together and see ourselves as on the same team. Our finances have improved dramatically since beginning recovery, because we are finally working toward common goals.

"We are closer than ever before, and are having more fun together than we have had in years. We have developed hobbies like playing board games together and have made a point of involving more couples in our social life. We want our relationship and the hardships we have been through to be a resource for others, to show that a couple can recover from traumatic disclosures of addictive behaviors.

"If you are willing to be honest and accountable to each other, you can make it through this. Honesty is the key for rebuilding trust in a relationship. But you cannot do it alone, so involve others to help keep you both accountable. Find trustworthy people and bring them into the situation and shine some light on your relationship. Other people have gone through the same thing and can relate to your pain.

"Shame was a key driver of my addiction, and shame kept my wife and me isolated from other people. Dealing with the sense of shame that we felt as a couple was a key part of our recovery. I have learned to accept who we are and to love the unique qualities of our relationship, rather than wishing we could be the model couple I thought we should be. We are not perfect people, and our relationship will never be perfect. It is, however, perfect for us."

Joe and Nicole, Texas

Gary and Karen's Story

"Our success story began when I decided to listen to God and my pastor. That is when I had enough peace to be able to quiet my mind enough to see that this was no isolated incident of someone being unsatisfied and looking outside the relationship. It was something much larger and out of control. This realization was an eye opener for both of us that led us into a faith-based twelve-step recovery group—me, because I thought he needed it, and him, because he was honest enough and desperate enough to want help. It was the best thing we ever did, and yes, I needed it, too. Once I admitted that and worked the program, I was able to release him to pursue his recovery without trying to force or orchestrate it.

"Four years later I have written and published a book about my experience and we speak to groups in our area as a recovering couple. My husband actually feels free for the first time in his life. He has made and continues to make positive changes and exhibit accountability and maturity. I have been freed of the low self-esteem and codependency that drove my life and controlled my decisions. Sometimes the worst experiences bring the greatest blessings.

"Our relationship now is real. Before the addiction came to light it was superficial and almost desperate. Now we disagree and argue like a normal couple. We also share our struggles. We could never have done that before.

"Don't give up. The struggle is real and ongoing, but it can be managed and conquered. Get help in the form of counseling and a twelve-step group. Both of you need accountability partners you can call on when you are struggling. Always remember, your spouse is not the enemy, the addiction is. Fight it, not each other."

Gary and Karen, Arkansas

Hugo and Karen's Story

"Through the years, my husband has been to many treatment programs. We have had multiple separations. Then we took a different path. Without a doubt, our intensive work in the States helped me start the painful healing process rather than go backwards. Without this, we wouldn't be together. I couldn't have continued to live with always questioning, wondering, and worrying. We did a full disclosure followed by a polygraph.

"I have found a good therapist who has helped me heal from my trauma. We both attend twelve-step meetings and continue to return to the States periodically for aftercare work and follow-up polygraph exams.

"A variety of things have helped, including: doing simple every day things and learning to take it easy, my husband telling me the whole truth for the first time in his life, medication for depression, telling a couple of trusted friends who worked in the therapy field or had their own experience, allowing myself to grieve, getting a handle on finances, blocks on computers and television, relationship workshops, reading recovery books daily, and meditation.

"Our relationship has certainly changed. We are both in recovery. We are calmer and more realistic. We both value our family and spend important time with them and each of the children. Our communication with the children seems to be better and we are probably more available to them emotionally. Both of us look after ourselves more.

"With follow-up polygraphs, I feel that trust is rebuilding at its own pace. I don't know how long this needs to continue, but for now,

it feels comforting. We are able to relax together more and have a better way of communicating. We are less 'dramatic' and respond more than react. We have a more mature relationship. And we are still working our way through it. The bruising is still in the process of healing.

"We both know that we are together because we want to be, even in the hard times (of which there are quite a few), and that we could survive on our own if necessary. Our sex life has decreased. There is less need for a 'fix' in that way. With us working on our relationship when it's less painful, I feel that this will be a part of our lives we enjoy even more.

"We both enjoy and value the simple things much more. We are less judgmental and more honest with each other. It is only fourteen months since we did the 'full' disclosure and it feels like the last three years have been a long journey. We are sorting out our finances together and focusing on our separate healing.

"Don't make any big decisions in the first year. Go to twelve-steps meetings and find the ones that help you. Go to a therapist who is qualified in sex addiction and trauma. Do courses to help release some of the emotion. Do a lot of research into material to help you and to understand what your partner is going through.

"Don't pretend you're not angry, devastated, or even suicidal. Talk to your doctor straight away and get some help for sleeping in the meantime. Temporarily separate if that helps for a time until you have a support structure up and running. Look out for yourself! This applies to you both. Take time to read, relax, exercise, and attend to nutrition—all those things people tell us which feel impossible early on.

"Most important, when you are ready, get a full disclosure with a professional and a polygraph whether you want to stay in the relationship or not. The sooner the better. What I realize now is that this is the biggest healing journey of my life. It felt like my life was shattered and I didn't think I could survive. Taking each step has been incredibly hard or in some cases wonderful.

"What has happened is that I have healed and dissolved many of my wounds from my past as a result of this, and I now have better relationships with my family and some friends. When I see my husband with our children, I am very grateful I didn't let go of our marriage. We have more compassion and understanding for each other and others. I never thought I could get through this but I have, and I know that there is so much more of the good stuff to come.

"Each stage passes and as you deal with each part and get whatever help you need during that time, it feels like putting together the jigsaw puzzle of your new (and better!) life. Forgive yourself as you are on a difficult path. You deserve to be loved and to love yourself. I know how hard this is. I've experienced it and I wouldn't wish the pain on anyone, but it can heal and you can come out the other side happier than you have ever been."

Hugo and Karen, London, England

Mike and Jennifer's Story _____

"I had always suspected something. I did not want to believe it was true. When I got a call from the health department I realized I could not stay in denial anymore. My husband had a problem, a big problem, and now it was a family problem.

"After two weeks of being in shock, I started doing some research. I did not find many resources I felt would be of help to us. Because my husband was a pastor he was well connected to the counseling community in our area. I knew conventional counseling was not the answer. I found our individual and couples' therapists online. They specialized in sex addiction and helping traumatized partners of sex addicts heal. After weeks of reading everything I could get my hands on regarding sex addiction I realized we needed people who specialized in this area. I truly believe that if we had just gone to a 'marriage counselor' neither we nor our marriage would have survived this ordeal of sex addiction.

"I gave my husband an ultimatum. Either we go to the three-day intensive now or it's over. I was surprised that we could not just

go for the counseling sessions. Our therapist required that we were both safe and emotionally able to start this journey. After seeing my family physician and meeting some other requirements, we faced and survived the three-day intensive therapy program. The road has been long and hard, and we are still fighting for our marriage. We made a commitment before God with our vows. We are both committed to staying on this path and fighting for our marriage. Prayer, our trust in God, and commitment to each other and the process of fighting for our recovery and restoration, along with professionals in the field of sex addiction is what has kept us together.

"To be affirmed by feelings that were so foreign, but are natural in this area of trauma and be part of a phone support group and study for a spouse were life savers. During the beginning of our recovery journey I was also going thru breast cancer. My Tuesday phone group with my therapist was so empowering for me. Her sweet understanding voice on the end of a phone when I was so desperately sick was so encouraging. My advice to anyone entering this journey would be to seek out those who are trained and specialize in field of sex addiction.

"I would describe our relationship now as growing. It feels like the seasons. There are seasons of new growth with everything bursting through the soil and blooming, then things wither and become dormant with the cold harsh winds of winter. Then the sun comes out and everything grows again and in some areas, bigger and better than before. It is a continuing cycle.

"It's not easy, we have good days and bad days, but it has been worth it. It would have been much easier to walk away, and some days I wish I would have, but I am glad I stayed."

Mike and Jennifer, Kentucky

John and Amy's Story

"Our path has included many things, including individual and couples' counseling, as well as twelve-step meetings for both my wife and I. This is still ongoing. It also included a three-day intensive program, a follow-up visit, and two polygraph tests. We are about to make a twelve-step meeting for couples part of our recovery.

"There were several difficult parts of this journey. The first was breaking all communications with the person I had an affair with. Next, was eliminating online pornography and this took several months. Finally, I had to give my wife enough time to heal, which meant not pressuring her into having sex with me.

"Even though my wife and I are still trying to find out a way to reconnect sexually we are closer now due to increased communication. You learn what is really important in your life. Sex for a sex addict is important, but in the overall picture there are many other things that are more important, such as keeping my family intact and having them trust me, and maintaining my professional stature in the community. Carrying on affairs brings too much danger and the excitement has worn off as I've learned more about the disease. I have also discovered how many people suffer from this disease, and it is mind-boggling.

"Building back trust can be a long road but it is worth it if you both love each other. Think about your lives together and the other lives you are a part of. It can be a long road and my wife and I are still a work in progress. We just celebrated our thirty-first anniversary. Three years ago when I disclosed my indiscretions to my wife I would have bet we would be divorced by now. Having the partner of the addict also work in recovery is a major step toward mending your relationship. If both are willing to work and understand the addiction you have a much greater chance of saving your relationship. Recovery has been worth each step."

John and Amy, Rhode Island

Michael and Barbara's Story _____

"When we married—my second marriage, his third—I knew he had problems with pornography but I didn't think much of it. We both believed it would be better after marriage and neither of us knew we were up against sex addiction. I had never heard of it. For eight years we lived in hell. I had two children from a former marriage; he had hoped to fill the void of not having a dad in our home but was rejected. The more he was rejected, the more it sent him into his addiction. Our home was being destroyed and we all were being damaged and torn apart. He relapsed badly. We sought help from counselors, pastors, psychiatrists, and other professionals with no success (I could write a book on this). The addiction flourished and his acting out kept getting worse. We separated.

"In 2006, I began my own recovery and in the fall of that year we went to Colorado Springs for an Intensive. It was life changing. We learned the missing pieces of the healing process. Michael was treated and so was I. A polygraph wiped the slate clean; we both dug back deep into our pasts to heal the infection within and off we were on a journey of healing; physically, mentally, emotionally, and spiritually. The process took three years before I felt the Lord tell me to move back and another three years before I witnessed a change and healed heart, not only in my husband, but in me. My family was restored.

"We are committed. My husband is sexually sober. We have been blessed beyond measure. We both lead recovery groups. We communicate, we rarely argue, we discuss feelings. Our family has been restored. We still experience some issues, but nothing like it used to be, and we are moving forward.

"This is what I would like to say to others who are on this journey: Be patient. Work your own recovery. Set protective boundaries. Give up control of your partner. Recovery is about you! Detach from addiction. Pray! Learn all you can about emotions. Spend quality time with your spouse. No lies.

"This has been one of the hardest journeys of my life, but I am grateful for it now. We are living a life with God in control, serving him, helping others, and feeling joy and peace. It doesn't get much better than that!"

Michael and Barbara, New York

Rob and Carol's Story

"Rob and I were church leaders when he confessed to me that he was struggling with sexual addiction, which had nearly led to an affair. At that point he was desperate to change. He was at the end of his rope living a double life. I was angry, but he was very repentant, which helped. We got some couples' counseling but the turning point for us was training on the subject of forgiveness. We began to understand that the roots of addiction and codependence came from our families of origin and our reactions—both spiritual and emotional—to our parents. My father was a sex addict and it was no coincidence that I married one. Rob's father was an alcoholic, so the roots of addiction ran deep in his family as well. By forgiving our families, as well as each other, we began a significant healing process.

"We had little peer support during those early years, and we were unsure with whom we could safely share our story. We had no access to a trained therapist or any counselor who knew anything about sex addiction. It was lonely having no one who could relate to what we were experiencing. I never really disclosed to anyone what I was going through, which I marvel at now. The one close friend in whom I tried to confide reacted in a hostile way to Rob, which didn't help me in my healing process. I had a hard enough time working through my own anger toward him!

"What is our relationship like now? Well, we work side-by-side and share elements of our story on a regular basis. We are currently Licensed Professional Counselors and sex addiction therapists and have begun our own sex addiction practice. He is my best friend and there is a true sense of victory when we are able to go back and help others through something that almost destroyed us. Our relationship is not perfect but it is solid. We have been through a lot together and have a bond that is deep as a result.

"For those who are just beginning this journey, we want to say that there is hope and it's worth the journey. I've never regretted staying with Rob and the relationship that we have now is worth all of the heartache of those early years. It was a hard-won battle. Perhaps we'll write our own book some day!"

Rob and Carol, Michigan

Stephen and Jean's Story _____

"After leading a life of lies and confusion, feeling lost in deadly shame, my wife and I both entered recovery. Making progress through the years in recovery initially, I had yet to realize a life that was more than the emptiness I had always known. A marked amount of energy was required to maintain "sobriety." After seven years of meetings, retreats, therapy, and the appearance of 'success' in recovery, I spiraled out of control into a place I had never been, even in my past wretched sinfulness. My sex addiction devoured me. I contemplated suicide before reaching out to my therapist from seven years prior at an inpatient treatment center in Arizona, where I started my journey. She counseled me and advised me to not just save my marriage and family, but to save my life.

"My wife declared she was leaving; she had been humiliated to a point of non-repair. She had been abused by my behaviors and lies for the last time over our twenty-eight years of marriage. I contacted a therapist who agreed to accept us for a three-day Intensive. My wife agreed to stay in the home until our weekend was scheduled. That was an agonizing time. I thought of dying daily and the sordid details of my lies and actions continued to leak out. I did manage to dig deep into my conscience and listed every sinful act I had ever committed, even the ones that were unspeakable or unthinkable. I slept in another bedroom and cried uncontrollably most nights in pain over my shame and my actions against my family and God. After three months I had a legal pad filled with my sexual history. Arriving for our intensive, we prepared for my disclosure. At the disclosure, the look on my wife's face was one of death and pain. I read my list of horrendous behaviors including those before our marriage. This seemed to go on forever and with each confession and exposure, the life drained from her more.

"After the hour barrage of my disclosure I had nothing left inside nor did my wife. Any chance for a life with this woman I had been given to love and cherish was gone. I had gone far over the line with her, and certainly with God. As soon as this was completed I was taken to a small room where I met a forensic polygraph examiner.

We talked for several minutes and I continued to confess even more shameful things I had done. After being attached to the machine with electrodes, blood pressure cuff, and respiratory monitoring, I felt as though I would explode with fear and anxiety. The fear now was not trying to cover lies, but to make sure the truth was known and verified. My therapist told me that the truth would, for the first time, offer integrity that I would never have thought possible.

"As the test was ready to begin, my heart rate lowered and a strange peace came over me. I was going to tell the truth without deception for the first time in my life. The next twenty minutes were a blur, but I remember what happened back sitting in front of my wife and our therapist when the polygraph examiner walked in and whispered to the therapist. He turned to my wife and revealed that I had gone through the process with no evidence whatsoever of any deception. In spite of my fears I had been honest at all costs for the first time in my life. With my marriage and life in shambles, I felt a peace I had never known. In the midst of the potential loss of everything worldly, even though faint, I had finally found some integrity.

"With the truth on the table and devastation from my disclosures, trust was the single biggest concern. Without trust there can be no relationship. My toxic shame began to dwindle as I worked hard to look at the lies that had culminated in my sinful behavior and deadly shame. My wife and I both worked on ourselves and traveled to another outpatient clinic. We spent several weeks there, though not together. I dealt with my shame and fears through intense work. Our therapist from the Intensive continued to monitor the process. There was freedom and peace in submission.

"Over the past four to five years I have a relationship with my wife that is unhindered by lies and shame. I ask God daily to create a clean heart in me. My wife has blossomed. There is a comfortable peace in our home. Our children began their healing process during this time. They will break this cycle."

Stephen and Jean, South Carolina

Keith and Valerie's Story_____

"I discovered my husband's first affair after thirteen years of marriage. He had been having an affair with a friend of ours who was also married. Our children were twelve, nine, six, and three at the time. We tried several support groups but Keith did not make it a priority. Six years later, I again discovered my husband was having an affair with another married friend. This time we went to a three-day Intensive with a counselor who specializes in sex addiction and both of us started attending support groups. We also went to weekly counseling sessions for one year, then every other week for another year, and monthly for another year. We worked really hard, prayed a lot and read books, and made new boundaries in order to rebuild trust and the relationship.

"The most difficult part of the journey was forgiveness and rebuilding trust, which included setting the boundaries that we needed to put in place to keep Keith accountable. The sex addiction also did damage to some of our friendships. It was awkward to keep distant from friends who might be triggers for Keith. For me, the hardest part was to let go and not try to control Keith or set his boundaries. It was difficult to allow him to move at his pace in recognizing what boundaries needed to be made in order to rebuild the relationship. It was hard to give him the space to work on his own stuff without me taking control.

"Our relationship today? It's great. God is good! We are not perfect, but we communicate better. I trust him and don't worry about him acting out. We are more open and honest. It no longer feels like the past is the present. We are different people and a different couple than we were then.

"I have learned that anything is possible with God as long as the spouse with the addiction is willing to put everything into making the changes necessary to rebuild the marriage. Forgiveness is possible! Hearts can be healed, trust can be rebuilt and love restored. It can happen. It takes work and requires patience and you must rely on your faith. I think it's vital to read books on the subject because they *can help normalize your feelings and give you support and hope. Get with a good counselor, and the offending spouse definitely needs to be in an accountability group."*

Keith and Valerie, California

Earl and Lynn's Story_____

"Since an initial disclosure in 2001, we have sought help from various sources. We attended a couples' weekend for sexual issues, completed the Twelve Steps in Celebrate Recovery, and took on local leadership roles in this program. Yet, I (Earl) could not achieve long-term sobriety. After being out of recovery groups for over a year, a series of increasingly severe relapses threatened to jeopardize both our marriage and careers. You see, we are both in ministry, and I serve as pastor of a church.

"When Lynn found incriminating files on my laptop and confronted me, we again sought help. Against the advice of others, we shared our full story with our church leadership and their wives who, amazingly, extended us grace and a commitment to help us seek restoration. Searching on the Internet, we found information about the three-day Intensives. We pursued this path and completed the Intensive and subsequent three-month and one-year aftercare visits with our therapist and then began seeing another therapist for continued aftercare.

"At our therapist's recommendation, Lynn joined a women's support group that met by telephone. When the group ended, Lynn sought certification as a Life Coach. She is now leading support groups for partners of sex addicts. She is pursuing a Master of Arts in Counseling [she has now graduated] and hopes to obtain licensure as a LPC. She actively serves in local church ministry. I continue to pastor a small church. Last year, I obtained certification as a Pastoral Sex Addiction Specialist, and helped organize a local twelve-step sex addiction recovery group—the first in our region. I maintain a website for ministry personnel seeking sexual integrity (www.sainministry.org) and I am currently seeking accreditation as

a life coach, specializing in addiction coaching. We hope to one day work together on couples' recovery efforts.

"We have tried to maintain a recovery-focused lifestyle, which includes attending daily meetings and following the regimen suggested by our therapist. We pray morning and evening, do daily intimacy exercises, and schedule regular recovery nights. We live one day at a time, enjoy one moment at a time, and seek to maintain open communication.

"However, we give all credit to God for the restoration of our marriage and the intimacy we enjoy. For me, the most difficult aspects since our Intensive have been dealing with depression and childhood trauma. For Lynn, the most difficult parts have been setting and maintaining healthy boundaries after my early slips and a minor relapse, as well as the added trauma of my struggles with severe depression.

"We enjoy a wonderful relationship that includes honest communication, loving respect, and delightful sexual intimacy. We've had our share of bumps in the road to recovery, but we are currently enjoying the benefits and blessings of sobriety.

"Here are some words of encouragement for couples that are going through the painful process of restoring their relationship after sex addiction. Be willing to surrender everything. For the addict, this means submitting to and dedicating yourself to treatment and recovery efforts. For the partner, this means maintaining healthy boundaries, yet willingly surrendering pride and personal expectations for the sake of your relationship. Don't give up, even if a relapse occurs. Keep working toward recovery."

Earl and Lynn, Illinois

Roy and Marnie's Story

"My husband started in this destructive behavior when he was twelve years old—first masturbating, then being a peeping tom, and then visiting prostitutes. He was caught in a sting in 2009 and charged with solicitation of prostitution. This was the first time I found out who he truly was and it devastated me. I had PTSD and was off work for six months trying to put myself back together.

"I still shared the same bed with him but it wasn't the same any more. I lost all trust and was always angry with him. I had gone to the doctor for assistance finding a counselor for him and was given two names. My husband decided which one to go to and made an appointment. After he had a few visits, I ended up in hospital with what I thought was a massive heart attack from stress, and he went to his psychologist who told him to tell me the truth because he would end up killing me. Fortunately, it was only a massive panic attack.

"After his disclosure I met with a marvelous counselor who had experience in addiction treatment and went to her for over a year. I also went to yoga and meditation classes to relax and center myself. Today, I am in a Mindful Meditation class, which helps people live in the moment, and helps me to put things aside.

"The things that contributed most to my success were finding an excellent psychologist who specialized in EMDR therapy (Eye Movement Desensitization and Reprocessing) and addiction, learning how to meditate, and do yoga. I also had hypnosis along the way. I still have difficult moments but they are fewer and fewer as time goes on.

"I had to weigh the strength of our relationship before and after the disclosure, and decide whether it was worth staying or moving on. It was a difficult decision because it seemed our whole time together was based on a lie when truly it was only a partial lie.

"I had wonderful friends who helped me through the worst of my healing process—some who gave great feedback and others who wanted me to move on. I was told that if you move on too quickly without considering everything you might regret it in the future. I was glad I kept that advice in the back of my mind when I wanted to call it quits. We also have an RV that we use all year long on weekends and getting away from the house has been a blessing. No phones, no memories, and no people.

"The most difficult parts of my journey were the flashbacks and the thoughts about what he did with these women. Nothing seemed sacred anymore. I had many anxiety attacks and remained on antidepressants for years trying to get some normalcy back in my life. Not being able to trust was also very difficult. I never knew what he was up to when he went out but I could not keep asking.

"None of our family or children were told about the problem and that created a large strain between one of our kids and me because they didn't understand why I was always so angry with their dad. Maybe one day they will be told but the time never seems right and I don't want them to lose their relationship with their father.

"Our relationship now is sometimes difficult (10 percent) but mostly a lot stronger (90 percent) than it ever was. My husband now helps around the house and is someone who listens to what I say, which never happened in the past. The difficult times mend themselves as long as I stay in the present and don't ruminate over the past or future. I am more content now and have a lot more trust in him, although there are times distrust enters into my mind.

"What encouragement can I give to others? Take your time with your healing. Look at all your options for self-care and choose the ones that are right for you. The biggest thing I never agreed with is the idea that I was codependent. I was told to not listen to such 'buzz words.'

"I found EMDR to be one of the biggest assets because it enabled me to heal faster than just talking about it. Start involving yourselves in more healthy activities that don't include a lot of other people. Don't take the easy way out and end the relationship. If you've been together a long time think about benefits vs. the costs of staying together. Be honest with each other even though it might hurt, and try to not be judgmental.

"This is a very hard journey and I would not wish this on anyone. It only takes one to destroy a relationship but two to build it back up, if there is willingness on both parties."

Roy and Marnie, British Columbia, Canada

Stewart and Anne's Story _____

"As I tell our story, I thought it might be useful to list the things that were most helpful for us during this journey.

- *Stewart's willingness to get help and not blame me; he did the research and found a place for us to go.*

- *We did a three-day Intensive where there was a disclosure followed by a polygraph.*

- *We both began attending meetings: SAA and COSA. We both worked the Steps and found sponsors with recovery themselves. Stewart did a 90/90.*

- *We both attended any informational seminars offered in the area, as well as open SAA meetings.*

- *Stewart's therapist was no-nonsense and held him accountable for doing his work.*

- *Upon completion of the Steps, Stewart began to sponsor others.*

- *We attended the annual conventions for both SAA and COSA. We got to hear the journey others had been on.*

- *We asked the three-day Intensive therapist to schedule follow-up sessions for us. They were not part of that program but we felt that they were necessary.*

- *We each got counseling separately. We did not do counseling together.*

- *We both created circles of appropriate and inappropriate behaviors.*

- *Anne established an accountability relationship with a close girlfriend.*

- *Stewart did amends with all Anne's friends and families (sixty-plus conversations!).*

- Anne kept half of the sobriety medallion with her at all times, as did Stewart. This demonstrated a shared commitment to recovery.

- We did intimacy-building exercises nightly for the first several years.

- We began doing daily prayer time at morning and night.

- We celebrated monthly and eventually annual sobriety dates.

- We had weekly recovery check-ins.

- We wrote up a postnuptial agreement.

"We realized that recovery needed to be a lifestyle and not just a series of meetings. We learned to celebrate the progress we made, talked through issues together, found couples and individuals who were role models for good recovery. Another important factor in our recovery was our faith in God."

Stewart and Anne, Texas

Vince and Elizabeth's Story_____

"Our marriage came crashing down in July, 2011 when I discovered my husband had been looking at Internet pornography. It was the third time, and the last straw for me. I gave up and asked for a divorce; meanwhile I checked out books from the library on sex addiction and researched it on the Internet. This discovery was followed by a full disclosure from my husband four weeks later, of thirty-two years of sexual acting out with over a dozen women, two affairs, strip clubs, and heavy use of pornography. This caused me to crash further and made me feel crazy. While I wanted to run away, I also knew that this had to be a mental illness, and so I was ready to learn and to try to help him heal, even if our marriage did not survive.

"I vacillated many times between wanting to go forward and wanting to end the pain by ending the relationship. My first step *was to physically separate (about five times) both within the house and having him leave the house. Then I asked for a legal separation because I felt I could not trust him. He had already spent some of our joint funds on prostitutes and affair partners. But both of us continued to work on understanding what happened and took steps toward healing such as attending counseling, couples' workshops, reading, and many hours of talking. I had to take medications for anxiety and sleeplessness. The more my husband opened up, the less defensive he became, the more our relationship improved. Both of us eventually added Buddhism to the mix of things we were doing, which helped us to understand and accept even more.*

Here are the things that contributed most to our success:

- *My husband's undaunted dedication to his recovery from sex addiction and his determination that our marriage be restored*

- *His remorsefulness and honesty*

- *His willingness to give me a legal separation without resistance*

- *My dedication to understanding sex addiction and willingness to give healing time*

- *Attending two couples' workshops, and doing some excellent telephone counseling sessions for each of us with sex addiction experts*

- *Becoming involved in the local Buddhist Center and studying and practicing Buddhism. We are also Methodists and we found Buddhism to be complementary and supplementary to our Christian faith*

- *My husband's regular attendance at twelve-step programs and completion of an online recovery program. He considers both programs to be crucial to his recovery*

"The following list details the most difficult parts of the restoration process:

- *My anger and resentment, anxiety, depression, and suicidal thoughts. Also, my grave disappointment in my husband and marriage, and how it felt like a death with all the grieving that goes with that*

- *My initial belief that my husband has never loved me; my difficulty in believing that sex addiction is a real disease; my perception that my husband is a promiscuous philanderer never to be trusted*

- *The legal separation was difficult, but necessary*

- *The necessary step by my husband to give himself up to the truth of the betrayal; to give up denial that what happened was not really so bad. This was essential in understanding the depth of the trauma and pain caused both to me and to him.*

"Today, our relationship is growing and rebuilding. We live together in the same home we have had for years. We are still legally separated while we work out new terms of our marriage. My husband is very respectful to me and I am cautiously evaluating his changes and trustworthiness. We have a healthy and fulfilling sex life. I still am having problems with mood swings into depression that may last two weeks and then subside. These are getting less and less frequent. We do not take each other for granted. We realize the other has feelings and we are careful with our interactions. We go places as a couple and entertain friends in our home. We take trips together. We regard ourselves as a couple once again and will continue to try to strengthen our relationship into the future. We feel it is an absolute miracle that we are still together after all the trauma and hurt, and it must be because we realize that we have always loved each other.

"Success is possible if the wounded spouse can get beyond the hurt, which can be tremendous, and if she can believe that sex addiction is a disease. For those of us who have never had an addiction to sex or anything else, sex addiction is very hard to comprehend and the wrongs done are hard not to take personally. The greatest healers are time, attending couples' workshops led by professionals, and reading psychology.

"We read in the sex addiction literature that the rate of recovery from sex addiction is dismally low. This can be extremely discouraging *for both the offending spouse and for the partner. In our case, it was cause for the wife to ask in the early stages of the husband's recovery 'what is the use? He will just try this and fail and I will be hurt again.'*

"But recovery can be 100 percent, provided the right conditions are present. First, the sex addict must truly want to change. He must dedicate himself to recovery as the number one priority in his life. He must seek help through counseling, engage in recovery groups, read recovery literature to understand what this is all about, seek support from real friends and from his partner, develop a desire to look within himself, and develop himself spiritually. We know true recovery is a lifelong quest, and that recovery, love, trust, and respect for each other will be the basis our lasting relationship.

"I am convinced that sex addicts, in their self-centeredness, are not totally aware of all the potential harm they are causing in their acting out. They believe they can keep their sex lives a secret, and thus no one is harmed. Sex addicts are insecure, needing affirmation of their manhood (or womanhood) from almost anybody who will give it through a sexual encounter. It grows into an addiction for sexual stimulation and gratification that to them resembles love, affection, and affirmation, even from images on a screen. It makes them feel real because inside they don't feel like real men and women.

"This is so difficult for spouses who are mature and secure to understand. It really is true that a sex addict can hide a secret life from his spouse for decades—I am proof. They can lie and hide and keep secrets with great stealth. For spouses who grew up decades ago, this seems like unimaginable behavior in another adult. However, in spite of this, this immature adult can be jolted into awareness by having to face grave consequences for his behavior, and realize that in his emotional immaturity his actions have done great harm to others. I have seen my husband's growing maturity as a result of this awakening, which complements his other excellent qualities and accomplishments. The feeling of recovery is one of finding out you can be even better than you thought you were!"

Vince and Elizabeth, Colorado

John and Rhonda's Story

"Our success story has been many, many years in the making. The first discovery of his sexual acting out, in the form of cybersex, occurred seven years into our marriage. At that time, we knew nothing of sex addiction. We fumbled through our marriage trying to restore it, but I had no idea what was really happening. Over the years, there were several other discoveries of acting out, but always on the Internet. I read a book about cybersex to learn more and realized this was a very serious problem.

"We lived in a small country town in Oklahoma at the time. My husband called several counselors looking for help for sex addiction. He was humiliated on more than one occasion by counselors' offices hanging up on him and some even telling him not to prank call them like that, that they were a professional counseling office to help people with real problems. After a while, we pretty much just went on with life. We prayed about it at church, and asked for prayers for undisclosed issues. It was just a matter of time before I made yet another discovery that he had acted out.

"It had been about twelve years since that very first discovery and I had run out of hope. We now lived in Tucson, Arizona, and John had finally started counseling. It was with a female counselor who was certified as a sex addiction counselor. However, I felt betrayed all over again. Here was my husband going to see a female counselor in private who was single and telling her things he would not share with me, his wife of nineteen years. I was going out of my mind. One day, when John was not home, I stooped to a low point again and picked up a workbook he was completing for his counselor. There I read that even though my husband had always promised and swore that he had never physically cheated on me, he lied. He had in fact physically cheated with six other women. My world went black and that was by far the lowest, darkest, loneliest, scariest moment of my life. In one of the books I was reading I found the name of another therapist who did three-day Intensives, and I told my husband I was willing to give that therapist a call, but this was the final straw.

"Going to our three-day Intensive was the beginning of our recovery. Finally, someone acknowledged the trauma I had been through, and affirmed that I didn't do anything wrong and this was not my fault. I was also able to participate in a women's phone support group; a tremendous help to my process of recovery. It has been a very long road.

"In the midst of all this, John was diagnosed with Parkinson's and was medically retired from his job. I have to credit this a bit for helping in his success in recovery, in that he used to stray outside our marriage in connection with his job and its required travel away from home. I consider our story a success because we are willing to give each day to God and ask for His guidance. There are still some dark days that require extra time with God to get through, but with His guidance there is always hope!

"There are a number of things that contributed to our success. Number one is God. I do not believe our marriage could have been restored without God's mercy, grace, and love. This experience has tested my faith to the core. Having my trauma acknowledged and validated, reading about and understanding the PTSD symptoms I was having, and learning healthy coping strategies to help deal with and overcome the triggers was critical for me. Our two therapists were both invaluable resources for our journey. Without either of them, I can honestly say we would probably not be together today. With their guidance and love, we celebrated a beautiful twenty-fifth wedding anniversary.

"The most difficult part of this process was learning the whole truth. I still have haunting thoughts of those truths from time to time. Dealing with the numerous emotions and the emotional rollercoaster of having many of those emotions simultaneously or consecutively all in one day and learning how to work through them in a healthy way was incredibly challenging. Even though my husband had this addiction long before I ever met him, he blamed me, and I believed him and blamed myself for it. Every now and then I still struggle with those feelings of inadequacy. I have to remind myself that God made me enough and that is all that matters. Trust and forgiveness were also a very difficult part of the process to get through. Trust is still an issue and I have to give my insecurity to God and put my trust in Him.

"I lived in denial and the fairy tale was crushed. We have both worked through a lot of issues and still have work to do both individually and together. To me, it will be a work in progress every day for the rest of our lives, till death do us part.

"For others going through this rebuilding process I would say, be patient. I don't believe it can be done without God. My faith has played a huge part in our recovery. Don't give up as long as you are both willing to put in the time and effort. It is so worth it! At those darkest moments, know there are others who have been there and have survived, and you will too. You are much stronger than you know. It's okay to feel all the emotions and work through them. Be kind and patient with yourself. Love yourself. Don't look for a finish line. There isn't one. Every day we can learn something new, do something better, love someone more, share our love in more ways, and never, ever stop learning."

John and Rhonda, Arizona

John and Rachael's Story

"It was mostly about the lies, not the sex for some reason. I fell in love and that has never changed. After he told me that he needed help, I could only feel awful for him. He is such a proud person and his accomplishments are so far beyond even his expectations. After we had our three-day Intensive, our life changed for the better. We became equal partners in everything; we became open with each other with no secrets.

"After our Intensive I promised myself that I would not check up on him, I would not look through his personal stuff, and I would not worry about his cheating. All of those things will eat you alive if you let them. I vowed to have trust until I had reason not to. I went through a three-year battle with cancer and during a stay in the hospital he had a slip. He was viewing porn on the Internet and told me, at that time I was too sick to care, but as soon as I felt good enough we went back to the therapist who did our Intensive and John retook the polygraph and passed.

"In the analysis of this whole process, I believe it's the polygraph that gives me peace of mind. I know the truth will come out, and he knows he is being held accountable. If you honestly love your partner, you will understand that this is an addiction; an illness. If John had not done his recovery work or gotten a sponsor I would have been disappointed, and the last thing he wanted to do is to disappoint me again. He wound up sponsoring other people through the program. That showed me his intent and made it easy for me to trust him.

"Several things contributed to our success, including not dwelling on him and taking care of myself. Another thing that helped me was knowing that I can't make him stop—he has to do it. I never questioned him outside of our set time for him to do a weekly check-in with me when I could ask questions in an open-ended way. In the past, for example, I might have said, 'You were gone an hour longer than you said you would be; where were you?' Instead now in our check-in I say, 'the other day you were gone an hour longer; what happened?'

"The polygraph exams that he takes periodically have allowed me peace of mind. The most difficult part of the journey for me was getting comfortable with sex again. We had a very fun sex life. It became silent which made me wonder what he was thinking. We eventually talked through it and it's fun and warm again.

"Our relationship today is great! We have both grown a lot. If you BOTH want to restore your relationship you can. So often, the strength of love is not there. But if you have it, then use it. Set aside a safe time to talk. Address the issues; if there is a slip, make an appointment and let the professionals do their thing."

John and Rachael, Florida

Jeff and Judi's Story_____

"I was a pastor when we began recovery. Our story of recovery has experienced a full range of emotions, successes, slips, and even relapses. Neither of us were even aware of the existence of sex addiction. I had battled with pornography for over eight years while being engaged in full-time ministry. My wife was aware of my struggle with pornography but neither of us knew how to get help and who to talk to about this. It was not until my wife looked online and found a program offering three-day Intensives that we discovered there was such a thing as sex addiction.

"I took a test on the website and sure enough I met the criteria for being a sex addict. A few weeks later I attended a men's retreat that deals with sex addiction recovery. We then completed the three-day Intensive and flew home to our church where I continued to serve as pastor for another three years. I started attending a twelve-step program in our area and got a sponsor. I later found a therapist within our area that specialized in sex addiction. The combination of finding a support group, a sponsor, and a therapist was instrumental to my recovery and the healing of our relationship. We later attended the follow-up meeting with the therapist who conducted our Intensive and continued to do recovery work together and attend support group meetings.

"The primary resources that contributed to my success were finding a sponsor that was fully engaged in my recovery work, attending support group meetings like SAA and SLAA, and doing personal work with a therapist who specialized in sex addiction. Ministry for me was very isolated and isolating; attending recovery support groups was the first time I was vulnerable with other men and women who were all on the same journey. My wife and I started attending another support group together called RCA (Recovering Couples Anonymous). These group meetings were instrumental in establishing healthy relationships with others where there was no judgment, criticism, or shame.

"Our most difficult challenge in the restoration process was rebuilding trust in our relationship. I had not only been caught in the trap of

porn addiction for several years but I had acted out with several women before entering recovery. I wish I could say that my recovery journey has been without flaws, but I acted out with another woman after entering recovery. This was damaging to our relationship as I once again broke my wife's trust, and it was very difficult for us to go through another full disclosure at another outpatient treatment center for two weeks. It was probably the most difficult two weeks of my life, but it was key in my recovery as I began to do some real work/therapy around my family of origin and difficult experiences I had throughout childhood. A new light of hope began to shine in my heart as I started to connect the dots as to when, why, and even what may have led me to act out in these ways. Although those two weeks were difficult to experience, I am grateful today for the opportunity to do that necessary work.

"Our relationship is like a flower blossoming each and every day. There is new life, fresh hope, and with every challenge we find ourselves prepared to do the work together as we check-in with one another often to share our thoughts, emotions, hopes, and challenges. We are a team that understands our flaws/weaknesses and is willing to do the work necessary to better ourselves as individuals and as a couple. Our self-awareness has increased 100 percent, as well as our awareness of each other's needs and desires. We have so much more work to do, but without the support of so many on our recovery journey we would never be where we are today.

"My words of encouragement to other couples in recovery and even to those who are deciding whether it is worth the work to start a journey of recovery is: Do not sell yourselves short. The work is hard and the journey is long but the results are worth every tear, all the heartbreak, the sleepless nights, and even the fear of failure. I did not coin the phrase but I often encourage myself with its words, Failure is never final. Failure only occurs when I give up. Failure gives me the opportunity to start again. As often as I have failed in my marriage and fallen in my recovery, I made a choice to GET BACK UP.

"Life is full of challenges and this has been the biggest challenge yet, but I am grateful for the opportunity to get back up and start again. If you are struggling with sex addiction, get up, shake off the shame, do the hard work, and see what lies ahead as you start again. I will not promise you an easy journey but I can say with confidence that if you are willing to do the hard work and invest yourself in recovery you will be a better person for it. Without the skilled therapists that worked with us and the friendships of so many good people from SAA, SLAA, and RCA, I probably would not be in my marriage today.

"Today, I'm back in school full-time and will soon graduate with a PhD in psychology. I plan to help other couples who have struggled with sex addiction. The training I have received, as well as our own story of restoration help equip me for my new career."

Jeff and Judi, Virginia

Chris and Mari Beth's Story _____

"We went to a one-week Intensive after the discovery. I would highly recommend that to everyone going through this. That experience truly jump-started the healing process for us. Once we came back home, we began doing most of the things our therapist suggested, in addition to seeing a psychologist regularly. These things were time consuming and expensive, but well worth it. The alternative would be divorce and that is way-more costly in so many areas, not just financial. My advice is to avoid divorce at all costs and commit to staying together to work on things for at least one to two years and then go from there. In our case, complete healing was reached by three years. Long, hard, and expensive, but so, so worth it in the long run. Try to look at the big picture, choosing not to focus only on the hurt and anger of the now. Feelings will change, so don't base major life-altering decisions on how you feel at the beginning of all of this.

"From where I am right now, looking back on everything that has happened over the last five years, I can honestly say that I am so

glad I stayed in the marriage. I didn't want to stay. I was leaning toward separation or divorce and didn't think I would ever be able to completely forgive my husband. It is still hard to believe we got through it, and that we not only survived, but thrived.

"At the beginning, and even in the middle of this odyssey, I just could not see a way for our marriage to survive such a huge blow, and it wouldn't have survived if I had given in to my feelings of despair and given up on us. If my husband had thrown in the towel and had not been willing to do the hard work and pay the price for his actions, we wouldn't have made it. But, wow, it's so crazy and really almost unbelievable that we have the beautiful marriage that we have now, and that our family is intact! I never would have believed it could have turned out this way when this first happened.

"This past Christmas gave me such pause, because I stopped and realized how thankful I was that our kids have been able to come home for the holidays with both of their parents. I reflected on how happy they were to be with us, and how ecstatic we were to be with them. Keeping the family together is such a worthy pursuit. It was then and there that I realized how glad I was that I hadn't run away from the marriage, that I didn't run away from the pain and hurt and hard work that was ahead. If I could say anything to wives like me, who are at the terrible beginning of this process, it would be: I know you may want to quit. I did too. But, trust me when I say, if you give it enough time, and you hang in there, you will be shocked by the forgiveness that can come and surprised by the joy that will come from having your family intact.

"I think the most important ingredients to our success were:

- Passage of time. Forgiveness came with time, although it didn't seem possible at first

- Our relationship with God

- My husband's steadfast patience with my healing process. It was my healing to have, and he needed to and ultimately gave me the breathing room to go through it, and do it my own way

- My husband's sheer determination to do whatever it took to get me to stay, regardless of how it would make him look to others

- My husband's complete and utterly repentant heart. He knew he broke my heart and had gambled our marriage and our health. The stark realization of what his actions had done caused his heart to break. From the breaking of his heart came change and repentance

"The most difficult times were after the dust settled from the initial shock. When the shock wore off, I had to work through anger and grief—it seemed unbearable. My husband had to be patient with me and let me be angry at him, let me ask tons of questions, and talk about whatever I wanted to talk about, whenever I wanted to. He struggled with patience. He was so scared I wasn't going to stay with him and that I would reject him completely, that he could barely wait for me to just be okay again, and love him again. It was so hard for both of us during that phase, and it lasted at least two years.

"I can't believe, after everything that he did, and after everything we went through to get here, that I can actually say this, but it's true— our relationship now is even better than before. We are each other's best friends again. We enjoy being together, doing life together and spending time with our children together. We have a beautiful, deep marriage that we both treasure and guard closely these days. Trust has been restored as well, which was another thing that I never thought would return. If someone had told me all of this at the beginning of this journey, I would not have believed it to be possible.

"If you are just beginning this journey, don't quit. No matter how hard and unbearable things get, do everything within your power to stay together, and if you do, with the passage of time, and good counseling, you will be surprised at how much better you and your marriage will become."

Chris and Mari Beth, Illinois

Kangaroos and Emus

On Australia's Coat of Arms, there are two of the nation's indigenous animals, emus and kangaroos. One unusual quality of both of these two animals is that they seldom back up. Emus have strong legs and can run fast but the joints in their knees seem to make it difficult for them to move backwards. Kangaroos, because of the shape of their body and their broad, long tail, also find it difficult to go backwards. Australia has chosen these animals for their coat of arms as a symbol of their nation's desire to always move forward.

The journey through sex addiction, healing from the trauma caused by it, and seeing relationships restored is long and tedious. Many things threaten to derail recovery, healing, and restoration. Our hope and prayer is that you will continue moving forward. We hope the stories of success inspire you to continue to strive for restoration in your relationship.

Whether you have just discovered that you or someone you love is a sex addict or you have been living with the reality of sex addiction for many decades, there is hope. As you can see from the stories written here, the hope is real and freedom is possible. Relationships can be restored and in many cases become better than a couple had ever dreamed.

Don't give up! Make a commitment that regardless of how difficult the journey, you will move toward healing. There is no quick fix for sex addiction or for relationships that have been badly damaged by acting out. But healing and restoration can come for you, as it has for many others.

We hope that this book has given you the courage you need to move forward in recovery from sex addiction and in healing from the trauma that comes from being in relationship with a sex addict.

HOPE

FREEDOM

APPENDIX A

Finding Frequently Asked Questions (FAQs) and Answers at a Glance

Chapters not listed here contain no FAQs.

CHAPTER 1: THE ROLE OF FAMILY OF ORIGIN

- Addiction seems to run in my family. Three of my four grandparents are alcoholics and my brother is a drug addict. Am I at greater risk of developing addiction?

- I think that my mother's trauma and my father's inability to deal with it greatly affected their relationship with me. Is it possible that this lack of bonding contributed to the development of my sex addiction?

CHAPTER 2: ABUSE

- When I was ten, I found some soft-core porn magazines hidden in my father's dresser. I would sneak them out and masturbate to the images every time I was home alone. How do I stop feeling guilty about doing that?

- I was brutally whipped by my father many times until I was a teenager. Could this abuse be partly responsible for my sex addiction?

- Both of my parents used to slap me a lot when I was a child. I don't remember acting out sexually until I was about fifteen. Why didn't I develop sex addiction earlier?

CHAPTER 4: OTHER RISK FACTORS

- Is there an "addiction gene"?

- My therapist said I should see a psychiatrist. Why would he suggest that?

- My wife is convinced I have ADHD. Could this cause my sex addiction?

- Will taking my medication for ADHD eliminate the need for me to attend twelve-step meetings?

- What part does depression play in sex addiction, and how does sex addiction affect depression?

- I have been diagnosed with bipolar disorder. How does this impact my sex addiction?

- I'm sure my husband is a narcissist. Is narcissism related to sex addiction?

- What is empathy and how do I do it?

- How did I become a sex addict?

- If I think my husband may have a personality disorder or some other form of mental illness, what should I do?

- I think I may have an abnormally high sex drive. Could my sexual behavior be a hormonal problem?

CHAPTER 5: THE ROLE OF PORNOGRAPHY

- Is addiction to pornography different from sex addiction?

- Can pornography cause erectile dysfunction (ED)?

- Can pornography harm my marriage?

- As a sex addict, how do I determine if masturbation is healthy or not?

- In recovery from sex addiction, when is masturbation considered a relapse?

CHAPTER 6: THE PROGRESSION OF SEX ADDICTION

- There is a lot of talk about whether masturbation for sex addicts is healthy or not. If your spouse is all right with masturbation and you are both open about it, is it okay?

- I just found out my husband has been having sex with men. I am more devastated by this than by learning he's had sex with many female prostitutes. How can I compete with a man? Does this mean my husband is gay?

- Does sex addiction lead to homosexuality?

- Does past sexual abuse impact gender preference in sex addiction?

- My husband condemns inter-racial relationships, same-sex relationships, and viewing child pornography. Now I find out these are his acting-out behaviors. Can you explain this contradiction?

- My husband is a sex addict and I am worried he may harm my teenage daughter. Is she at risk?

CHAPTER 7: GENERAL QUESTIONS ABOUT SEX ADDICTION

- How common is sex addiction?

- Is sex addiction a real disease?

- What are the criteria for diagnosis of sex addiction?

- Why is sex addiction not listed in the DSM-5?

- What is the difference between sex addiction and love addiction?

- What is the difference between sex addiction and being polyamorous?

- Is there a relationship between IQ and sex addiction?

- Is there a relationship between wealth and sex addiction?

- What makes it so difficult for people with sex addiction to ask for help, even when they obviously need it?

- What is the difference between guilt and shame?

- What is being done to educate the general public about sex addiction?

- How could I have participated in behaviors that are so contrary to my faith and values?

- How does sex addiction affect a person's self-esteem?

- If I become successful at not acting out, will I still always be a sex addict?

CHAPTER 8: QUESTIONS ABOUT SEX ADDICTION FROM PARTNERS

- Why didn't I see the signs before? How could his addiction remain hidden for so many years? Am I a fool or naive to not have seen it earlier?

- How could he have hidden the electronic tracks of his acting out so well?

- Is there anything I could have done to prevent him from being unfaithful to me?

- Why would my husband want to have sex with others rather than me?

- Why does my husband prefer an unattractive prostitute to his beautiful, loving wife?

- Can you explain the irony of a sex addict who is unable or unwilling to have sex with his wife?

- Why didn't he ever think of me and our children and the damage he was causing by his acting out?

- How can he prefer masturbation to having sex with me?

- Why did I end up in this relationship?

- Will my husband always feel like he needs something more?

- Why do so many churches seem to blame the wife instead of addressing sex addiction?

- If this is an addiction and the addict's sexual acting out is compulsive, how is it that sexual liaisons are often carefully planned in advance?

- I just found out that my husband is a sex addict. Am I in danger?

- I don't like my husband going to twelve-step meetings. He tells me that many of the men there continue to act out.

- Should I be concerned that female sex addicts attend some of my husband's twelve-step meetings? Isn't this like pouring gas on a fire?

- Is there anything I could have done to prevent this?

- Can a sex addict ever stop?

CHAPTER 9: IS THERE ANY HOPE?

- Is there hope for me?

CHAPTER 11: GENERAL QUESTIONS ABOUT RECOVERY

- I have just acknowledged that I am a sex addict. How can I slow down my sex addiction?

- How long does recovery take?

- Am I going to have to fight with this every day?

- Do the cravings or urges ever go away?

- When am I at the greatest risk of acting out?

- How do I stop lying?

- How do I stop feeling shame about what I have done in the past?

- How can I truly learn to let go of the past and forgive myself for my lustful thoughts and actions?

- Will I ever be normal?

- Does my sex addiction define me?

- How do I know which is the best way to get help for my sex addiction?

- I just started attending twelve-step meetings and have been shocked by how many of the men are really telling my story when they tell their own story. Are sex addicts really that similar?

- I live in an area that does not have any sex addiction-related twelve-step meetings. How do I do recovery without them?

- If you are a non-believer how can you turn to a higher power?

- When someone has multiple forms of addiction (sex, alcohol and other drugs, and gambling), what should be addressed first and how is recovery different?

- I never had wet dreams as a youngster but since entering recovery I have had several of them. Is this normal?

- I have been in recovery for two years and have remained sober but I still sometimes have sex dreams. I wake up in a cold sweat, fearful that I've acted out only to find it was a dream. When will this stop?

- If someone is doing well in recovery and has been sexually sober for a year, is it okay to take a break from recovery?

- How long does it take to regain your self-esteem?

- Do I need to work with a therapist?

- How do I find a good therapist?

- My wife and I have had two previous therapists who said we just needed to have more sex with each other. Why don't they know better?

- How can I integrate more of the spiritual aspects of recovery into therapy?

- Can medication help my sex addiction?

- What is the best blocking and tracking software for safer Internet use?

- How do I remain sober in a culture inundated with sexual messages?

- I believe God has delivered me from sex addiction. Why do I still feel pressured to continue in recovery?

CHAPTER 13: WHY DID HE DO IT?
- What did I do wrong?

CHAPTER 15: MOVING FORWARD

- What are the most helpful steps to take to move forward?

- Is it okay (safe) for my husband to maintain friendships with other addicts?

- How do I know he's really stopped?

- How do I know if he is really in recovery or still lying and just faking it?

- Is this marriage salvageable?

- Should I leave or should I stay?

- Now that I know, what should I do?

- How do I deal with my grief?

CHAPTER 16: QUESTIONS ABOUT RECOVERY FROM PARTNERS

- Did my spouse ever love me?

- How could he love me and carry on relationships with other women?

- Does he really love me now?

- Since our relationship was based on a lie and I really don't know who he is, why do I still really love my husband?

- How can I learn not to loathe my partner even though I love him?

- How do I confront my spouse about his sex addiction when he says he is not a sex addict?

- I know my partner is a sex addict but he will not get help. What am I supposed to do?

- How do I get him to understand how he is killing our marriage?

- What is the practical difference between supporting his recovery and enabling him?

- How does enabling differ from support?

- How can I support my spouse when he goes through recovery without opening myself up for more hurt?

- How do I detach from the addict so I can recover?

- He relapsed again. When should I think about leaving?

- How do you navigate finding a good therapist?

- How long will it take me to heal from what he has done to me?

- When do I need to separate for my own health?

- I just found out my husband has had affairs throughout our marriage. I want to leave him but I have four kids and never finished college so I could support him while he completed his education. What do I do?

- I feel I need to separate from my husband but I have to stay in our house for the sake of our children. How do I set up an in-house separation?

- Why do so many partners report that the emotional abuse they experience gets worse when the sex addict goes into treatment?

- What is "acting out" for wounded partners?

- How can I help my therapist and others understand where I'm coming from regarding codependency versus relational trauma?

- At what point does a woman extend her forgiveness?

- How can I ensure that this doesn't keep happening?

CHAPTER 17: COPING WITH TRAUMA

- How do I deal with my triggers and flashbacks?

- When does the underlying constant feeling of sadness lift?

- How do I get off the emotional roller coaster?

- Does the pain of betrayal ever completely heal?

- How do I set healthy boundaries?

CHAPTER 19: QUESTIONS ABOUT RESTORING RELATIONSHIPS

- How can I begin to better understand and empathize with my wife's feelings?

- What am I supposed to do if I've been working really hard on my recovery, but my wife still doesn't trust me?

- When should I start marriage counseling with my wife?

- What are the chances of our marriage truly recovering?

- When are major life changes (e.g., relocating geographically, new job, new church, a totally new start) necessary?

- How involved should a spouse be in defining what a sex addict must do to recover?

- What boundaries are recommended for couples to put in place after discovery?

- How do you counsel a man who sees no benefit in pursuing recovery since his significant other is deeply affected by her own issues (PTSD, anxiety, depression, etc.) and refuses to see a counselor or get other help for herself?

- What can partners realistically expect from the recovering addict during the first year?

- The walls between us are up and I can't imagine how they can come down any time soon. Is there any real hope that we can learn to love each other again?

CHAPTER 21: QUESTIONS ABOUT DISCLOSURE

- Why do I need a therapist to do a disclosure? Why can't I just pick a night when my wife would be most receptive and tell her myself?

- I am working on my disclosure to my wife. I'm willing to disclose everything but I don't want to tell her I have given oral sex to prostitutes. Is that okay as long she knows everything else?

- When should a disclosure be done immediately?

- Is it ever a good idea to wait on doing a disclosure?

- Are there ever cases when it is inadvisable to do a disclosure?

- My husband is going to do his disclosure to me very soon. I know I can ask questions afterward. What things should I ask about?

- In his disclosure, will my husband reveal to me the names of the people he has had sex with?

- The Ninth Step talks about making amends to people unless it would injure them or others. Does doing a disclosure go against Step Nine if I think it will injure someone else?

- Should disclosures include sexual thoughts and fantasies, in addition to actual incidents of sexual acting out?

- How many marriages end after disclosure?

- Do I need to do a disclosure to my children?

- Should I do a disclosure to my parents? What about my in-laws?

CHAPTER 22: QUESTIONS ABOUT POLYGRAPH EXAMS

- How reliable are polygraph exams?

- Can a sex addict be trusted to tell the truth about anything, including his recovery and sexual sobriety, without a polygraph?

- Why is it so important to use polygraph exams in conjunction with a sex addiction therapist?

- Why should I do polygraph exams subsequent to the disclosure?

- How do we make arrangements to get polygraphs exams?

- Is there training available for sex addiction polygraph examiners?

CHAPTER 23: REBUILDING INTIMACY

- I am working on my Ninth Step. How do I make a proper amends to my wife?

- In making amends to my wife, is it possible to have the wrong motive?

- My husband wants his amends to me to include renewing our vows. He wants to do this publicly, and it seems to me he is interested in putting on a show for others. Am I wrong for not wanting to do this?

- How do I make amends to my children?

CHAPTER 24: HEALTHY SEXUALITY

- What sexual behaviors are healthy?

- How will I know if he is still thinking about someone else when he is having sex with me?

- What boundaries can a wife set with her husband to feel safe about trying sex again?

- What am I to do if we have been in recovery for over two years but my wife still will not engage in sex because of her anger toward me?

- My husband blames me for our lack of a sex life because I am not patient when he fails to get an erection. Before I knew about his sex addiction, his erections seemed to be instantaneous and now nothing works. My mind automatically goes to: I no longer excite him; I am unattractive and undesirable; I am less than his previous sexual experiences. What are we supposed to do?

- Is there still room for "play" that includes sexy lingerie and marital aids in our sex life or will that hurt a sex addict's recovery?

- Does "no" ever mean "well maybe" or "yes?"

- My husband has not wanted to be sexual with me for more than three years. He used to find me attractive. I am in good shape and I take care of myself. Why doesn't he find me appealing now?

- Over the past few years, I have developed a significant problem with premature ejaculation. Where can I go for help with this?

CHAPTER 25: GENERAL QUESTIONS ABOUT SLIPS AND RELAPSE

- Why do I repeatedly slip despite my resolve not to?

- Is there still hope if my husband has a relapse?

- What are the signs that my husband may have had a relapse?

- If I think my husband has had a relapse, what do I do?

- My husband has just told me that he relapsed. What should I do?

- My husband has had yet another relapse. How many relapses before enough is enough?

- What is the relapse rate for sex addicts?
- Is it worth it to continue to work on a marriage with a sex addict given the risk of relapse?
- When I have a relapse, I tend to binge for a few days. How can I pull myself out of that spiral?
- How do I deal with relapse without giving up on recovery?

CHAPTER 27: PREVENTING RELAPSE

- What are things I can do if I recognize I am on the road to a relapse?

RECOVERY PROGRAMS AT HOPE & FREEDOM COUNSELING SERVICES

www.hopeandfreedom.com
713-630-0111

THREE-DAY INTENSIVES

Three-Day Intensives are short but concentrated programs that focus on a particular aspect of recovery. They are not a "Three-Day Cure." There is no such thing. Rather, it is to do intensive recovery work in order to develop a solid foundation for recovery or to address a specific recovery need.

Hope & Freedom Counseling Services offers a variety of Three-Day Intensives that are especially helpful for persons who live in geographical areas where sex addiction therapy is not available. These are particularly good for individuals or couples first entering recovery and are an ideal forum in which to deal with the crises that may have precipitated recovery. Intensives are also good for anyone who has not been able to maintain long-term sexual sobriety or has experienced a slip or relapse.

These are not the treatment of choice for every individual or couple where compulsive sexual behavior is a factor. We accept fewer couples than apply for this treatment program. A number of factors may not make this the treatment option of choice.

Persons considering a Three-Day Intensive must be willing to work hard. They must be prepared to do whatever is necessary to stop the destructive behaviors related to sexual addiction and be willing to take extraordinary steps to restore their relationship. For the Intensive process to be successful, it requires couples to be willing to participate in the three-day experience, and also willing to work hard on rigorous assignments that are included each evening. In short, the Intensives we offer work best for highly motivated clients.

A prerequisite for participating in an Intensive is for both partners to be stable emotionally. Clients with untreated obsessive-compulsive disorder or bipolar disorder may not be good candidates for Intensives. After these disorders are stabilized with medication and therapy, they may be ready for the rigorous Intensive process. Additionally, persons in danger of harming themselves are not appropriate for Intensives.

Couples who are approved for participation in Three-Day Intensives must make an unqualified commitment to stay in the relationship after the Intensive. This is crucial since disclosures typically reveal additional acting-out behaviors or details about them. This new information usually traumatizes the partner. When the pain associated with trauma starts, the typical response is to look to anything to stop the pain, including ending the relationship.

We ask partners to make a commitment to stay in the relationship for a minimum of 12 months after the Intensive, regardless of what the disclosure reveals. We ask sex addicts to double the commitment and to stay in the relationship a minimum of 24 months after the Intensive, regardless of their partner's anger or disappointment. Couples must agree to enter a contractual agreement with that goal to participate in the Hope & Freedom Three-Day Intensive.

Couples who come to Intensives must be willing to devote total effort to recovery for the full three days. This includes not conducting any "business as usual" during the Intensive. We also ask that contacts with home and family be minimized for the duration of the Intensive.

People interested in Intensives first must complete an online application before they are carefully screened to make sure that they are appropriate for an Intensive and there is a reasonable expectation they will benefit from it. The content of the Intensive is customized to the specific needs of each client. Intensives are offered for couples as well as individually for men. However, if the client is in a committed relationship, we will only work with them as a couple, because successful recovery depends on both partners being involved in the recovery process. (Information and applications about Intensives may be found at www. HopeAndFreedom.com.) The following is a partial list of Intensives offered through Hope & Freedom Counseling Services as well as by Certified Hope & Freedom Practitioners.

RECOVERY FOUNDATIONS INTENSIVE

Recovery Foundations Intensives are designed for men and couples at the beginning of recovery and give participants a broad understanding of sex addiction and what is involved in recovery. There is an emphasis on understanding the origins of addiction and the factors that contribute to sex addiction.

These Intensives focus on integrating recovery routines into daily life, and to begin to reestablish trust in the relationship for couples. Relapse prevention is also a significant focus. The Recovery Foundations Intensive culminates with each client drafting a Personal Recovery Plan.

RESTORATION INTENSIVE FOR COUPLES OR FOR INDIVIDUALS

This Intensive is structured for couples where the sex addict has had some time in recovery but has had a slip or a relapse. Attention is given to understanding the cause of the relapse and preventing further relapses. A significant focus of this Intensive is dealing with the issue of trust. The couple is introduced to a process of trust rebuilding that requires significant commitment from each. It offers a high success rate. A similar Intensive is offered for individuals who are not in a committed relationship.

SURVIVORS INTENSIVE FOR COUPLES OR FOR INDIVIDUALS

This Intensive is designed for couples where one or both partners have experienced significant past trauma. The trauma may go back to childhood, or may be connected to recent or current sexual acting out. This Intensive focuses on the impact the trauma has had on the relationship, and has each partner begin the significant work needed to heal. A similar Intensive is offered for individuals who are not in a committed relationship.

STEP-DOWN INTENSIVE FOR COUPLES OR FOR INDIVIDUALS

This Intensive is designed as a step-down treatment for couples where the sex addict has just returned from inpatient treatment or from an extended intensive outpatient treatment facility. The emphasis is on life re-entry. Clients learn to identify and deal with daily triggers as well as learn new thought and behavior patterns to replace dysfunctional thoughts and behaviors. Relapse prevention and developing a Personal Recovery Plan round out the Intensive.

SPECIAL TOPIC INTENSIVES

We offer special topic Intensives designed to fit specific clients' needs. These deal with a number of topics related to recovery such as multiple addictions where addiction is present for both husband and wife, recovery issues involving the family, or religious abuse.

HIGH PROFILE CLIENT INTENSIVE

Individuals with high public profiles face special challenges entering recovery. If they go into a therapy office, they risk revealing their struggle with compulsive sexual behavior. To address this concern, we take the Intensive to the client. This Intensive is good for any high-profile person including senior executives, professional athletes, politicians, actors, broadcast personalities, and other celebrities. These are offered at a discrete location in the United States or Canada. Special arrangements can be made to have these Intensives in Europe or Asia. The content is customized to fit the needs of the individual or couple. The location is chosen to allow for an extra buffer of anonymity not available for high-profile persons or celebrities who enter well-known treatment centers.

Additional Intensives are offered to meet the special needs of physicians and clergy. These Intensives are highly individualized to deal with the specific issues involved.

PREPARING FOR INTENSIVES

Clients preparing for Intensives are encouraged to make adequate preparations to ensure the success of their concentrated work. First, they are encouraged to spend time thinking about the events that have contributed to the need for the Intensive. For Intensives dealing with sexual addiction, it is important to make a complete, detailed list of all acting-out behaviors. The more detailed and complete this list, the more effective the Intensive.

Clients who participate in a Three-Day Intensive are encouraged to take care of all business and family matters before coming to the Intensive and not to conduct any business during the Intensive. Frankly, we have found that clients who conduct "business as usual" during an Intensive get limited benefit. For this reason, we strongly encourage clients to schedule an Intensive when they are able to devote their full concentration to continuous therapy over three days.

To maximize the effectiveness of this time, we have the following stipulations:

- Leave cell phones, pagers, Blackberries, PDAs, iPods, laptops, and other electronic devices at home.
- Refrain from conducting business during the duration of the Intensive.
- Limit phone calls to one per day to check with family or to check on dependent children.
- Do not drink any alcohol for the 30 days preceding the Intensive.
- Refrain from all alcohol use during the Intensive.
- Do not watch television or read newspapers during the Intensive.

The total focus of the three days is to concentrate on individual recovery and strengthening the relationship. Distractions must be kept to a minimum. Nothing should be allowed to hinder the important work that takes place during an Intensive.

It is beneficial for clients to stay an extra day or longer after the Intensive to process with their partner what they have learned and accomplished during the preceding three days. This time can be important as couples make plans to reenter life and consider how their restored relationship may be different in the future.

AFTERCARE INTENSIVES

A rigorous aftercare program is an important ingredient in any recovery treatment program. After the initial three days of work, we encourage couples to come back for periodic One-Day Aftercare Intensives. These are mini versions of a Three-Day Intensive. During Aftercare Intensives, couples receive a combination of individual and couples' therapy. Aftercare Intensives are used to check up on recovery progress, and for the couple to learn additional tools of recovery and work on communication issues. A follow-up polygraph exam may be used to verify that acting out has not recurred.

The first of these one-day follow-ups is scheduled three months after the initial Three-Day Intensive. They are scheduled every six months for an additional eighteen to thirty-six months, depending on the couple's needs. Thereafter, many couples opt to schedule an Aftercare Intensive annually as a checkup on the relationship and to monitor progress in recovery.

Additional information about Hope & Freedom Three-Day Intensives, as well as many free videos can be found at www.hopeandfreedom. com. Dr. Magness can be contacted at www.milton.magess@ hopeandfreedom.com.

SPECIAL NOTE TO THERAPISTS

Our training program for therapists is called the Certified Hope & Freedom Practitioner (CHFP) training. In a typical year, one or two therapists who are already outstanding in their profession and have significant experience and training in working with sex addiction are selected for this training. Therapists who are interested in applying for the CHFP program can find an application at www.hopeandfreedom.net.

RECOVERY PROGRAMS & RESOURCES AT A CIRCLE OF JOY

www.acircleofjoy.com

For Women Partners of Sex Addicts

FREE PHONE CALL

Our team offers a free phone call to every hurting woman who reaches out to us, giving women the opportunity to share their stories with someone who understands and cares. For many, this is the first time they've told another person about their experience. This call also provides a venue for asking their many questions, and to hear what options may be available in their communities to help them begin to heal.

A CIRCLE OF SISTERS ONLINE COMMUNITY

A Circle of Sisters is an affordable online community where partners of sex addicts can connect with other women and be embraced with respect, compassion, and open hearts. It's a place where partners of sex addicts can freely ask questions, tell their story, and share in complete safety, knowing what they share will only be read by other women on this journey.

Telephone Support Groups

JOURNEY TO HEALING & JOY SUPPORT GROUP

These twelve-week telephone support groups give women an opportunity to share and process their pain with a trained facilitator and three other women in a supportive, healing environment. Participants learn important skills and make mental shifts to empower them to see their lives differently. They learn to use new tools that begin to help them move forward, whether their marriages heal or end.

JOURNEY TO HEALING & JOY FOR PARTNERS OF THE SAME SEX ATTRACTED

Journey to Healing and Joy for Partners of the SSA offers a safe place to process your pain among women who have experienced similar hurts. Working through Marsha Means' *Journey to Healing & Joy* workbook, this twelve-week telephone support group focuses on personal healing. Topics include healthy self-care, setting boundaries, exploring forgiveness, and finding joy—all in light of SSA issues. Whether you are still married, seeking to remain in and rebuild a relationship, separated and unsure of what steps to take next, or single again but just trying to make sense of it all, this group will help you heal.

HEALING THROUGH JOY

This group builds on the foundation of healing laid in *Journey to Healing & Joy*. It provides a deeply healing way to resolve unhealed trauma from your partner's sex addiction. Using the Life Model principles introduced in *Journey to Healing & Joy*, this group combines neuroscience, Attachment Theory, and Biblical principles to take us further in our healing. Together we give our brains what they need to help us heal. And as we do, our hope, our peace, and our joy increase. This group meets for ninety minutes each week for twelve weeks.

BOUNDARIES IN MARRIAGE

When we live with an addict of any kind, boundaries become particularly important. But when we live with a sex addict, they become imperative! If this is an area where you'd like to do some focused work and growth, we invite you to join us for the Boundaries When You Love a Sex Addict support group.

Most of what we process as a group is focused on the special challenges we face as we strive to live out healthy boundaries with the sex addict to whom we're married. These groups follow the same format used in the Partner's Healing Journey telephone support groups. We meet for 90 minutes each week for fourteen weeks and limit the groups to four women so each participant has plenty of time to share and integrate the material into her life.

LEARNING TO TRUST AGAIN

When you have been betrayed how do you know you're ready to trust someone again? How do you move past the pain of your past and learn how to re-enter a significant relationship? Whether you're trying to restore a current relationship or begin a new one, this support group will help you:

- Reinstate appropriate closeness with someone who broke your trust

- Discern when true change has occurred

- Re-establish appropriate connections in strained relationships

- Restore former relationships to a healthy dynamic

- Learn to engage and be vulnerable in a new relationship

Using John Townsend's book, *Beyond Boundaries*, you will find the answers that move you toward the closeness and intimacy you've been longing for. This twelve-week telephone support group applies what we learn to setting healthy physical, mental, emotional, and spiritual boundaries with healthy men so we know how to feel safe enough to risk male relationships again (and, perhaps in time, marriage).

JOURNEY THROUGH CRISIS OF FAITH

Many women who discover the man they love has a secret, also discover their foundation of faith is shaken and cracked. Has the discovery of your husband's sex addiction challenged your faith—or perhaps caused you to want to find faith for the first time in your life? If so, we encourage you to take part in this group that provides a safe place to share and explore those feelings, and to begin to work through them.

During thirteen weeks together this group will talk about, and learn, new ways to connect with God, as you continue to heal and grow.

TOOLS IN MY TOOLBOX

We all need a toolbox, and we all need to know how to use the tools we collect. If you've done a *Journey to Healing & Joy* support group, you've already learned one set of tools. But did you know there are more? Add to your empowerment and confidence as a woman in recovery by joining our coach and three other women for this twelve-week, "Tools in My Toolbox" support group. Each week our coach will creatively help you identify empowering recovery tools that you can use for those challenging life situations. And she will teach you how to use them. By the time your group comes to an end, we promise you will feel much more empowered for what lies ahead.

MARRIED & ALONE: LOVING AN EMOTIONAL ANOREXIC

This support group meets the needs of the many women who find that even after their husband gains sexual sobriety, he is still stranded in intimacy anorexia. Living with unmet emotional needs inflicts deep pain and a lack of connection. But life can feel good again if we can learn to live it on different terms, and create other fountains for joy. Join us if you are among the millions of women searching for a way to thrive in this painful isolation.

MY STORY

Using Dan Allender's life changing book, *To Be Told*, this group helps you discover God's fingerprints in your story, even in your life's most painful chapters, including your husband's sex addiction. It will invite you to discover how the pain in your story has uniquely equipped you to encourage others in your life as they face their own heartaches. If you want to see God turn your tragedy into your treasure, this group will help you do just that. Our coach facilitates this group, drawing on her own life tragedy that God has turned into beautiful treasure.

JOURNEY TO HEALING & JOY AS TRAINING FOR WORKING WITH PARTNERS OF SEX ADDICTS

Marsha facilitates these phone-based training groups for four women at a time. For three months these groups meet for two-hour weekly sessions as Marsha models how to use the *Journey to Healing & Joy* workbook effectively. Each session includes extra time for questions and answers, as well as teaching-point take-aways for the participants as future support group facilitators.

A CIRCLE OF JOY ONLINE FACILITATOR TRAINING SITE

A Circle of Joy Facilitator Training Site was developed as an online resource for women who have healed from the pain of their husband's sexual betrayal, who now want to help women in their locale find healing, too. Filled with live and recorded resources, archived articles, and an interactive forum, this site is a rich and affordable resource for any woman who wants to help other women heal.

WOMEN'S INTENSIVES

Marsha Means, MA, partners with another team member to provide three to five-day individualized healing Intensives for up to five women at a time. These Intensives offer focused healing for women who feel stuck or in need of more help than a support group can offer. The Intensives are held in beautiful, peaceful settings to maximize the benefits they offer.

COUPLES' RESOURCES

Pathway to Intimacy Retreats are offered in a bed and breakfast setting in the tree-covered mountains of Oregon. Facilitated by husband and wife team Coach Steve and Coach Kristie, these four night/five day retreats for four couples at a time focus on helping couples rebuild intimacy once sexual sobriety is in place. In addition, Steve and Kristie offer individualized couples' coaching.

Men's Resources for Healing and Growth

BOOT CAMP

If you're a guy who struggles with sexual integrity, we invite you to join us weekly with facilitator Coach Steve and a group of men facing the same struggles. We call this group Boot Camp because it is our basic, entry level group that empowers men with the tools and encouragement to begin and sustain real recovery. We use Darrell Brazell's *New Hope for Sexual Integrity* workbook, which incorporates strong recovery principles, plus the Life Model of emotional maturity, to help you grow in your ability to form healthy emotional intimacy with your wife, children, and other safe men. This group meets for 90 minutes each week for 16 weeks.

INTIMACY 101

Facilitated by Coach Steve, these twelve-week groups help men learn how to identify and gain release from past wounds, understand their current emotional/spiritual maturity level, and begin experiencing genuine joy that flows into their lives through intentional, life-giving relationships. The concepts learned and the growth achieved lay the foundation for true intimacy in men's lives.

INTIMACY 201

This twelve-week group builds on Intimacy 101, taking an honest look at our Creator's original design for marital intimacy. As participants stretch and grow, a new ability to connect intimately with their wives is developed. The group uses *Reclaiming Paradise*, written by Coach Steve.

WORTHY OF HER TRUST

Using the text, *Worthy of Her Trust*, co-authored by Stephen Arterburn and Jason B. Martinkus, we focus on the nine non-negotiables of rebuilding trust in the marriage relationship and how to incorporate them in your recovery journey. This group will help you rebuild your wife's trust after it was shattered by sexual betrayal.

MY STORY FOR MEN

This is a twelve-week group that uses the life-changing material contained in the book, *To Be Told*. Is the goal of a man's life to live free of addiction, or is there more? In this challenging group, each man will be equipped to discover who he really is, as well as the purpose for which he was individually designed by his Creator. We have been designed for far, far more than to simply survive. God has made us to thrive! In "My Story," each man will discover how he can thrive in his daily living.

You can find more information about all of the programs in A Circle of Joy at www.acircleofjoy.com. Marsha Means can be contacted at marsha@acircleofjoy.com.

FREEDOM

HOPE

ADDITIONAL SEX ADDICTION RESOURCES

TWELVE-STEP PROGRAMS FOR SEX ADDICTS

Sex Addicts Anonymous (SAA)
800-477-8191
713-869-4902
www.saa-recovery.org

Sex and Love Addicts Anonymous (SAA)
210-828-7900
www.slaafws.org

Sexual Compulsives Anonymous (SCA)
800-977-HEAL
www.sca-recovery.org

Sexual Recovery Anonymous (SRA)
www.info@sexualrecovery.org

Sexaholics Anonymous (SA)
866-424-8777
www.sa.org

TWELVE-STEP PROGRAMS FOR PARTNERS OF SEX ADDICTS

COSA
866-899-2672
www.cosa-recovery.org

Infidelity Survivors Anonymous (ISA)
www.isurvivors.org

S-Anon
615-833-3152
www.sanon.org

TWELVE-STEP PROGRAMS FOR COUPLES

Recovering Couples Anonymous (RCA)
877-663-2317
www.recovering-couples.org

CHRISTIAN-BASED TWELVE-STEP MEETINGS

Castimonia
www.castimonia.org

Celebrate Recovery (CR)
www.celebraterecovery.com

WEBSITES TO LOCATE THERAPISTS THAT SPECIALIZE IN SEX ADDICTION

www.findachfp.com
Certified Hope & Freedom Practitioners

www.sexhelp.com
The International Institute of Trauma and Addiction Professionals

www.sash.net
The Society for the Advancement of Sexual Health

INTENSIVE OUTPATIENT SEX ADDICTION TREATMENT PROGRAMS

Center for Healthy Sex
Intensives for men, women, and couples with the goal of moving clients into healthy sexuality
10700 Santa Monica Boulevard, Suite 311
Los Angeles, California 90025
www.thecenterforhealthysex.com
310-843-9902

Psychological Counseling Services (PCS)
One- to three-week intensive outpatient program for men, women, and couples with a heavy focus on individual therapy
7530 E. Angus Drive
Scottsdale, AZ 85251
www.pcsearle.com
480-947-5739

INPATIENT SEX ADDICTION TREATMENT CENTERS

Pine Grove Behavioral Health and Addiction Services
2255 Broadway Drive
Hattiesburg, MS 39402
www.pinegrovetreatment.com
888-574-4673

Keystone Center
2001 Providence Ave.
Chester, PA 19013
www.keystonecenterecu.net
800-733-6840

Life Healing Center
25 Vista Point Road
Santa Fe, NM 87508
www.life-healing.com
866-806-7214

Gentle Path at the Meadows
1655 N. Tegner St.
Wickenburg, AZ 85390
www.gentlepathmeadows.com
800-632-3697

The Ranch
6107 Pinewood Road
Nunnelly, TN 37137
www.recoveryranch.com
888-477-8953

Santé Center for Healing
P.O. Box 448
Argyle, TX 76226
www.santecenter.com
800-258-4250

Sierra Tucson, Inc.
39580 S. Lago del Oro Parkway
Tucson, AZ 85739
www.sierratucson.com
800-842-4487

CHRISTIAN-BASED WORKSHOPS

Bethesda Workshops
Workshops for men and women
3710 Franklin Pike
Nashville, TN 37204
www.bethesdaworkshops.org
866-464-4325

Be Broken Ministries
Three-day workshops for men
1800 NE Loop 410, Suite 401
San Antonio, TX 78217
www.bebroken.com
800-497-8748

Faithful & True Ministries
Three-day workshops for men, women, and couples
15798 Venture Lane
Eden Prairie, MN 55344
www.faithfulandtrue.com
952-746-3880

SEX ADDICTION RECOVERY-RELATED WEBSITES

www.CelebritySexAddict.com
Intensive outpatient programs for persons who cannot visit a therapist without becoming the subject of media scrutiny.

www.GotToStopIt.com
A YouTube channel with many videos related to sex addiction and recovery.

www.GuardUrEyes.com
For Jews who struggle with compulsive sexual behavior.

Sex Addiction Information Videos—Milton Magness, DMin.
www.sexaddictioninfo.com

Sexual Addiction Resources—Patrick Carnes, PhD
www.sexhelp.com

www.HopeAndFreedomU.com
Online sex addiction recovery education that includes streaming video courses.

www.iCANstop.com
Online sexual addiction recovery education.

www.iMUSTheal.com
Online recovery course for partners of sexual addicts.

www.InternetBehavior.com
Provides cybersex addiction research and resources. This site also includes a screening exam for persons who think they may be addicted to cybersex behavior.

www.PhysiciansInCrisis.com
Intensive outpatient therapy for physicians who struggle with sexual addiction.

www.ProvidentLiving.com, www.salifeline.org, and www. overcomingpornography.org
Resources for persons who are members of The Church of Jesus Christ of Latter-Day Saints.

www.RecoveryApp.com
Recovery-related applications for iPhones and iPads.

www.RecoveryOnTheGo.com
Brief audio books, MP3 downloads for getting started recovery.

www.SAATalk.org
Gives a list of SAA meetings that take place by electronic means.

www.StopSexAddiction.com
For partners who wonder if the person they love is a sexual addict.

www.WoundedClergy.com
Brief intensive programs for clergy struggling with sexual addiction.

OTHER WEB-BASED RESOURCES

iRecovery Addiction Recovery Tracker
This iPhone™ application is designed to keep track of recovery activities and plot the user's progress. The tracking process is also designed to be an encouragement to think about recovery daily.

Main Features

- Assigns recovery points to typical recovery activities
- Charts those activities and compares progress from week to week
- Users can add their activities and assign a point value for each
- Preloaded affirmations with counter
- Users can also add their own affirmations
- User defined "Red Light," "Yellow Light," and "Green Light" behaviors

- "Contacts" button takes users to list of their Circle of Five contacts
- Recovery points can be customized to meet individual recovery plans as directed by counselor or therapist
- iRecovery is also available in a specific iPad™ application. www.RecoveryApp.com

INSPIRATIONAL AUDIO MESSAGES FOR SEX ADDICTION RECOVERY

Audio messages, each approximately twenty minutes in length, narrated in a professional yet relaxed and encouraging tone, dealing with the following areas:

1. Am I a Sex Addict?
2. Lost in Cyber Space
3. Intensive Preparation for Her
4. Intensive Preparation for Him
5. Getting Started in Recovery I
6. Getting Started in Recovery II
7. Disclosure
8. Accountability in Recovery

These audio messages are particularly beneficial when the sex addict or partner could benefit from a caring, professional voice giving them reinforcement for the path they have taken to freedom from addiction and are available at www.RecoveryOnTheGo.com.

TWELVE-STEP FELLOWSHIPS FOR OTHER FORMS OF ADDICTION/COMPULSIVE BEHAVIORS

Alcoholics Anonymous
www.aa.org

Cocaine Anonymous
www.ca.org

Crystal Meth Anonymous
www.crystalmeth.org

Debtors Anonymous
www.debtorsanonymous.org

Food Addicts Anonymous
www.foodaddictsanonymous.org

Gamblers Anonymous
www.gamblersanonymous.org

Marijuana Anonymous
www.marijuana-anonymous.org

Narcotics Anonymous
www.na.org

Nicotine Anonymous
www.nicotineanonymous.org

Overeaters Anonymous
www.oa.org

Spenders Anonymous
www.spenders.org

Shopaholics Anonymous
www.shopaholicsanonymous.org

Workaholics Anonymous
www.workaholics-anonymous.org

The Twelve Steps of Sex Addicts Anonymous[76]

1. We admitted we were powerless over addictive sexual behavior – that our lives had become unmanageable.

2. Came to believe that a Power greater than ourselves could restore us to sanity.

3. Made a decision to turn our will and our lives over to the care of God as we understood God.

4. Made a searching and fearless moral inventory of ourselves.

5. Admitted to God, to ourselves, and to another human being the exact nature of our wrongs.

6. Were entirely ready to have God remove all these defects of character.

7. Humbly asked God to remove our shortcomings.

8. Made a list of all persons we had harmed and became willing to make amends to them all.

9. Made direct amends to such people wherever possible, except when to do so would injure them or others.

10. Continued to take personal inventory and when we were wrong promptly admitted it.

11. Sought through prayer and meditation to improve our conscious contact with God as we understood God, praying only for knowledge of God's will for us and the power to carry that out.

12. Having had a spiritual awakening as the result of these steps, we tried to carry this message to other sex addicts and to practice these principles in our lives.

---

76 Copyright by the International Service Organization of Sex Addicts Anonymous. Used by permission.